ALL KIDS CAN THRIVE

A Holistic Education Resource for a Successful and Conscious Classroom

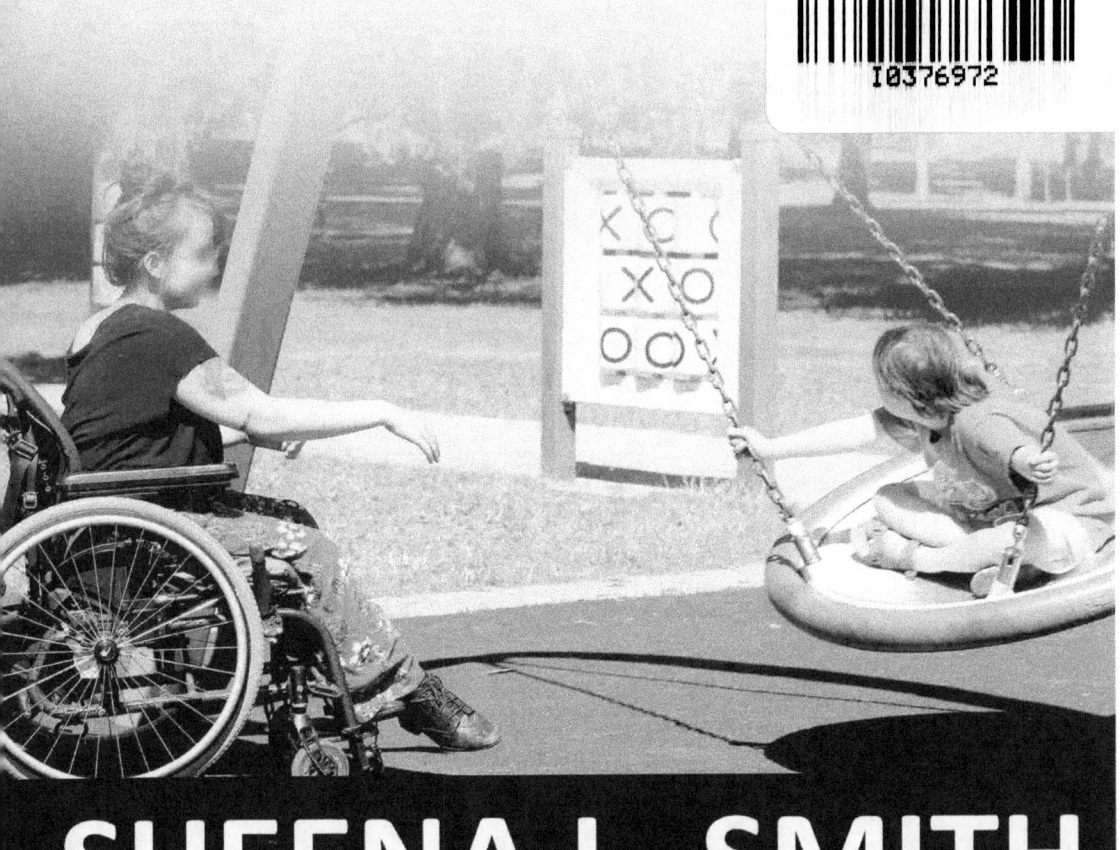

SHEENA L. SMITH

Foreword by Debra Poneman
Bestselling author, Award-Winning Speaker and Founder, Yes to Success, Inc.

All Kids Can Thrive

A Holistic Education Resource for a
Successful and Conscious Classroom

By Sheena L. Smith

— PRAISE FOR *ALL KIDS CAN THRIVE* —

"ALL KIDS CAN THRIVE is a must read for anyone working with children. It is a practical user-friendly resource that incorporates a variety of concrete classroom strategies with the holistic visions of a wide variety of experts from Coloroso and Covey to Hay.

Ms. Smith stresses the importance of incorporating and modelling mindfulness and reframing in the classroom. Her personal experience with Down Syndrome and Spina bifida gives the reader greater insight into the challenges faced by these children.

I think that this book should be required reading for those planning to engage with children in any field."
~ **Jan Fluke**, B.A. Reading Specialist, Children's book author

"As exemplars for teaching students about life, moral values, education, and unity consciousness you have a tremendous opportunity in your hands. I know you will enjoy this resource filled with valuable wisdom, useful tools and insights for teachers, educational assistants, and support staff alike. Thank you, Sheena, for your wonderful insights for our youth."
~ **Dr. Sue Morter**, Author of The Energy Codes: The 7 Step System to Awaken Your Spirit, Heal Your Body and Live Your Best Life, international speaker, master of bio-energetic medicine and quantum field visionary.

"Neuroplasticity is more than a buzzword; it is a blessing to know that learning potential is endless with the application of re-patterning and brain enhancing exercises. Sheena's book provides you with an introduction to some of the many proven and effective techniques for improving the functioning of your brain to consistently rewire your brain for lasting positive changes. Sheena has the beautiful gift of being able to see children as whole and complete exactly the way they are which enables her to help them reach their full potential. I believe there are angels on this planet tapped to do the work Sheena naturally does in this world and her work is very needed at this time."
~ **Lisa Garr**, host of The Aware Show and Being Aware, author of Becoming Aware: How to Re-pattern Your Brain and Revitalize Your Life.

"Sheena Smith offers a powerful system for helping students live happy, thriving lives by discovering how to be self-reflective, resilient, and empowered. "All Kids Can Thrive" is a valuable resource to help guide your students to shine brightly in their own unique ways."
~ **Marci Shimoff**, #1 NY Times bestselling author and Featured Teacher in The Secret.

"The teacher of the future will be more of a coach. You will need skills to "coach" your students to become the best version of themselves. "All Kids Can Thrive" will help you build a child's confidence and self-esteem. Through use of strategies students can discover how we are all connected by our similarities and yet valued for our differences and unique contribution. I encourage you to read this thoughtful and valuable book and use its suggestions to lead with your heart and intuition."
~ **Suzanne Lawlor**, M.A.-Master Coach, Director of Coaching for Your Year of Miracles

"I really enjoyed reading "All Kids Can Thrive" written by Sheena Smith. The information Sheena shares is invaluable to all adults working in a scholastic environment. In reading this book, we can all learn more strategies that will help every child reach their potential! I give this book an A+"
~ **Laura Arella**, Grade 6 Teacher (OCT)

"Sheena's book, All Kids Can Thrive speaks to those who have believed this all along. Sheena champions this belief through her informative, thought provoking personal and professional journey. Bravo Sheena"
~ **Shelley Miller**, Developmental Social Worker, BA., Special Educational Assistant and former School Councillor

"Sheena Smith's book encompasses any child as a whole individual. I have worked front line in the field of mental health for over twenty-five years in several capacities. I have too often borne witness to special needs children being misunderstood or overlooked entirely. Sheena's book identifies the significance of the body mind and spirit connection needed, to fully thrive and live life to our fullest potential. Sheena's book is a must read for anyone entering a career working with children as it provides valuable insight and strategies to help children reach their full potential. Bravo Sheena well done!"
~ **Korin Maier**, MSc, BA, CYW

"All Kids Can Thrive is right on the mark. As a former School Principal I recognized that when a teacher is attuned to the pulse of children in their class as they arrive, they can turn a day around. All teachers have the ability to empower every student to realize the potential and purpose in learning and to take on its challenges. The role of a teacher is a critical one on the path of a child's development. That children be given a sense of belonging can significantly affect the learning environment as a whole, and as such, teachers have a vital role in shaping a society. This can have a serious impact on learning and affect the direction a child will take in life."
~ **Rose Bresolin**, former School Principal, writer and Personal Life Coach. You can visit her on her website: rosebresolin.com

"In all the years that I have known Sheena Smith, I've been constantly inspired by her dedication, integrity, calm, and patience as a parent, educator and coach. I've seen first-hand how she walks her talk and have been impressed with her dedication and on-going support helping others in their pursuit to children thriving each and every day. This book is a must read for anyone working with children."
~ **Beth McBlain**, writer, publisher, entrepreneur

"My mom's All Kids Can Thrive is a valuable resource. I know from first hand experience of the many tips, tools and strategies used in this book. All readers will benefit from the excellent book"
~ **Tessa Kayleen Troch**, 23 year old, third child

Copyright © 2021 Sheena L. Smith

All rights reserved. No part of this publication can be reproduced, distributed, or transmitted in any form or by any means, including photocopying, recording, digital scanning, or other electronic or mechanical methods, without the prior written permission of the publisher, except in the case of brief quotations embodied in critical reviews and certain other non-commercial uses permitted by copyright law.

To request permission to excerpt or to contact the author:
54 Wellington St. West, Sault Ste. Marie, Ontario, P6B 3Z1 Canada
Email: allkidscanthrive@gmail.com
Website: sheenalsmith.com

Published 2021
Printed in Canada
ISBN 978-1-7776219-0-2

All company and/or product names may be trade names, logos, trademarks, and/or registered trademarks and are the property of the respective owners. All Kids Can Thrive was written as a source of information, and should not be considered a substitute for advice, decisions, or judgement of a qualified mental health professional. This book does not dispense medical advice or prescribe the use of any technique as a form of treatment for physical or medical problems. The intent of the author is to offer you information to help you in your quest for a successful and conscious classroom.

All efforts have been made to attribute quotes, information, techniques to the correct source.

The author and publisher disclaim responsibility for any adverse effects arising from the use or application of the information contained within this book.

All links to websites and resources were working at the time of publication. If any links become inactive after publication we apologize in advance.

Website & Cover Design: Dalton Fluke
Portrait photo credit: anna@kevanna.com

This book is dedicated to Marianna

Also to all the other wonderful teachers and educators who are laying awake at night worrying and wondering how they can help a child solve a problem, have a better life, find their gifts, and believe in themselves. You are their reason for hope! Thank you for helping children thrive! Your efforts do not go unnoticed and are truly life-changing for future generations.

My beautiful friend knew the secret to helping a child thrive, as she put it best:

"Love is all that matters"

— TABLE OF CONTENTS —

CHAPTER 1: TEACH p. 15
- A. The New Education and Conscious Classroom Benefits
- B. The Future is NOW!
- C. The Whole Child Approach to Teaching
- D. Success, Social and Emotional Learning
- E. Your Emotions, Feelings and Those of Others
- F. Mindset: I can! I will! Watch me!
- G. Educate Me by Modeling: I Want You to Show Me the Way
- H. Rebel with Applause: Managing Disruptive Behaviour
- I. Reasons for Negative Behaviour: Communication Breakdown
- J. Social Skills: I Get by with a Little Help from My Friends
- K. Recess
- L. Responding versus Reacting
- M. Teach: It's Your Turn!

CHAPTER 2: HONOUR p. 47
- A. Honouring Your Students' Basic Needs
- B. Safety is the Key to Wellness
- C. All Systems Go!
- D. Polyvagal Theory
- E. The Six Ghosts of Fear
- F. How You Can Help a Grieving Child
- G. Culture and Heritage
- H. Making Sense of Sensory Needs
- I. Types of Sensory Needs
- J. Individual Preferences and Uniqueness
- K. Honour: It's Your Turn!

CHAPTER 3: RESPECT p. 85
- A. Judge Not! Meet the Needs!
- B. Mental Health Issues: A Rising Trend
- C. Anxiety and Children
- D. Calming Activities
- E. Be Grounded: Meditation
- F. Coping Skills
- G. Your Thoughts Can Control the Outcome
- H. Meet the Needs
- I. Learning Styles
- J. Universal Design for Learning
- K. Brain Dominance—Seriously, Learning Isn't All in Your Head!
- L. Multiple Intelligence Styles
- M. Sense of Belonging and Attachment
- N. Children Learn What They Live
- O. Respect: It's Your Turn!

CHAPTER 4: INSPIRE p. 112
- A. Courage, Confidence, Compassion and Inclusion
- B. How to Boost Your Confidence and Build Your Courage Muscles
- C. Inclusion versus Integration
- D. Teaching Styles and Classroom Management
- E. Class Environment: How to Have a Proactive and Well-Managed Classroom
- F. The Power of Focus
- G. Behaviour Planning and Prevention
- H. The Red Choice/Green Choice Booklet
- I. Positive Home and School Communication
- J. Goal-Setting and Class Culture
- K. Choices, Rules and Consequences
- L. Dealing with Negativity
- M. Resilience
- N. Inspire: It's Your Turn!

CHAPTER 5: VALUE p. 141
- A. Relationships and Connection: The Power of Thoughts
- B. The Value of Play, Movement, and Exercise
- C. Rhythmic Movement
- D. Top 10 Signs Your Brain is Running on a Paradigm
- E. Value Yourself: Self-Love
- F. Thoughts are Things: How to Love Yourself
- G. Self-care
- H. Burnout
- I. Value: It's Your Turn!

CHAPTER 6: ELEVATE AND EVOLVE THROUGH HOPE p. 165
- A. Begin Where You Are With What You Have
- B. Raise Your Vibration
- C. Happiness: It's Truly Your Choice
- D. Letting Go
- E. Ho'oponopono
- F. Emotional Freedom Technique
- G. Being an Empath and Expressing Empathy
- H. Tips for an Empath on Achieving Balance and Happiness
- I. Advice for an Empath: How to Help Yourself be Less Affected by Others and Manage Your Anxiety!
- J. Seek First to Understand Through Active Listening Skills
- K. Be Present. Develop Mindfulness: It's Your Gift to Yourself and Others
- L. Mastering Your Emotions to Empower Yourself
- M. Elevate: It's Your Turn!

REFERENCES AND RESOURCES p. 189

ACKNOWLEDGMENTS p. 206

— FOREWORD —

From the moment I met Sheena Smith in 2015, I knew I was in the presence of someone extraordinary. That meeting took place when she was a participant in a four-day retreat I was leading with Marci Shimoff, my co-founder of the personal growth phenomenon, Your Year of Miracles.

During the individual introductions I learned that this bright and gentle soul who had the same name as one of my favorite fictional characters of the 80's, Sheena, Queen of the Jungle, was an educator who cared as passionately about the children of the world as the fictional Sheena cared about the inhabitants of the wild.

As the retreat went on and there was more time to share, Sheena mentioned in her unassuming way that besides working in the Canadian school system, she has two step daughters and four children of her own, one with Down syndrome and one with spina bifida—oh, and in her spare time she went on humanitarian trips to Africa.

Sheena and I have become close over the ensuing years and I've watched her as she lovingly parents and grandparents her ever-growing brood. I especially marvel at her skill at raising her beautiful, fiercely independent daughter whose spina bifida hasn't stopped her from graduating from college and living on her own. I also can't help but smile whenever I think of the smart, funny, mischievous, creative, and curious Connor whose Down syndrome is no barrier for Sheena and her husband to make sure he is unconditionally cherished and given every possible opportunity to thrive.

Sheena wrote this book based on her own experience over the last four decades raising not only her own children to be compassionate, kind and self-aware human beings and her experience with the thousands of other children she has nurtured as they moved through the various institutional and educational systems where Sheena has worked or volunteered.

The conclusion Sheena has come to is that truly all kids can thrive if given the proper guidance and love, and if they are surrounded by adults who model the types of behavior they'd like to see in those entrusted to their care.

All Kids Can Thrive is also filled with specifics.

Sheena has done extensive research and shares time-tested tools and techniques that educators (and parents!) can use to help children to flourish. Those include being mindful and respectful of others, reaching out to those with differences, being self-aware, developing critical thinking, being effective communicators, exhibiting emotional competence, and believing in themselves.

Perhaps even more importantly, she also offers ways that educators can create environments where our young ones feel honoured and respected for exactly who they are.

In my own life, I remember the day that my brother received his acceptance letter in the mail from Harvard University. The children of immigrants, neither of my parents had ever gone to college. Harvard was a big deal. Yet as various aunts and uncles, neighbors and friends, came over to congratulate my parents on raising a son who would soon but on his way to the #1 University in the U.S. my mother's response was, as always, about me and my brother, "As long as they are good human beings, that's all I ask."

At a time when our educational system and our world as a whole desperately need people for our children to look up to who exhibit positive behaviors like taking responsibility for their choices, mastering their emotions, seeking to understand, speaking the truth, and practicing forgiveness, we have the ultimate handbook for becoming those people in All Kids Can Thrive.

We are also fortunate to have the ultimate role model in Sheena Smith, who, in my humble opinion, is the embodiment of a good human being.

Enjoy your journey of personal growth through the pages of this amazing book and thank you for your desire to contribute to the future of our planet through enriching the lives of our precious children.

Debra Poneman
Bestselling author, Award-Winning Speaker and Founder,
Yes to Success, Inc.

— INTRODUCTION —

"I shall pass this way but once; any good that I can do or kindness I can show to any human being; Let me not defer, nor neglect, for I shall not pass this way again."
— Stephen (Etienne) Grellet, Quaker missionary

I have worked with children for 40 years and, for as long as I can remember, I always wanted to teach. I love being with kids, they are amazing to observe, so perfect and delightful to be around. I began my journey as a Child and Youth Worker and through placements and job opportunities I gained experience in many different settings including day care centres, the adolescent girls' unit of a psychiatric hospital, a detention centre, group homes for youth, and a children's aid receiving home. Later on, I became a Special Educational Assistant and have continued to work in this role for over 20 years.

I have devoted my life to discovering tools to enable my children, my daughter who was born with spina bifida and my son with Down syndrome, and my students to be the best possible version of themselves. I've left no stone unturned. I've taken courses, seminars, and training around the world, all with the aim of helping children thrive. Along the way, I also learned that my own self-care, self-love and higher states of consciousness were essential pieces of the puzzle.

There were often times in the beginning that I forgot myself. I was constantly putting the needs of my students and my children first. I was burnt out, tired, exhausted and found myself living a life of daily pain. Depression and disconnect were the result. When I learned the value of self-care and implemented it miracles happened. Complete miracles! This is possible for you as well. It is my hope that by learning and implementing the strategies and techniques described in this book you will find new ways to connect with students while implementing deep levels of self-care for yourself so that you may experience the true joys of teaching.

When my daughter was born, the doctors painted a grim future—she wouldn't walk, there might be brain damage; there would be surgeries and lots of challenges. I was positive that was not how our story would go. I knew that there had to be answers and more possibilities for potential. I counted on miracles, prayer and my own determination that this wasn't how her story would unfold. I knew my child would survive, and more than that, she would thrive. In that dimly lit, slightly chilly hospital, I held her perfect dainty little hand through the tube of the incubator. She was recovering from her first surgery, performed less than 24 hours after she was born. In that moment, looking at her darling face, I made a promise that I would do everything and anything to help her experience life to the fullest potential. That beautiful baby is now a college graduate, and a young lady living on her own, pursuing her dreams. We are so blessed! I am so proud of her! She inspires me as much today as the day I made the promise to do my best.

My sweet friend Marianna was a teacher that led with her heart. Sadly, she passed away in July 2014 and will be forever missed by the many students who loved, treasured and adored her. She was a well-respected teacher who elevated so many students through her wisdom, encouragement and belief in their abilities. She believed in them until they believed in themselves. Marianna was one to build a student's self-esteem. She truly appreciated their efforts and she valued their cultures, learning styles and interests. She engaged students and made learning fun. She was able to make each student feel wanted, safe, and welcome. She encouraged each child to participate to the best of their ability. She was great at adapting and modifying lesson plans. Without knowing it, Marianna embraced Shelley Moore's bowling analogy for education and aimed for the outside pins, enabling her to reach everyone. While she seemed to be a unique and one-of-a-kind teacher, I know that with conscious efforts we can all be that great teacher, that great educational assistant, educator, or support staff member. We can all show unconditional love and appreciation. Marianna knew how to develop and maintain relationships and connection. Her students will remember her kindness and selfless generosity forever. My dear friend was an inspiration; this book is dedicated to her.

In her book, **Happy for No Reason**, my mentor Marci Shimoff says, "The best way to keep relationships happy, healthy, and supportive can be summed up in one word: appreciation. What you appreciate, appreciates. When we demonstrate our appreciation for the support we receive from others, it reinforces that behaviour and deepens our connection to them."

This book asks you to consider the whole child: mind, body, spirit, emotional capacities, their unique learning styles and abilities. By truly appreciating them for who they are, you will empower them to shine, to bring out the best in themselves, to want to discover, learn more and grow in their own knowledge and understanding. You get to be part of igniting their spirit! To me, that's inspiring and exciting. At the start of my day, I will often say a little prayer, "God, please, show me how to serve today. Show me how I can inspire and lift someone up today." Some days I'm handed really tough assignments, others days it's as easy as simply smiling at someone.

Both my son's and my daughter's conditions put me on the true path of discovery. In looking for answers to best help them, I also began a journey of self-discovery. The answers I found for myself, and for my children, can also immensely benefit children within the school system. It's no secret that education has changed over the years and we are in a new era—a time where the world is rapidly changing. Old school methods of teaching are outdated. It's crazy to hear that the jobs that exist now may no longer be the same when the younger generation grows up. Where will they begin? More importantly where shall we begin? Begin with the end in mind. Begin with where the child is at, right now. Begin with teaching the whole child: mind, body and spirit. Begin with you where you are at right now. Begin with this book—may it help you to find your bliss, deepen your happiness and sharpen your strengths so that you, and the children you teach, can truly thrive.

CHAPTER 1 - TEACH

"We cannot teach people anything, we can only help them to discover it within themselves." Galileo Galilei

Have you had enough stress?

Overload, overwhelm, frustration, and an ever-present feeling of being underappreciated define the environment that so many teachers and support staff live within day in and day out. No wonder employee burnout rates are so high. Teachers spend far too much time managing negative behaviour.

Work-related health issues, stress-related depression and discontent are commonplace. Principal's offices have become the place to moan, whine and vent frustrations. Staff rooms have become complaint departments. Students are left behind despite programs and suggested strategies to enhance their educational curriculum experiences.

There is worry, doubt, fear and dread of each day. Just walking through the school doors can cause anxiety and stress. Not just as a result of interactions with students but also with teachers, educational assistants, and other support staff. Although the problem may seem like an outward one, it can be managed inwardly by conscious choices. There are laws of success that can be implemented by you to allow you to have your ideal day, your dream classroom and positive interactions with students who are eager to learn. By choosing your thoughts consciously, and actively employing conscious behaviours, you will make a difference that will change your life and the lives of your students both now and in their future. This is exciting!

Did you catch yourself agreeing with any of the above? Were you commenting in your head with positive or negative thoughts? Were you thinking: "How can I add anything else in my day? My school doesn't have funding for anything extra! We do not have time for anything else! I can barely think as it is!" Perhaps you even went a step further: "Kids don't care. They show up because they must. There's nothing that I can do. I've tried everything!"

I get you! I feel your frustration and disappointment in the systems. As someone who has worked with children of all abilities for over 40 years (20 years within the education system) I have seen the changes through the years first hand. Cultures are changing. Systems are changing. Our education system is changing. Know this—there truly is a better way and I can show you how it is possible through the suggestions outlined in this book.

You can have your spirit renewed along with your faith and belief that schools are the best place for children to learn skills, connect, interact with others and be loved unconditionally for who they are. Your class can go from chaos to calm. You can have a conscious-based classroom. And the best part is that it all begins with you! You can be the person that makes a difference and helps a child thrive. Are you ready for some fun?

All kids deserve a chance to have an environment that is set up to provide them with success, growth and learning. You have a valuable role in their life to do just that. You are their mentor, their role model and their teacher. You are also their protector and provider of unconditional love.

Many of the tips, strategies and tools that I feature in this book are not new, although they may be new to you. They are science-based, time-tested tools that have been proven to work effectively. My hope is that by compiling them into one resource, you as a teacher, support worker or educational assistant, will be able to apply these tools and see how you can help a child thrive.

A. The New Education and Conscious Classroom Benefits

"One looks back with appreciation to the brilliant teachers, but with gratitude to those who touched our human feelings. The curriculum is so much necessary raw material, but warmth is the vital element for the growing plant and for the soul of the child." - Carl Jung, psychiatrist and psychoanalyst

I look forward to possibilities! Although some may think it's scary to look towards the future and see how a classroom is going to evolve, I feel optimistic and curious to see how things will unfold. The successful teachers will be those that are prepared for the changes.

Ch. 1: Teach

Cathy N. Davidson has written an interesting book entitled ***The New Education:*** *How to Revolutionize the University to Prepare Students for a World in Flux*[1]. She is a founding director of the Futures Initiative and a professor in the Doctoral English Program at the CUNY Graduate Centre. Davidson traveled to universities to study what educators were doing to revamp education to make it more adaptable, creative, collaborative and flexible for students to learn and thrive in our ever-changing society. I believe these changes in teaching need to be implemented earlier than university, so that children can develop emotional intelligence, an understanding of learning styles, communication skills, problem solving skills and self-awareness.

Davidson pointed out that while Google is most widely identified as a company that would want you to be highly trained in STEM subjects—science, technology, engineering and mathematics—a recent study of their employees showed that there are other soft skills that are more valuable for success in the company's workplace. Essential soft skills listed for employees' success included effective communication, active listening, and problem-solving abilities. Knowing how to be a critical thinker, being open-minded, understanding different values, views, and opinions were also highly valued.

Children need to be socially and emotionally competent in core areas: they need to have self-awareness and social awareness; they must be able to regulate emotions, and have the knowledge of basic relationship skills. They also require the know-how for proper decision-making with regards to safety, ethics, respect for self and others. That is a great deal to know and learn, it cannot begin being taught only at the university level. These abilities and skills are learned throughout one's life at home and at school. In the following pages I share some essential tools and suggestions to help you bring these skills into your classroom.

---

[1] Davidson, Cathy N. *The New Education: How to Revolutionize the University to Prepare Students for a World in Flux*, New York, Basic Books, 2017.

[2] Strauss, Valerie. *"The surprising thing Google learned about its employees—and what it means for today's students."* The Washington Post. December 20, 2017. www.washingtonpost.com/news/answer-sheet/wp/2017/12/20/the-surprising-thing-google-learned-about-its-employees-and-what-it-means-for-todays-students/

B. The Future is NOW!

"Education is the passport to the future, for tomorrow belongs to those who prepare for it today." - Malcolm X

I would like to think that anyone teaching or working with children and adolescents has the ultimate goal of helping them become the best version of themselves, so that the students can go out into the world prepared and resilient enough to face life's challenges and adversities with strength, wisdom, and the innate knowingness that life is good and that it supports them to grow and live happy and fulfilling lives.

Up until now, education has mostly been designed to create labor force workers. This is no longer the way it will be. By 2030 the current kindergarteners will be graduating, and they need to be life-ready not work-ready. New research states that students will have a better future if they have strong social and emotional foundations.

Here's what the McKinsey Global Institute has to say: "The fastest growing occupations will require higher level cognitive skills in areas such as problem solving, critical thinking, and creativity, and 30 to 40 percent of jobs will require explicit social-emotional skills ... globally, about half the work people are paid to do today could be automated by existing technology by 2030, and up to 375 million people may need to switch occupational categories between now and then."[3]

---

[3] Microsoft and McKinsey & Company's Education Practice. *"The class of 2030 and life-ready learning: The technology imperative."* A Summary Report: edudownloads.azureedge.net/msdownloads/13679_EDU_Thought_Leadership_Summary_revisions_5.10.18.pdf

Research from multiple sources, surveys of 2000 teachers and 2000 students in Canada, Singapore, the United Kingdom and the United States. This research paper included in-depth interviews with over 70 thought leaders, including educators, policy makers, researchers and technologists. It is also part of an in-depth review of 150 articles of existing research. To get the White Paper: info.microsoft.com/ww-landing-McKinsey-Class-Of-2030-Whitepaper.html?lcid=en-us

Ch. 1: Teach

The development of people skills is critical. Teachers play a priceless role in this change. Education will become more personalized learning, centred on the student. There will be more focus on the student's ability to make choices, discover and reach their potential. Teachers will be more like coaches guiding and motivating students to their greatness within.

Methods of teaching should meet the needs of the student through a variety of experiences in a more active-learning environment: personalized learning for deeper understanding, project-based learning, inquiry-based learning, challenge-based learning, phenomenon-based (real life) learning. This will be a huge change from the traditional subject-based learning we are used to in our Western world. The assessment is no longer based on a final result but is based upon the process throughout. Finland has already implemented some of these changes to their education system and the world is watching.

Jobs of the future will include software developers, care providers, and construction workers. There will be less office support staff, less clerks, less production workers, and less equipment operators.

Soft skills will be woven into learning programs and there will be a switch from standardized teaching to student centred with the use of technology programs. Grading and assessments will be more automated. Students will experience their learning through our physical world and virtual reality world. They will connect more with students across the world.

A current example of this mixed reality model of learning can be found at Lifeliqe. This is a science-based curriculum for visual learners that features 3D-reality experiences and over 700 lesson plans that increase cognitive growth and enhance social and emotional growth. There is no doubt that more and more of these programs will become a big part of the future. Children can be and do anything they choose to be. Technology has changed the present and future potential to create unlimited possibilities for our children.

---

[4] *"How is Finland building schools of the future?"* QS Asia News Network. April 19, 2018. qswownews.com/finland-building-schools-future/

[5] For more information visit: lifeliqe.com

C. The Whole Child Approach to Teaching

"Showing our humanness is key to developing those relationships with our students. And relationships matter. They are foundational to learning."
- Rebecca Alber, Edutopia consulting editor

Education researcher Maria del Carmen Salazar, PhD, is an Associate Professor of the Teaching and Learning Sciences and Teacher Education Program at the University of Denver's Morgridge College of Education. She has authored numerous publications on culturally responsive teaching and effective, equitable teaching. She has developed theories and practices of teaching humanness within the teaching for success. Salazar suggests four ways to improve interactions and relationships with students.

1. Listen to the students with regards to their interests and concerns. Check in with them to get their views and opinions. Children want to feel like they belong. Help create a sense of community for them.

2. Be aware of the home lives of your students and check in frequently with how each child is doing. It gives you an opportunity to build rapport and assist children with feelings and emotions they might be experiencing through empathy, compassion and genuine caring. Noticing and getting to know when a child is out of sorts is important.

3. Model qualities that show you care and respect the child: kindness, respect, and patience. Keep a calm voice and tone. Refrain from using sarcasm and try to be fair. Do your best to keep everyone's dignity intact.
I cannot tell you how many times I have witnessed a teacher tearing a child down with blunt sarcasm and disrespect. Children need to be seen and understood. As a child, I felt very invisible and can only remember a few teachers who attempted to engage me in conversations to show me that I was valued and an important part of the class.

4. Check in daily to see how students are feeling. A check-in list or chart is a useful tool. You could use a visual chart showing pictures of emotions. Some teachers use paper plates with actual pictures of children displaying the particular emotion (anger is illustrated with an angry face, for example). Children then attach a clothespin with their name to the emotion that they are feeling at the time. Ask how the child is feeling and what they need to feel better. Share how you are feeling too, it allows children to see your humanness too.

5. Allow frequent movement breaks to raise energy levels. Doing a mini dance-a-thon frequently is great for stretching and energizing.[6]

Build strong foundations and then get moving!

D. Success, Social and Emotional Learning

"Empathy and social skills are social intelligence, the interpersonal part of emotional intelligence. That's why they look alike." - Daniel Goleman, author and science journalist

More and more research is proving that for children to have success in school and in life they need to be supported in the areas of self-awareness, self-management, and social awareness. They also need to have relationship skills and problem-solving abilities.

These skills can be learned with practice, through modeled behaviour and interactions with others. Essential social skills include learning to listen (understanding not just responding), exhibiting empathy and showing compassion. Understanding how to resolve problems, conflict resolution, and effective communication are also important.

Learning to resolve problems relates to issues that need to be solved or answered. The need for conflict resolution arises from differences in perceptions, ideas, opinions, and the motivation of others. Strategies for conflict resolution can vary from a stance of co-operation to a stance of un-cooperation. These strategies may include: defeat (or avoidance) where one has given up and/or avoids the issue. It's not an ideal strategy because the issue is not resolved. Accommodation is less than an ideal solution too because although it may keep the peace so to speak it still may leave issues unresolved. The strategy of competition is also less than optimal as a choice because the aim becomes just to win and get one's own way. Collaboration is the most effective strategy for a win-win. This method shows true leadership where each is contributing and co-creating together.

---

[6] Alber, Rebecca. *"Embracing the Whole Child"*, Edutopia. March 12, 2018, www.edutopia.org/article/embracing-whole-child

The term "emotional intelligence" was originally coined and defined in a 1964 paper written by Michael Beldoch. Two psychologists, Peter Salovey and John Mayer later published an article in a small academic journal that outlined their formulation for emotional intelligence. The concept of emotional intelligence gained popularity in the 1990's when Dan Goleman, a science reporter at the *New York Times* released his book **Emotional Intelligence** in 1995.

Emotional intelligence (EI) or emotional quotient (EQ) is defined as "the capacity of individuals to recognize their own, and other people's emotions, to discriminate between different feelings and label them appropriately, to use emotional information to guide thinking and behaviours, and to manage and/or adjust emotions to adapt to environments or achieve one's goal(s)." [7]

Supporting social and emotional learning (SEL) and development is the key to the success of a child and is also instrumental in the success of other programs including violence prevention, anti-bullying, character development, leadership-skill building, drug prevention and school discipline programs. SEL is the umbrella that arches over all the others. In a school setting, social and emotional learning are not just used with the goal of reducing and eliminating problems, it is also a vital tool for improving the overall climate and environment of the school.

I believe many schools are realizing the value and benefits of programs that support social and emotional development and learning. In fact, schools around the U.S. and Canada are adding these social and emotional learning support programs as part of their day. One program that I highly recommend is called "Leader in Me", designed as a whole child approach to assist students in becoming life ready. It is an evidence based approach with proven teaching methods, classroom techniques and social and emotional learning systems. My current school is the only "Lighthouse" school in our city that offers this program at this time. I am excited about the future potential of a whole school community of children raised on this proactive approach to developing students to be competent in critical thinking, learn valuable leadership skills, self-management, self-awareness, relationship building and empowerment through goal setting. It enables the learners to work through their paradigms. Find out more at leaderinme.org.

---

[7] *"Emotional Intelligence."* Wikipedia, Last modified December 21, 2020, en.wikipedia.org/wiki/Emotional_intelligence

Ch. 1: Teach

"If you want small changes work, on your behaviour; if you want quantum leap changes, work on your paradigms" - Stephen R. Covey

I love how researchers are discovering more and more about how the brain works and how learning is affected by the ability (or inability) to self-regulate emotions and control behaviours. They are realizing it is more than simply self-control and the old "he can do better if he tried" style of teaching. The brain under stress freezes and the child cannot do better even if he wishes to do so.

Goleman says: "In 1995 I also proposed that a good part of the effectiveness of SEL came from its impact in shaping children's developing neural circuitry, particularly the executive functions of the prefrontal cortex, which manage working memory—what we hold in mind as we learn—and inhibit disruptive emotional impulses. Now the first preliminary scientific evidence for that notion has arrived. Mark T. Greenberg of Pennsylvania State University, a co-developer of the PATHS curriculum in SEL, reports not only that the program for elementary school students boasts academic achievement but, even more significantly, that much of the increased learning can be attributed to improvements in attention and working memory, key functions of the prefrontal cortex. This strongly suggests that neuroplasticity, the shaping of the brain through repeated experience, plays a key role in the benefits from SEL."

The success of programs designed to enhance social emotional learning is dependent upon more than just the program. True success is based on the person teaching the skills.

Children need to be shown how to become calm and manage their emotions. At age appropriate levels of understanding, they need to be presented with how to recognize their own unique strengths, emotions, and abilities through self-awareness. Next, they need to understand how to manage these emotions; especially the powerful negatives ones. They need to know how to control their behaviour and understand their behaviour patterns.

---

[8] Goleman, Daniel. www.danielgoleman.info/topics/emotional-intelligence/

Linda Lantieri is the Director of the Inner Resilience Program. It was created for parents and teachers in response to the needs of students following the traumatic events of September 11, 2001 in New York City. The program focuses highly on the self-care and wellness of the teachers in order to support the resilience and inner strength of children. With over 40 years' experience with education, mindfulness and SEL programs, Lantieri is a member of CASEL[9] (Collaborative for Academics Social, and Emotional Learning). She has also written a book entitled **Building Emotional Intelligence: Techniques to Cultivate Inner Strength in Children**.[10] She highly stresses the value of children knowing how to manage their emotions, becoming calm while learning to identify and manage how they are feeling. The principles outlined in Lantieri's book are based on modern brain research. She teaches self-regulation through exercises that are designed for each developmental stage. Although social emotional learning is developed from the outside through interactions and experiences with others, it can be a powerful complementary tool to the discovery and implementation of mindfulness, which is an inside job.

---

[9] *Casel: Collaborative for Academic, Social, and Emotional Learning (CASEL)*. I have included a free guide in the resources section.

"Educating Hearts. Inspiring Minds" is the motto on the CASEL website. They have a guide that lists programs they have approved as valuable and beneficial for use with students. It contains information on over 25 approved programs. To be included they must be well-designed classroom-based programs that support students socially and emotionally. The programs must allow for the student to practice and grow throughout their school years. Training must be provided. Each program recommended in the guide must be supported by an evidence-based report supporting its value through evidence of students experiencing positive results behaviourally and/or academically.

The approaches of teaching SEL have changed over time. Initially, teachers simply taught a lesson about the emotion and social behaviours. Now there is more of a blend of academic content and social and emotional learning. Others use instructional teaching and classroom management teaching techniques to set the environment for educational learning, social and emotional development. Methods include modeling and coaching students to recognize their feelings and emotions through the use of games, sports and interactions that involve teamwork and cooperation. One such group interaction could entail involving all students, teachers and support staff with the setting of rules together to support having an environment of mutual respect of self and others. Involving parents is important too to maintain communication and discuss the strengths, weaknesses and areas to focus growth on.

[10] Lantieri, Linda. *Building Emotional Intelligence: Techniques to Cultivate Inner Strength in Children*, Sounds True, 2008

Ch. 1: Teach

E. Your Emotions, Feelings and Those of Others

"When you control your thoughts and emotions you control everything."
- Marshall Sylver, motivational speaker and author

In Redwood City, California at the Summit Preparatory Charter High School students from Grades 9-12 attend a class with a program of developing systematic habits of success as well as social and emotional learning skills. It's called HCC (Habits, Community, and Culture) class and is designed to increase respectful community building and cultural understanding. Students have routine practices of starting their day with visualization and mindfulness. Parts of the curriculum include a variety of activities that are engaging, interesting and foster friendships and communication. Some of the activities include:

1. Sharing an emotion. Students take turns stating in one word how they are feeling at the current moment.

2. Writing away your stress. Students draw or write down what's bothering them, rip it up and throw it out.

3. They also engage in an activity that I call "Triple 'A' sharing". At the end of the class each student is invited to share their "a-ha" moment from the day, something they appreciate about someone, an appreciation from their day's learning or an apology to someone. The others are encouraged to snap their finger if it resonates with them as well. If it is emotionally charged, they also shake it off by shaking both hands and releasing the energy.

4. Sharing a baby photo. Students bring in baby pictures of themselves and tell something about their childhoods. [11]

---

[11] For the full article, view: www.edutopia.org/article/13-powerful-sel-activities-emelina-minero

F. Mindset: I can! I will! Watch me!

"Everyone is a genius. But if you judge a fish by its ability to climb a tree, it will live its whole life believing that it is stupid." - Albert Einstein

Carol Dweck, author of **The New Psychology of Success**[12] coined the term "growth mindset". A mindset of growth is how students perceive their ability; it plays a huge role in how motivated they are to achieve. Dweck's research shows that when a student believes intelligence can be developed, they do better than those who have a fixed mindset and believe their intelligence and ability to learn can't be changed. Those with a growth mindset understand that, more than hard work and effort, it's important to attempt new strategies when necessary and seek assistance and advice from others. It's okay to ask for help.

Model a positive mindset yourself

You can help your students grow their mindsets by encouraging them and asking discovery questions such as: "You did it this way and it didn't turn out as you wished it would. What is another way that you can try it?" The fun in asking these types of questions is that you are encouraging your students to understand that there is always a way and that there is more than one way to achieve a goal. This mindset empowers students to keep doing their best and striving for the success they want. Problems and setbacks then become opportunities for creativity and brainstorming.

There are many successful people that faced challenges and kept on going. Look up their stories and see what they overcame to make history. Some of these history makers include: Albert Einstein, Thomas Edison, Martin Luther King Jr., Steve Jobs, Nelson Mandela, and Mother Teresa. Make sure to share their stories with your students!

When a student is struggling with a setback be understanding and empathetic to their feelings of disappointment. Tell your own stories of setbacks and challenges. Create a sense of optimism for them. It helps them to see your humanness and they will relate to you as a role model.

---

[12] Dweck, Carol. *The New Psychology of Success* (New York, Ballantine Books: Reprint, Updated Edition, 2007).

Ch. 1: Teach

Provide a safe and positive learning environment. The environment needs to be calm. Calmness is created by your own sense of calm. Children are so great at picking up the energy of others.

Talk with your students about fixed and growth mindsets. With a fixed mindset, you get stuck and decide you can't learn or succeed. Teach students to be mindful of making excuses. Whatever they are telling themselves may not be true. It might be a perception that they believe because of a past experience or event. A fixed mindset is okay in balance but not necessarily when it shuts you off from achievement.

Develop a routine for the end of your school day where the students use a success journal to record the successful moments of their day. Here are a few examples of starting lines:

- What I liked most about today …
- What I learned today that I enjoyed …
- My favourite part of the day was …
- Three things that I'm happy about today are …

I encourage students to use a different starting line each day.

The students taking the HCC class that I detailed a few pages ago are also asked to complete a "success folder", detailing what they learned, the wisdom they gained, what they accomplished, as well as what they are proud of as they reflect on the day's activities. It can be done digitally but I believe that it is more powerful to write or draw it out. There is power in the written word when it is expressed in its positive form too.

Another powerful form of appreciation can happen verbally. This is an activity that I learned from Marci Shimoff and Debra Poneman during the Your Year of Miracles self-development program. The exercise is designed to show appreciation for each other, and is an excellent morale booster during a staff meeting, at home with your family, and even in the classroom. One person starts by completing the phrase: "What I appreciate about you is …" and listing a few characteristics about the person. (Examples would be: What I appreciate about you is your ability to actively listen. What I appreciate about you is how you helped me clean up that mess in the classroom. What I appreciate about you is the way that you smile at me every time I walk in the door.) Using the same phrase, the next person then describes the person who has just spoken.

Teachable moments happen all the time. When you hear a student putting themselves down, help them understand how valued they are and how important they are to your class.

Discuss feelings, what it's like to be challenged and how to find other solutions. Share how great it feels to meet your goals, solve your problems, and discover answers through new strategies and exploration. Feel the feelings of excitement, happiness and joy! Bam! Success creates a rise in positive vibrational energy.

Do not give up! Lisa Nichols[13], motivational speaker and author of **Abundance Now** encourages her audiences to have a reset button that gives you 1000 chances. When you get to effort number 999, press your imaginary reset button and go again. Revamp your plan if you need to, but don't give up. Keep going! Quitting is not an option. Rest, but do not quit!

With a growth mindset, you can discover that your choices, attitude and behaviours can and will transform your life and experiences. This is true for you, the teacher, and for your students. Take on challenges and persist until you are successful. Be willing to wonder, to let your creative juices flow. As you celebrate your wins and the wins of your students you raise self-worth and empower the students with the knowledge that they can do anything if they set their minds to it.

A fixed mindset makes me wonder if it is actually "fixed" (rigid) or if it is functioning in survival mode and unable to access other areas of the brain for input. For example, when criticized, a person with a fixed mindset may become angry or upset at you rather than accepting feedback and input. They won't use this as an opportunity for growth and allow another person to have their own opinion without judgment. Your brain can get stuck in a fixed mindset. If you are in a fight or flight mode it is hard to access your frontal lobes where you can draw upon your skills of reasoning.

---

[13] Lisa is the founder and CEO of Motivating the Masses. She is an incredible storyteller and speaker. Her journey to abundance and wealth is an inspiring one. Check her out at: www.abundancenowonline.com

[14] Nichols, Lisa. *Abundance Now* (New York, Dey Street Books, 2016).

Ch. 1: Teach

A child who has been criticized or felt put down may accept the negative as truth and hang onto it. The condition becomes chronic and often the child is continuously operating from this mode. This, in turn, will affect learning confidence and future self-esteem, which can then develop into a fixed mindset where they will avoid trying new skills and learning. It is crucial to trust and let the child know they are safe. When you help a child to feel secure, they can more easily operate in other areas of the brain rather than fall back into survival mode, which wants them to be on guard to be ready to fight or run. With your guidance and modeling they can learn how to discuss, question and discover.

A child can sense how you feel about them based upon your body language, your energy that you are emitting, your posture, tone of voice and avoid use of finger pointing at the child as you are stressing your point. Your disapproval can be devastating. These actions hurt and go straight to a child's spirit. Over time the repeated actions can potentially crush a child's spirit, causing them to shut down and harbour feelings of low self-worth. This can lead a child to develop beliefs about themselves, usually negative ones, such as I am bad, I am dumb, I am not worthy, and I can't learn.

Children are intuitive, and they know if you like them or not. They feel your energy and react to it in a variety of ways from shutting down to defiance, disruptive behaviours and exhibiting a negative attitude. Building a positive rapport with children and having open discussions helps them to understand mindset and communication.

Teaching and building positive mindset skills can begin at an early age. Modeling is the first way children learn. Help children to have positive self-talk and to know that our habits create what we see. Teach them to be kind to themselves as they would to a good friend.

The brain is very fascinating; so much is still unknown about how it operates. The incredible discovery of recent times is neuroplasticity, which means that it is capable of changing during a person's entire life. Neuroplasticity is exciting because it is about the brain's ability to reorganize itself through new connections and new neural pathways. Creation of these pathways compensates for injuries, disorders, and diseases. Some of the ways that neuroplasticity changes happen are through behaviour, environmental stimuli, neural processes, even your thoughts and emotions. Again this is why mindset and understanding cognitive dissonance are important. Cognitive dissonance is when you experience discomfort due to having a discrepancy between your behaviour and your thoughts/beliefs.

When you are able to change your thoughts, your behaviour changes, and the brain will do what it can to assist with resolving the inconsistencies, enabling you to feel more content and calm. Keeping your brain active, enjoying activities that require focused attention and having new experiences are important for changes. For example: some activities that are beneficial if you or your student is experiencing anxiety include: crosswords and memory games, yoga, juggling, and mild to moderate exercise. Even learning a new language is believed to be helpful! The reorganization within the brain happens in response to movement and activity. Learning, memory, recovery from a brain injury and healthy development are also associated with activity-dependent plasticity.

Interestingly enough, a growth mindset and neuroplasticity are two concepts that mirror each other. Growth mindset consists of using approaches of positivity, possibility, and determination that create new pathways. Neuroplasticity is the ability to reorganize through creating new pathways. I have a child with Down syndrome and I find the latest research to be fascinating and encouraging. This is unlike the old mindsets of 25 years ago where it was believed that children with special needs couldn't learn and they were put in institutions. People never knew their potential because they weren't given opportunities. Children were stuck in playpens and had limited stimulation; they weren't provided the appropriate environment to flourish, grow and develop properly or to their potential.

The future is bright for so many individuals. I know people with illnesses associated with brain loss and memory loss. This research is exciting and it is only the beginning!

G. Educate Me by Modeling: I Want You to Show Me the Way

"Example isn't another way to teach, it is the only way to teach."
- Albert Einstein

As a teacher, your job is to educate by drawing out and allowing the child to develop to their full potential through inner knowing, skills, and talents. Two Latin words are represented in 'education': educare (to train or mold) and educere (to draw out or lead).

How does a teacher, educational assistant, or support worker do this?

Ch. 1: Teach

There are many ways, especially if you teach in a way that supports your students' learning styles and types of intelligence. Everything will be explained in greater detail in the following chapters.

The first step in helping a child is to teach by example. It is, therefore, critical that you be happy, content, and grounded. In order to feel this way, it is important to make yourself a priority and ensure that your needs are being met. Times are challenging for teachers; not only are we working full-time, many of us are running households and raising our own children. Self-care must be practiced on a regular basis to maintain balance in your life to avoid burnout.

For children to learn by example they need to see you caring for and about yourself. Self-care is not being greedy or selfish. It's just like when you are on an airplane, you need to put your own oxygen mask on first before you can help anyone else.

In a school setting you have many opportunities to model throughout the day. You can model communication, positive behaviour, the value of having a good attitude, coping skills, respect for belongings and others, resilience and ways to bounce back from setbacks, flexibility, appreciation, forgiveness, consistency, fairness, safety, character values, responsibility for choices, opportunities for reflection, self-discovery, and participation as a way to feel valued and loved as part of your class.

Often children have to be shown how to behave and act through repeated situations and practice. The "Model Me Kids" video series[15] is effective, evidence-based material for students with Autism, Asperger syndrome, developmental delays, and for younger students, to show social skills, turn taking, working as a team and how to wait in the context of a variety of school settings. These videos are great to use with the whole class. It's a great rainy day filler with a very useful purpose!

For all these teachable moments to be recognized and modeled without causing yourself complete exhaustion and burn out you need to be very kind to yourself. Make quality self-care a daily priority (more on this later).

---

[15] *Model Me*™ : Evidence-based modeling resources for children with autism shows improvement in social competence and a decrease in behaviour that is considered anti-social. For more information visit: www.modelmekids.com/index.html

H. Rebel with Applause: Managing Disruptive Behaviour

"Behind very challenging behaviour is an unsolved problem or lagging skill."- Ross Greene, PhD, author of **Lost at School**

Have you ever had a student whose behaviour demanded your attention and took you away from teaching a lesson to students who were interested in learning? Has this particular student done it time and time again: interrupted your class and caused you to become frustrated, annoyed and even angry? Did you think to yourself "How dare this child disrupt my class? Who do they think they are?" How mad did you get? Did you decide to ignore them only to discover they got louder and more disruptive?

As the late Wayne Dyer said: "When we change the way we look at things, things change."

This attention-seeking behaviour is usually the result of a child who is unable to express themselves appropriately. Rather than looking at it as "attention seeking", reframe it as "connection seeking"; this can give you a whole new lens to view the situation. Teachers and educators encounter communication problems daily. Communication challenges exist with mainstream children as well as those with special needs. I've learned that things are often not always as they seem—acting out isn't just for attention, although it may seem like it is. So many are looking for love and connection. Relationships with your students are a valuable resource.

I'm sure you have heard that behaviour is communication. The mystery then becomes what is the child trying to say? That's where your role as a teacher comes in.

When the behaviour occurs, you get to be a detective. Ask yourself: why are they speaking out, acting out, misbehaving? What is the student attempting to avoid or escape? In a conscious classroom setting you can use your intuition as a lead as to why they are behaving as they are. The reasons can be numerous, or it can boil down to something simple such as the student didn't get a turn at something they thought they should have. It might be a perception of injustice or unfairness on their part. It's great when you can ask a child what's going on and they are able to answer you. But, even when a child can verbalize, what they are saying isn't always the true reason. Knowing your students is important: what matters to them, what they love, and what motivates them. Know what they are experiencing in their home lives and their school environment.

Ch. 1: Teach

Apart from avoidance or escape, one reason students act out is that they don't understand the lesson being taught. Rather than admit to it and possibly embarrass themselves in front of their peers, children will act out in attention-seeking ways.

Some children act out or become the class clown simply to be noticed; any attention in their mind is better than no attention. Children might also be affected by certain medications. Depending upon their age, they could also be doing drugs that are not prescribed. A child could also be having a problem with a peer who is doing something to distract or annoy the child behind your back.

Have they had breakfast? Do they need to go to the bathroom? Gas! Is it gas?

They also could be having problems at home or at recess that is drawing their focus away from the lesson. What are you noticing? Is it happening at the same time every day? Only on certain days? During one specific topic or multiple topics? Sometimes it may seem that there is no reason ... but there is almost always a reason. What could it be? The most common functions of behaviour are: attention, escape, wanting a tangible item, and self-stimulation.

Throughout this book, you will see that I highly stress 'noticing'. By being present you can often discover what's going on with a child that is exhibiting negative behaviour. The simple A-B-C model[16] is beneficial to follow and can help to detect trends and commonalities to outbursts of negative behaviours and aggression.

A. Antecedent: What happened just before the behaviour occurred? What triggered this situation?
B. Behaviour: What was the reaction? What is the child attempting to say through his behaviour?

---

[16] The A-B-C (Antecedent-Behaviour-Consequence) model is a simple tool to use to explore behaviours and triggers to change behaviour. Find out more www.betterhelp.com/advice/behaviour/understanding-the-antecedent-behaviour-consequence-model/

C. Consequence: What happens after the behaviour occurs? After the situation has resolved itself it is important to assess what happened (Why was Johnny mad, what behaviour occurred such that the student was screaming, yelling and throwing the pencil crayons, what's the end result to avoid reinforcing it to occur again.) This could involve assessing the results and outcome of his behaviour and the appropriate time to discuss his behaviour. The point is discussions have to take place so it's not "if" there will be a discussion but "when". Problem-solving to avoid future issues is important. Possibly Johnny could have access to his own pencil crayons.

Reasons for challenging behaviours can include and not be limited to: lack of understanding of a situation, changes in routines at home (exposure to parental conflict, divorce, arrival of a new baby, family moved, trauma, and abuse). Other reasons for challenging behaviours at school may include: sensitivity to noise levels in the class, lighting (fluorescent), being told "no" to a specific request, not being listened to, having to stop a preferred activity or task, transitioning to a non-preferred task or activity, being given a directive by a staff member that the student doesn't prefer. Always consider and rule out health issues first: hunger, thirst, bowel routine changes, headaches (vision problems, especially children with glasses and ADD).

I. Reasons for Negative Behaviour: Communication Breakdown

"Human beings have enormous power to enrich life. We can use words to contribute to people's enjoyment, their wisdom. We can use words that can make life miserable for people. So our words are very powerful. We can touch people in ways that give great pleasure, great nurturing, support. We are powerhouses, and there's nothing we enjoy doing more than to use that power to enrich lives. So isn't that wonderful that we have this power and the joy it brings when we use it? That's to be celebrated. Wow! And the more we celebrate that, the less we will be willing to do anything else."
- Marshall B. Rosenberg, PhD, developer of non-violent communication

A possibility for consideration if communication is an issue is that the child has not reached the developmental stage where they can express themselves in an appropriate way. Skills may be lagging.

For communication to be empowering and effective, children should be shown at an early age how to express themselves. If your students do not know how to have the following conversation, make a point of teaching/modeling it to them as soon as possible.

Ch. 1: Teach

This conversation is an example of how you can teach a child to express their emotions to another. This is an exercise that parents can teach at home too.

Conversation:

Two children are playing outside in a sandbox at recess. One is kicking sand on the other's toy cars.

Child who is upset: "(Name) I don't like it when you (describe an action). It makes me feel (describe an emotion)."

Second child who was kicking the sand then says: "I hear you saying that you don't like me kicking the sand because (repeats the action voiced by the first child) and it makes you feel (repeats the emotion voiced by the first child) and you would like me to stop doing it."

The child who spoke up for themselves can then agree with how the other child reflected their request and how the actions affected them.

The second child can also apologize.

The children can then shake hands or high five. The second child can simply acknowledge that they understood and agree to not do the action again.

And then it's time to move on with having fun!

Teachers can model this style of communication until the children can independently do it on their own. There may be rules listed for certain behaviours and the child who breaks a rule will have to comply with the consequences of their actions. This teaches children the concept of accountability and responsibility.

The above is presented in a simple form that can easily be modeled for children as young as kindergarten or even preschool ages. Another 4-part style of problem-solving communication is called the Non-Violent Communication Process, developed by Marshall B. Rosenberg, PhD. It is an empowering method to consciously communicate to another so that the other person understands what we are asking for in a non-violent manner that bypasses yelling, hitting, bullying, or hurting altogether. It is a way to improve communication, increase safety, connect with empathy and build trust. It can help you feel heard and have your feelings validated.[17]

---

[17] Non-violent communication is a powerful four-part process for communication and connection developed by Marshall Rosenberg is a PhD. A free pdf download is available on their website along with other valuable information:
www.nonviolentcommunication.com/aboutnvc/4partprocess.htm

Clearly expressing	Empathically receiving
how **I am**	how **you are**
without blaming	without hearing
or criticizing	blame or criticism

OBSERVATIONS

1. What I observe (see, hear, remember, imagine, free from my evaluations) that does or does not contribute to my well-being:

   "When I (see, hear) . . ."

1. What you observe (see, hear, remember, imagine, free from your evaluations) that does or does not contribute to your well-being:

   "When you see/hear . . ."

   (Sometimes unspoken when offering empathy)

FEELINGS

2. How I feel (emotion or sensation rather than thought) in relation to what I observe:

   "I feel . . ."

2. How you feel (emotion or sensation rather than thought) in relation to what you observe:

   "You feel . . ."

NEEDS

3. What I need or value (rather than a preference, or a specific action) that causes my feelings:

   ". . . because I need/value . . ."

3. What you need or value (rather than a preference, or a specific action) that causes your feelings:

   ". . . because you need/value . . ."

Clearly requesting that	Empathically receiving that
which would enrich **my**	which would enrich **your** life
life without demanding	without hearing any demand

REQUESTS

4. The concrete actions I would like taken:

   "Would you be willing to . . . ?"

4. The concrete actions you would like taken:

   "Would you like . . . ?"

   (Sometimes unspoken when offering empathy)

© Marshall B. Rosenberg. For more information about Marshall B. Rosenberg or the Center for Nonviolent Communication please call 1-818-957-9393 or visit www.CNVC.org.

To learn more please visit nonviolentcommunication.com

J. Social Skills: I Get by with a Little Help from My Friends

"The glory of friendship is not the outstretched hand, nor the kindly smile, nor the joy of companionship: it is the spiritual inspiration that comes to one when you discover that someone else believes in you and is willing to trust you with a friendship."- Ralph Waldo Emerson

All children need friends. However, many do not have the necessary social skills for acquiring and maintaining friends. Children need to practice and model social skills until they become natural to them. Throughout the day there are many opportunities for learning these skills. Recess is the best time to build upon them, encourage friendships and promote appropriate competences and communication for being a better friend.

If you, as an educator, are on yard duty be mindful and notice what's going on. Who is playing happily and cooperatively? Who is standing off to the side alone? Who is tattling every recess? Which student always seems to be fighting with everyone? Is anyone pouting? Crying? Mad?

Instead of just playing referee you have an opportunity to teach skills that children can use throughout their whole lives. Be especially mindful of children with special needs because recess is one of the best times to blend in with peers and do a joint activity that can benefit all. You can even use these times to build gross motor skills and fine motor skills depending upon the toys you have available. Opportunities for turn taking, sharing and cooperative play are numerous.

Ch. 1: Teach

Gross Motor Skills	Fine Motor Skills
<ul><li>Sitting-posture-strong muscles</li><li>Walking</li><li>Crawling</li><li>Balancing- balance beams low to ground</li><li>Climbing</li><li>Climbing stairs-up and descending</li><li>Sliding</li><li>Catching a ball</li><li>Rolling a ball</li><li>Bouncing a ball</li><li>Throwing a ball overhand/ underhand</li><li>Tag</li><li>Running</li><li>Jumping</li><li>Kicking</li><li>Hopping on one foot</li><li>Jumping jacks</li><li>Touching toes</li><li>Riding a bike</li><li>Hanging from monkey bars</li><li>Skipping rope</li><li>Hopscotch</li><li>Kicking a football</li></ul> *Ball skills are so valuable because you can be so versatile with skill-building.	<ul><li>Paper clips</li><li>Clothespins- opening and closing onto objects</li><li>Tweezers-picking up small objects</li><li>Straws-cutting</li><li>Stickers- peeling and placing</li><li>Toothpicks</li><li>Beading-on pipe cleaners, raw spaghetti strips</li><li>Lacing</li><li>Tracing</li><li>Pinching</li><li>Squeezing</li><li>Cutting</li><li>Tongs- picking up objects</li><li>Pom poms</li><li>Plasticine-modelling clay</li><li>Playdough - rolling, squeezing, pinching, (hide objects in it-marbles, pasta, buttons, etc.)</li><li>Rubber bands</li><li>Colour</li><li>Paint</li><li>Sorting skills</li><li>Puzzles</li><li>Tower-blocks</li></ul>

Social skills that are valuable and essential to learning include: listening, learning how to apologize, learning how to get attention appropriately, following directions, staying on task, waiting for turns, taking a turn, minding one's own business, asking for what you need, asking important questions, working with others, hand raising, asking permission to leave class, going the bathroom, and getting something from a backpack or lunch box.

Other skills that are important to learn are: accepting a compliment, disagreeing respectfully, accepting criticism, saying 'no' to peer pressure and learning to stand in the power of one's own choices, asking for help, asking the right questions for whatever you are attempting to learn, working as a team.

Students need to learn how to accept situations and changes that might occur instead of having negative reactions, meltdowns and temper tantrums. When students are able to express themselves and self-regulate they are able to have better focus, less distress. They are also able to participate more often, experience an improvement in attention and feel less distracted. Children that exhibit abusive behaviours such as hitting, biting, kicking and punching develop alternative coping skills and are more able to express themselves in more appropriate ways.

A wonderful program that I love to use is called Zones of Regulation®.[18] It was developed by occupational therapist and autism resource specialist, Leah Kuypers, and is one of my favourite programs to recommend for younger students, especially those students on the autism spectrum and students with ADHD.

---

[18] This resource has information on how to implement The Zones of Regulation for your whole school. There are links for free educational resources to use such as Zones of Regulation bingo and Zones Moment of the Week. I highly recommend buying the whole book which includes a DVD with colour printables. The website has pre/post data collection self-assessment worksheets. The company is progressive and always adding more to their site as well as having studies in the process of gathering quantitative data.

They also now have a game that teachers or educational support staff can play to enable group collaboration and problem-solving skills and strategies with visual support, "Navigating the Zones: A Pathway to Self-Regulation", for cooperative learning. For more information, visit: www.zonesofregulation.com/index.html

It's an easy to use curriculum-based program rooted in a cognitive behaviour approach that teaches students self-regulation and self-control. It is a practice based on evidence that includes activities and strategies for increased self-control, better problem-solving strategies and sensory regulation; students learn how their behaviour affects others and have an increased ability to consciously recognize feelings and emotions. It improves a student's ability to communicate their feelings in an effective and proactive way. When the student learns these tools and strategies, they can know that it's okay to have a variety of emotions throughout the day and will learn that they can shift between all the zones and that is perfectly okay too.

The four coloured zones are:

Blue represents lower states of alertness and feelings such as sadness, tiredness or boredom.

Green represents feeling calm, happy and focused.

Red represents intense feelings such as anger, rage, panic, and feeling out of control.

Yellow represents a higher state of alertness, stress, frustration, feeling anxious. It may also include when a student is feeling silly and acting "wiggly" or nervous.

What I love about this system is that students can learn to be more proactive about their emotions. They can learn to notice how they are feeling on a regular basis. They can discover what their triggers are and be empowered to take charge of changing those emotions and feelings. Children can create their own toolbox with visual strategies that work best for them.

The book includes a DVD with printable visuals to display. It is useful for children of all ages, even adults. This program can be used at home as well. It is a system that incorporates common terminology and language that can be used throughout the school with teachers and students for ease when transferring from one grade to another. The level of understanding and usage grows with each year of use.

Emotional regulation is usually a part of normal development but it can be impaired or delayed due to many factors including: ADHD, anxiety, autism spectrum disorder, learning problems, sensory processing issues, even DMDD (disruptive mood dysregulation disorder- characterized by the individual being depressed and irritable).

A child that has problems with emotional regulation and self-control tends to have tantrums, meltdowns otherwise known as "lid flipping". Lid flipping is a term coined by Dr. Dan Siegel who has a useful video on YouTube that shows how you can understand lid flipping and brain function. It's an easy way to explain it to children too.[19]

Children that "flip their lids" tend to have poor impulse control, low problem solving skills, difficulty self-soothing, may have a hard time expressing their needs verbally and often have trouble with delayed gratification (waiting for a reward). Once children are in a state of meltdown they are unable to access their prefrontal cortex as easily as they would when they are calm, which can make rational decision-making difficult.

You may now be wondering: are self-regulation and self-control the same thing?

Stuart Shanker, research professor, founder and CEO of the Mehrit Centre (2016) put it this way, "Self-control is about inhibiting strong impulses, self-regulation is about reducing the frequency and intensity of strong impulses by managing stress load and recovery. In fact, self-regulation is what makes self-control possible, or, in many cases, unnecessary."

Researchers have analyzed whether self-regulation would be a good predictor of resilience. This study ("How self-regulation can help young people overcome setbacks") shows that helping young people to bounce back from adversities through acquiring self-regulation skills such as setting goals and adjusting their path after a misstep, equips them better to do well in school and in life."

---

[19] Check out the video here: www.youtube.com/watch?v=f-m2YcdMdFw

[20] Frontiers. "How self-regulation can help young people overcome setbacks." *ScienceDaily*. May 29, 2017, www.sciencedaily.com/releases/2017/05/170529101502.htm

Ch. 1: Teach

Resilience is a key part of emotional regulation. Did you know that resilience involves your whole body, incorporating your physical, mental, emotional and spiritual states? All of these aspects include the ability to be flexible. You need to be physically strong and flexible to cope with physical challenges. The mental aspect of resilience involves being able to consider views of others, have a positive and optimistic world outlook. The emotional dimension of resilience looks at positive feelings, relationships, flexibility, and self-regulation. Spiritual resilience is associated with your ability to be flexible and tolerant of others, use your intuition, and be committed to your core values. In order to bring balance to resilience and enable you to recover from setbacks and not allow them to build up to stress overload it is useful to implement strategies to shift your emotions and attitude to a positive frame of mind. Learning to control your thoughts, feelings, and emotions are valuable tools for emotional regulation and resilience recovery. Negative emotions such as anger, irritation, sadness, shame, and blame add stress to your body and drain your resilience. Stress interferes with focus, concentration, judgment, decision-making and memory. A positive mindset, mindfulness and control of your emotions maintain balance and coherence in times of stress. As Dr. Rolling McCraty, director of research at the HeartMath Institute explains, "Emotion is the energy that gives resilience the power to flex and recover in the face of adversity."[21]

K. Recess

"A great recess is an essential building block for healthy school environments that help kids thrive socially, emotionally and physically." – Nancy Barrand, senior advisor on program development for RWJF - Robert Wood Johnson Foundation

Recess is a chance to play, escape, pretend, and explore. How can you help a child have friends and foster inclusion?

When my daughter was younger, she had a circle of friends that she hung out with outside of school for birthday parties and activities, the time she spent with these friends created priceless memories for my daughter. She and her friends spent recess time laughing and playing, enjoying each other's company and engaging in activities that my daughter in a wheelchair could do.

---

[21] McCraty, Rollin. "Perspectives on Resilience in These Changing Times", heartmath.org

For children with special needs or those you see who don't have friends, create a buddy system. This is how it works: the peers the child spends time with rotate, and the activities the child is interested rotate for variety.

One time I announced over our school PA system that I was looking to fill a position for a 'peer helper'. Interested students had to complete a one-page resume as well as indicate available times and days they would be interested in volunteering to help our student. Students got to check off the activities they would be interested in doing. All choices were activities that the student with special needs loved to do. By giving the volunteers choices, they had the freedom to still do 'their thing' on other recesses with other peers and also do fun activities with the student that they were helping. The position came with perks: invitations to special events (random celebration parties and birthday parties), snacks, and indoor recess during the cold winter months.

The volunteers knew there was no pay except for the benefit of kindness and experiencing the joy of helping another to have fun playing and laughing. The experience was truly priceless and so beneficial.

It was a win-win for all. Self-esteem building and sense of purpose were the benefits for those who volunteered. To this day some mention how much they enjoyed helping that student.

L. Responding versus Reacting

"I have come to the frightening conclusion that I am the decisive element. It is my personal approach that creates the climate. It is my daily mood that makes the weather. I possess tremendous power to make life miserable or joyous. I can be a tool of torture or an instrument of inspiration. I can humiliate or humour, hurt or heal. In all situations, it is my response that decides whether a crisis is escalated or de-escalated, and a person is humanized or de-humanized. If we treat people as they are, we make them worse. If we treat them as they ought to be, we help them become what they are capable of becoming." - Haim G. Ginott, **Teacher and Child: A Book for Parents and Teachers**

How often do you find yourself reacting to a situation impulsively?

Our part is to hear not just to respond. We must truly hear what others are saying to understand the situation. Conscious mindfulness is responding calmly, with compassion and interest, instead of reacting with sarcasm,

Ch. 1: Teach

anger, and assumptions that may be wrong. Many self-development experts including Jack Canfield, Marci Shimoff, and Debra Poneman underline the importance of being mindful of what can happen as a result of their reactions to an event. This gap in time right after something happens is critical because often your perception of an action and your response determines what the outcome will be. For example: it might seem that your student is throwing his papers on the floor to give you a hard time. When in reality, he is having a hard time and lacks the tools to appropriately express frustrations. The outcome of the situation will be very different depending upon what you choose to perceive. Also, your student will discover that it's not "if" you will confront them on their negative behaviour, it's "when". The "when" is important. Don't confront them when they are still agitated, not in front of peers and others. A positive relationship and timing is everything.

When the time is right, you can be supportive of a student in this situation by knowing your student from previous discussions and reminding them of their preferred ways of calmly asking for help when needed rather than acting out in frustration.

There is power in the gap—we get to consciously choose our responses.

Think about your reactions in the classroom: How do you respond to a student's negative behaviour? Does your response hurt or heal the situation? Can you think of a time where you responded impulsively? What was the outcome? What did you learn from that situation? What would you do differently next time?

M. Teach: It's Your Turn!

We can teach from our experiences but we cannot teach experiences." - Sasha Azevedo, artist and teacher azquotes.com/quote/667346

The world of teaching is changing and how you experience it will be within your own power through your own thoughts, attitudes and self-care habits. Success can be achieved in your class by empowering students to set goals, self-regulate their emotions through co-regulation and modeling. Guide them to be empowered leaders who accept responsibility for what they experience, and encourage the student to make conscious choices for a positive school environment and happiness.

As my dear friend Hal Price, international speaker and author of **Eli Benjamin Bear** - *A Heart's Journey Home and The Bear Essentials*, put it best, "We did not come here to lead ordinary lives," he reminds us that, "we can change the world by just being ourselves."

Self-reflection questions

- *What skills, insights, and wisdom did you discover in this chapter? What will you implement in your classroom?*
- *What will you explore for yourself? What will you research more about for better understanding?*
- *Where do you find yourself experiencing the most stress?*
- *Do you consider "the gap" when responding?*

 **CHAPTER 2: HONOUR**

"To nurture and educate a child it's essential to honour the whole child so that they can rise to their potential." - Unknown

What is the value and role of honour within a classroom as part of a whole child approach?

A whole child approach that honours your students would include not only honouring their mind, body, and spirit but also their emotions, feelings, fears, as well as their cultural differences and sensory needs. It enables them to experience an inclusive and equitable learning environment.

Inclusion honours the individual for doing one's own best.

To honour someone is to recognize their uniqueness and individuality as a human being. By appreciating differences and celebrating a diverse range of abilities, we give each student worth and dignity. It is an opportunity to lift others and enable everyone to work in partnership, leadership, cooperation and collaboration.

By honouring one's individuality, you are validating their existence. This form of validation is empowering and motivating to self-esteem, personal growth, fulfillment, and pride. These factors give the individual a chance to excel in their educational setting. Honouring others increases the sense of belonging. This is a basic need that we all have—within our society, within our culture, our community and our education system. Can you imagine a world where everyone was honoured and respected for exactly who they are? That would definitely add value to inclusion. In fact, it would help inclusion become a seamless habit that everyone naturally performed. Honouring and accepting a child as they are is a gift of love. Honour is a responsibility; it's our responsibility!

Learning to be non-judgmental is truly another skill that is an important part of honouring the child, because it involves letting go and not being attached to the outcome. If you can honour a student you are showing them that you value, care and love them just as they are. It's unconditional love!

A. Honouring Your Students' Basic Needs

"It rests in the hands of the common person as well as those with the power to shape humanities course towards a world where every child, woman and man's basic needs are met." - Forest Whitaker, actor

A child's needs are derived from Abraham Maslow's[22] hierarchy of needs that he developed in 1943. They include physiological needs (food, clothing, shelter), safety, love and belonging, esteem, and self-actualisation. He later added observations of a human being innately curious, highlighting the need to discover and explore. And no, despite what children and the Internet are saying, Wi-Fi does not qualify as a new, updated modern need!

As mentioned above, physiological needs for survival include food, water, rest, and warmth. So many children begin their day without adequate rest. They come to school before having any breakfast and are often not wearing weather appropriate clothing. Having raised four children, I know the daily battles of trying to get them to eat something before school, attempting to get them to sleep at a decent hour and reminding them to dress warmly and wear the clothes that they have. I've learned to choose my battles. As Barbara Coloroso[23] points out in her book **Kids are Worth It: Raising Resilient, Responsible and Compassionate Kids**,

---

[22] Wikipedia. "Maslow's hierarchy of needs." Last modified December 21, 2020. en.wikipedia.org/wiki/Maslow%27s_hierarchy_of_needs

For more on Maslow's Hierarchy of needs: www.simplypsychology.org/maslow.html

[23] Barbara Coloroso is an international speaker and author recognized for her works designed to assist parents and educators with discipline, parenting, and non-violent conflict resolution. She has been a classroom teacher and serves as an education consultant. Her wisdom and wit are valuable during these times of injustice, chaos, and confusion. She has free resources on her website including three kinds of families, parenting wisdom and wit, and parenting through crisis. I enjoyed her books when navigating through the teen years with my own children. She also offers her wisdom for stopping bullying at home, schools and communities.

Book: Kids are Worth It: Raising Resilient, Responsible and Compassionate Kids
shop.kidsareworthit.com/kids-are-worth-it-giving-your-child-the-gift-of-inner-discipline-KAWI.htm

Website: www.kidsareworthit.com Email: info.kidsareworthit@gmail.com

Ch. 2: Honour

if it's not life threatening, illegal or immoral, let it go. Teens especially learn some of these lessons the hard way when they wear running shoes to school in the winter and still have to go outside in the snow at recess and then must spend the rest of the day with wet, damp, and cold feet.

Proper rest is so important for a child to be able to focus and function at school. Knowing your students and their home lives allows you to have more compassion and a better understanding of the behaviours that you see. There are children that live such traumatic and unstable lives that often their sleep is disrupted by parents fighting, slamming doors, and violence. As a result they arrive at school exhausted from functioning in fight or flight response to trauma whether it is currently occurring or whether they are dealing with trauma from the past. Being compassionate when you know the child's home situation is beneficial in providing comfort and impressing upon the child that they are safe in your care at school.

Children aged 3 to 6 years old need 10 to 12 hours of sleep a night, children aged 7 to 12 years old need 10 to 11 hours of sleep and those aged 12 to 18 years old need a minimum of 8 to 9 hours of sleep.

Healthy food is a need that should be met at home. Children need proper nutrients, vitamins, minerals, protein, and essential fats. Far too often children's lunches are loaded with high salt, high fat, calorie-laden, nutrient-deficient, processed-filled junk. Brains cannot function long term on these types of food choices. Food choices matter because of the effect on energy levels, on the functioning of the systems in your body and on overall health. I understand that kids can be picky. But if parents slowly add in other foods and encourage trying bites of new foods, eventually children will find things that they like to eat.

At school it is great when you can do activities that involve eating different kinds of food. It's a good way to introduce students to new things. When I was in a kindergarten class, I would bring in fruit and veggies cut into little pieces and do "taste testing". The kids loved it. Many of the students would try something new and different because their peers were doing it too.

A resource I like that is useful for early education and elementary school teachers is a book called **Give It a Go, Eat a Rainbow** by Kathryn Kemp Guylay[24]. It contains a mixture of real-life photography and illustrations drawn by her 12-year-old son, Alex Guylay. Children are introduced to a character named Blake who is experiencing low energy and wishes to feel better. After meeting a magical leprechaun, Blake goes on an adventure to find a pot of gold that is a metaphor for good health and energy.

I am a nutritional consultant and know the value of proper nutrition. There is so much to know with regards to what is best to eat and how to get enough minerals and vitamins in your body. Hopefully, your school has a breakfast program or at least a nutrition program with healthy snacks available.

As a teacher, be mindful of behaviour changes from students after they consume certain foods. Some changes are instant and quite noticeable. For example, food dyes can cause behaviour changes. I've seen students become quite aggressive and defiant shortly after drinking fruit drinks with red dyes. Dairy milk and dairy milk products can also cause a similar effect. Some reactions to foods can include sinus problems, stuffy or runny noses, head congestion and digestive disturbances including diarrhea or constipation. These types of reactions are delayed reactions that may not appear until hours or even days after ingesting them. Common food allergens are seafood, citrus, dairy, eggs, peanuts, wheat, tree nuts (walnuts, almonds, pecans, brazil nuts), and soy.

Keep in mind that even with healthy foods children may have negative reactions.

---

[24] Kathryn Guylay is a heart-centred leader who loves to make everything fun. This multitalented mother and change-maker wears many hats including author, coach, consultant, non-profit founder, CEO, board member, podcaster and media personality. She has a diverse range of interests including nutrition, leadership, wellness, and publishing. She offers free resources on these topics on her website. She offers many interesting and informative podcasts: makeeverythingfun.com/mountain-mantras-podcast/

Links to her books including *Give it a Go, Go Eat a Rainbow*: makeeverythingfun.com/books/
Email: kathryn@guylay.com

Ch. 2: Honour

One time, I observed a shy student reading for a teacher. He was calmly and meticulously reading a story while consuming a few fresh strawberries. Within minutes he completely changed, he was speaking loudly and talking with different character voices.

Be a mindful observer. By being present and knowing your student through observations and daily conversations you can easily know when the child is not themselves or is having a hard time. Often students have something happen in their lives where they don't know what to think of a situation and it is helpful to have a caring listening ear to talk to. When a student trusts you they are more open to being honest and telling you about themselves. By observing physical changes: posture, stance, breathing, and emotional changes, as well as mood and behaviour changes, you can get clues to how a child is feeling even if they aren't expressing it verbally.

After working over 20 years in many different school settings, I have witnessed first-hand when children are not getting their basic needs met. Sadly, there are times when a call to a child protection service has to be made. But most often the educator and/or school can help support the child by ensuring that they have lunch or snacks available. So many parents live paycheck to paycheck and stretching food for a month can be challenging. It can be heartbreaking to witness. Poverty is real. Hunger is real. We all know that it takes a village to raise a child. By helping families get through the in-between grocery times or the lighter lunch days or even the no-lunch days, we are doing kindness to children who need to feel they are being treated like human beings.

Another basic need that children have is to belong. Children need to feel that they have a place in this world to feel worthy. By providing life experiences and opportunities to children you are contributing to the universal design of learning. This leads to growth and self-actualization which is a higher need that allows the child to reach their potential and have the ability to be creative.

B. Safety is the Key to Wellness

"If children feel safe, they can take risks, ask questions, make mistakes, learn to trust, share their feelings and grow." - Alfie Kohn, author and lecturer on parenting, education and human behaviour

Never underestimate the need for safety. Safety is an important precondition for learning. It truly is a basic need of utmost importance. A safe classroom provides opportunity for trust and respect. If your classroom can provide safety and an environment where strengths, different learning styles, and diverse cultural backgrounds are recognized you will have an amazing classroom filled with children that truly thrive!

Along with feeling safe in their environment children need to feel safe in their body. If they have experienced trauma that causes post-traumatic stress disorder (PTSD) children can become locked in their trauma by their body's responses to threats. Then, they tend to react to perceived threats as if it's a threat in their current reality. These reactions can become a patterned response. To them the threat is real! The child feels their very survival is being threatened. When survival is at stake, (real or perceived as a real threat), we engage in responses to regulate stress. A child that feels unsafe in their classroom may resort to hiding under tables, withdrawing and refusing to engage with other children to play and also refusing to engage with adults to express what they are feeling. Another child may have a meltdown seemingly over nothing and refuse to participate in class activities.

As humans we have four main defence strategies: fight, flight, freeze and fawn. Fawn is a term coined by Pete Walker, a C-PTSD survivor and licensed marriage and family therapist. It involves the defence of being a "people pleaser" often at the cost of sacrificing one's own needs and exhibiting poor boundaries. We also have a subconscious system for detecting threats and safety. This neurobiological subconscious system is called neuroception, a term coined by Dr. Stephen Porges.[25] To understand neuroception you must understand the Polyvagal Theory, which was introduced by Dr. Stephen Porges in 1994.

---

[25] Dr. Stephen Porges is a distinguished scientist at the University of Indiana. He is the founding director of the Traumatic Stress Research Consortium. He is the leading expert in developmental psychophysiological and developmental behaviourial neuroscience. Check out his bio on his website page. He is extremely intelligent and has a great deal of knowledge in his area of expertise. He developed the polyvagal theory that supports our desire and quest for safety and understanding of the workings of our social engagement system. He links the ANS (autonomic nervous system) to social behaviour. His wisdom has given me great insight and understanding of how children and adults get locked into set patterns and are simply unable to free themselves from autism, anxiety, depression, trauma, and other mental illnesses. His work enabled others to understand the unconscious connection between psychological experiences and physical manifestations within the body.

Ch. 2: Honour

C. All Systems Go!

"There is a wisdom in the body that is older and more reliable than clocks and calendars." - John Harold Johnson, American publisher and entrepreneur

Let's begin by talking about your autonomic nervous system (ANS).

Your body has two primary autonomic nervous systems: the parasympathetic (calming system) and the sympathetic (responding system). The sympathetic nervous system is the responding system. It works like a gas pedal in a car triggering the fight or flight response to perceived danger. The parasympathetic nervous system is your calming system and it is much like a brake in your car. It helps your body return to rest and relaxation when the danger is gone. The role of these systems is to provide safety, protection and homeostasis (balance). In order for the body to function effectively, these systems need to be balanced; as a result your immune system functions well, your digestive system works well, you are healthy and sleeping well. Both systems are beneficial and the flow between the two should happen smoothly. When your body is in a state of chronic stress like fight or flight mode however, you may experience adverse health effects that can include anxiety, chest tightness, digestive problems, chronic fatigue, and chronic pain. It's terrible to feel this way and if you have ever experienced chronic fight or flight response I'm sure that you can deeply empathize with children who are in this state daily at home and at school.

The following scenario illustrates how these systems work together.

Imagine you are happily driving in your car, zipping along 15 miles over the speed limit. You're drinking your coffee and singing along to your favourite rock and roll song on the radio—you are feeling great, so calm, and so happy. Suddenly in your rear view mirror, you notice a police cruiser with its lights flashing. You freeze for a split-second and then reacting quickly, you pull over. Coffee is put down into the cup holder, radio volume lowered.

He also created SSP (Safe and Sound Protocol—a listening program designed to reduce stress and auditory sensitivity while at the same time enhancing social engagement and resilience.

His book that I reference is called: *The Polyvagal Theory: Neurophysiological Foundations of Emotions, Attachment, Communication, and Self-regulation* (Norton, 2011).
Website: www.stephenporges.com/

At this point your heart may be racing, your breathing could become shallow and fear may have set in. You notice that your face is flushed. You are embarrassed and the heat in your body has caused your blood pressure to rise.

But, before the police officer can give you a ticket, he gets a call on his radio and needs to immediately get to the scene of an accident. He gives you a warning and then hurries to his car and speeds off. You are left exhaling a sigh of relief, your breathing returns to normal, you smile, take a sip of your coffee, pull back out on the highway at a normal speed (for now!), and calmly turn the radio up again and start singing.

You were designed to go between these autonomic nervous systems as needed and then return to a normal state of balance between the sympathetic and the parasympathetic. The above scenario is an example of your autonomic nervous system (ANS) in action. You were calm and relaxed, even while multitasking. The situation changed when a potential danger was perceived and it caused you to freeze and experience fear. Stress messengers, like cortisol hormones and adrenaline were released, cascading throughout your mind, heart and body. When the situation eased and resolved, you were able to go back to your state of calmness and balance. The return to a balanced state happens after about 20 minutes, but with the newest discoveries, recovery can be even quicker.

Children also get thrown out of balance and their nervous systems will protectively kick in too. When the stress is chronic and continual, children and adults get into habitual reaction patterns and have a harder time with recovery. The patterns of behaviour can be unconscious, and it becomes more difficult for the child to see how their behaviour resulted in the feelings and reactions they are experiencing.

Life can throw us off balance creating chronic stress, trauma, and anxiety. It is critical to know how to notice how you are feeling and wonderful to know strategies to help get and stay on track for your wellbeing. It is also extremely fulfilling to assist a student in their own awareness and empowerment when it comes to dealing with managing these systems.

Using the Zones of Regulation[26] (which were described in Chapter 1) really helps students to be empowered and understand their emotions. There are many ways that students can self-regulate, positively problem solve and move from one zone to another. You can also be in more than one zone at a time. For example, a student may not have slept well last night and feels tired and sad yet is now feeling anxious about an upcoming test at the same time. This is the ideal time to drink water and take some deep breaths.

There are two excellent breathing techniques I'd like to share with you: Lazy 8 Breathing and Four Square Breathing. Lazy 8 Breathing involves tracing along a lazy 8 (the number eight that's been set horizontally so that it resembles the infinity symbol) with your finger. First, breathe in on the first half of the eight and do one breath out on the second half, repeat until calm. Four Square Breathing is when you breathe in to the count of 4, hold for a count of four, breathe out to the count of four and pause for a count of four. Repeat until calm. A cut out paper square is useful for following along, the child can trace each line of the square with their finger as they breathe and count in their mind. An adult can help with this activity by co-regulating and counting out loud. Teaching children to breathe properly is vital. Too often we hold our own breath and do not breathe properly.

Depending on how your student is feeling and the emotions they are experiencing, allow them to choose the action that makes them feel best. These actions can be: taking a break, drinking water, eating crunchy foods or a snack, talking to an adult, holding a fidget toy or other sensory item, stretching, moving, jumping, hopping, using a trampoline, running on the spot, doing wall push-ups, carrying heavy things, thinking positive thoughts, asking for a hug, or rubbing their hands together.

---

[26] The Zones of Regulation™ is a systematic cognitive behaviour approach to self-regulation and controlling emotions in order to get needs met. It was created by occupational therapist, Leah Kuypers MA ED., OTR/L. It is recognized as one of the top programs for teaching social and emotional learning. The website offers webinars, training, resources, and some free downloadable materials. Check out the useful resources for Zones of Regulation ™ distance learning on the website too. They also have a book nook where you can find suggested books to help students better understand themselves through other books and stories. What I love about it is that the program can be implemented school wide, enabling staff and students to use common language through the school. There are also beneficial visuals to enhance understanding.

Website: www.zonesofregulation.com/index.html
Email: info@zonesofregulation.com

The student can also pause and gain some perspective about the situation and think of ways to change it or feel better about it. When a child is having a meltdown you can help them regulate by supporting and helping them feel secure. Again, relationships matter. Circle of Security[27] is a concept developed to help parents struggling with impediments to developing healthy attachments with their children. Developers, Kent Hoffman, Glen Cooper, Bert Powell and their associate, Christine Benton, created a resource book, **'Raising a Secure Child: How Circle of Security Parenting Can Help You Nurture Your Child's Attachment, Emotional Resilience and Freedom to Explore.'**

The foundation of this approach is based on research of the attachment theory in the 1950's by psychiatrist John Bowlby[28] and psychologist Mary Ainsworth. Their work focused on attachment and the importance of a secure and trusting mother-child attachment bond for healthy development. The quality of a bond can be affected for many reasons: abuse, poverty, lack of parental skills and knowledge (you can't give what you never received). The Circle of Security gives you strategies to build bonds and attachments through creating a safe haven and a secure base for your child, and even your students. It is designed to help them to be calm and curious enough to explore their world while feeling reassurance that they are safe. If something happens to cause fear and uncertainty and even meltdowns, the child can discover through your presence that they are safe. Comfort and support enable them to explore again and feel balanced.

---

[27] Circle of Security. Hoffman K., G. Cooper, B. Powell, and C. Benton, *Raising a Secure Child: How Circle of Security Parenting Can Help You Nurture Your Child's Attachment, Emotional Resilience and Freedom to Explore* (New York: The Guilford Press, 2017).

This is a great resource for understanding how to protect, nurture and parent your child to feel safe and secure while exploring their own independence and self-discovery. You can learn what a toddler is expressing through difficult behaviour. You will also learn how your own upbringing has influenced your parenting style.

www.circleofsecurityinternational.com/cos-books/books/

[28] John Bowlby was a British psychoanalyst with a keen interest in understanding the distress infants have when separated from caregivers, especially mothers. For further reading about the Bowlby Attachment Theory including information about the stages visit: www.simplypsychology.org/attachment.html

Here is a link for more learning about this theory www.psychology.sunysb.edu/attachment/online/inge_origins.pdf

Ch. 2: Honour

When the child is able to regain control from being in a dysregulated state such as anger, sadness or anxiety on his own, it is important that you allow it to happen. Through noticing you will understand when it is necessary for you to step in and help make sense of their emotions, meet a need, and come from a place of love and calmness.

In her book, '**Kids These Days: A Game Plan for (Re) Connecting with Those We Teach, Lead & Love**[29]', psychologist Dr. Jody Carrington explains "Always be bigger, stronger, kinder and wiser; whenever possible follow a need. Whenever necessary take charge." She continues on to say, "when the kid is losing their freaking mind, you need to dig deep in the core of yourself and figure it out **with** them." When safety is a risk or someone may get hurt, take charge!

I feel that our education system needs more training on trauma for educators including teachers, early childhood educators, educational assistants, bus drivers, and librarians—everyone who works with children within a school day. Too often, educators are at a loss as to how to help the students that they work with. Teachers learn about the educational aspect of teaching but often do not have the training for responding to children with trauma, abuse, special needs, FAS (Fetal alcohol syndrome), ADHD, ODD, or behaviour problems.

---

[29] Carrington, Jody, *Kids These Days: A Game Plan for (Re)Connecting with Those We Teach, Love & Lead* (Impress, January 2020)

I read this book through a book club offered by educator and consultant Shelley Moore. Through reading this book with many other educators we discovered so many great nuggets of information to use with students that we work with. Carrington really stresses the importance of us, as educators, being okay so that we are okay to love, support and hold "the babies" that we work with.

Course: How to Connect with Kids These Days. It is informative and educational with the opportunity to access a VIP Course with 20 hours of extra audio inspiration. I took this course in April and May of 2020. It was filled with many useful tips and strategies to consider when working with students who have experienced trauma. Carrington offers educational opportunities for school-wide training and learning about trauma, grief and loss, connection and relationships.

Website: www.drjodycarrington.com/
Email: jody@drjodycarrington.com
Facebook: www.facebook.com/drjodycarrington

Carrington offers extremely valuable training programs on mental health to educators through her company Carrington Connections Network (CCN). They created a model for creating resilience in schools looking after educators first. If those who are responsible for children are not okay our children will not be okay. Currently there isn't a consistent approach or common language for working with children with "mental health" problems. Statistically one in five have mental health problems.

"The CCN was developed out of a need to connect school divisions in a relationship-focused, trauma-informed practice. Educators do the holy work of raising and teaching our future generations, but like our children, educators have never felt more disconnected." No truer words were ever spoken: the disconnect is increasing; yet children need us more than ever. We, as educators, need to feel supported, heard, and understood. The CCN programs are designed for those in senior leadership positions and also the masses. For more information visit carringtonnetwork.com

D. Polyvagal Theory

"By processing information from the environment through the senses, the nervous system continually evaluates risk. I have coined the term neuroception to describe how neural circuits distinguish whether situations or people are safe, dangerous or life threatening. Because of our heritage as a species, neuroception takes place in primitive parts of the brain, without our conscious awareness." - Dr. Stephen W. Porges, distinguished University Scientist and professor in the department of psychiatry University North Carolina networkyogatherapy.com/stephen-porges/

If you have students presenting behaviour problems you will want to pay close attention to this next section of the book. It's the most exciting to me because of the information that I am going to share with you relating to the polyvagal theory. Learning about this theory has made my heart leap because it has helped me understand students who have a hard time regulating their stress responses and who go to fight and flight automatically and become reactive when they do not feel safe.

Porges, a distinguished scientist at the Kinsey Institute Indiana University Bloomington, developed the polyvagal theory based upon experiments with the vagus nerve. The vagus nerve works with the parasympathetic nervous system, which is responsible for calming the body and the mind. Vagus means "wandering" and interestingly the vagus nerve is one of 12 pairs of cranial nerves, it meanders in a zigzagging fashion from the brain, branches into the ear, goes down each side of the neck, and through the chest, into the stomach and intestines. It affects facial muscles, the ability to make facial expressions as well as vocal cord tone and patterning. It also assists with regulating body functions, breathing, blood pressure, heart rate, digestion, and even perspiration.

Porges coined a term for a third part of the nervous system that he discovered - the social engagement system. This social engagement system is set into motion by a unique nerve influence. His theory provides the link between psychological experiences and physical manifestations in the body.

This social engagement system requires safety. The feeling of safety is important for trust, coping, and being flexible within relationships. It's associated with the neuro-physiological foundations of attachment, communication, self-regulation, and emotions. This is a huge discovery that majorly affects students and their education.

It explains a great deal about the health of educators too.

Everyone has a varying degree of vagal tone. If someone has a strong vagal tone then their body can relax after a stress response. If the tone is low the recovery is less efficient. Low vagal tone is also associated with chronic inflammation. This increases our risks for diabetes, stroke, and cardiovascular disease too.

If the vagal tone is strong you release less stress hormones, have better health, your blood sugars are regulated and you will experience less depression and anxiety. With anxiety being so prevalent in our society this is an exciting theory to examine. Especially when you know that there are ways to help you be calmer, experience less pain, and less inflammation, and help you recover from stressful situations more quickly and easily.

When something happens that causes us to feel fear or freeze, it slows down or shuts down our vagus system (the dorsal vagus nerve in particular which is located in the diaphragm). This may cause problems with our digestive processes. You may become light-headed, experience muscle fatigue, even chronic fatigue. Your heart and lungs may be affected too. The vagus nerve is part of your "gut instinct" too, another reason you would want to have it operating properly for optimal health. A healthy body helps you be in tune with your own intuition and gut instincts more easily.

Many children have experienced trauma and have PTSD (post traumatic syndrome disorder) as a result. They are in a constant state of fight, flight or freeze. A child with a compromised social engagement system may withdraw socially or exhibit aggressive behaviours where hitting, kicking, punching, pinching, and freezing are their first reactions of defence due to activated brain circuits telling them that they aren't safe. Their neuroception may be faulty or it may be accurate. Not all environments are safe. Individuals that experience faulty neuroception may include those with anxiety, depression, autism, or schizophrenia as well as those who are maltreated or institutionalized children with Reactive Attachment Disorder. This is a condition where a child did not form healthy, stable social bonds with a parent or caregiver. Symptoms of this disorder manifest as the child having trouble managing emotions, problems bonding with others, they may be fearful, sad, rarely seek comfort, often avoid eye contact, may express anger, may even fail to show remorse or guilt. Children placed in foster care or orphanages experience this as well as children in homes where they are physically and emotionally abused.

Neuroception relates to how our neural circuits discern whether people or situations are safe or dangerous. Our brain subconsciously determines our response of which defence behaviour it will implement: fight, flight, or freeze. Even though cognitively we have not realized or decided that someone or something was dangerous, our body responds by a change in heart rate, flushed face, perspiration, and possibly by causing us to become dizzy, pale, and faint.

If a child's neuroception decides that they are safe they are able to be more prosocial with classmates and more able to share, play nicely, and get along with others. If the child's system detects danger and triggers physiological states of defence they may run, fight, push, shove, hit or pinch, as a protective response. For a child to effectively get out of a defensive mode his nervous system needs to assess the situation and decide if the environment is safe or not. He decides these things through his senses and nervous system.

When a child seems unable to hold back his defence reactions in a safe environment he may have faulty neuroception. With faulty neuroception the child incorrectly assesses the environment as dangerous or unsafe. He may also judge others as untrustworthy. You may be asking how does the nervous system know when it is a safe environment? Well, areas of the brain check out body language, facial expressions, and even vocal intonations to assess if they can trust and be safe in the setting.

Ch. 2: Honour

This makes me think of times when a parent drops their child off at school, especially kindergarten students. That child may cry and cling onto their parents with whom they have a strong social attachment. It seems like they were ready for school, they had talked about it all summer and even excitedly helped to pack their first day's lunch. Then upon arriving, their neuroception may have quickly and unconsciously determined that the situation didn't feel safe. The child didn't have to think 'I'm scared' to be scared. Their body just informed them that they were scared.

That is why it is so important for teachers and educators to be smiling, welcoming and reassuring. Even if the educator doesn't have an angry look on their face a non-friendly or non-expressive look can trigger a child's neuroception to signal danger or fear and as result the social engagement is compromised and they will react defensively in one of the three defence modes (fight, flight, or freeze).

Developing trust and relationships matter because an area in the cortex lights up when a familiar and safe person is seen. At this point neuroception will say it's a safe place to be and the defences won't jump in to rescue. This explains why children who are used to having the same teacher and same educational assistant every day may react aggressively or even run away when faced with a new staff member. Their neuroception has told them they are not safe and they spontaneously react. Once they can assess the environment and realize they are safe and secure they can relax and recover rather than have an outburst or meltdown over not feeling safe.

If you are put with a student that seems to be acting defensively, develop a rapport as quickly as you can, encourage their safety through reassurance, and if possible, get the child laughing to release oxytocin. In younger grades, if allowed, hugging helps release oxytocin. It is an activity that aids social bonding.

I noticed that, for myself, I had a hard time calming my body after being exposed to chronic long-term stress from raising two children with disabilities. I was in a state of constant overload from frequent doctor appointments, medical travel, health issues, dental emergencies, complications from my child having spina bifida, fighting systems for educational rights and safety, fighting for better accessible health care and even advocating for accessible transportation for my child. I didn't know how to stop. I didn't know how to calm down. I worked full time during the early child-rearing years, rarely taking leaves from work except for an out-of-town surgery. I cared for my children after working all day and getting them into bed. I took courses and training on everything from nutrition to alternative wellness and energy techniques. During that period, I was also coping with the death of my sweet friend, Marianna.

I didn't know how to stop or how to relax—I kept busy doing things that distracted me from being in the present moment. I used to play over 100 games of Yahtzee all at once and could not wait until I had free time to play. This resulted in a disconnection of my own social engagement system, which I now know, was compromised. My disconnecting was a shutdown for survival. Others who are in this state of disconnect might compulsively work out, rake leaves, or clean their houses. They don't know how to stop; they feel they must constantly be doing something and usually take that something to extremes. It becomes like an addiction.

Children can become disconnected by long amounts of exposure to technology. They become distracted, addicted, and focus obsessively on the next time they can play. It affects their moods, behaviour, and sleep patterns. A child that is stuck in disconnect can experience IBS (inflammatory bowel disease), rheumatoid arthritis, and even epilepsy. Teachers can watch for symptoms of depression, anxiety, and PTSD in children for clues as to how the child is coping and not coping with stress.

The fight or flight stress response is a survival mechanism. When it is chronically activated your health can be impaired and the immune system lowered dramatically. Chronic stress has long-term physiological and psychological effects on your body including increasing your blood pressure, depositing artery-clogging materials, inflammation, and changes to your brain resulting in anxiety, depression and addictions. Obesity can also result.

The best part about polyvagal theory is that it gives hope to many, because they can learn to change these responses and become more mobilized (having less temper tantrums, less melt downs, less fight/flight reactions) through a variety of activities to induce the relaxation response. You can help your students feel safe by engaging their social nervous system. The field of bioelectronic medicine offers Vagus Nerve Stimulation (VNS) as an intervention, but of course, as educators this isn't your area of expertise.

Ch. 2: Honour

Your students can become more resilient, less reactive, and have better impulse control. As Ross Green[30] says, "Kids would do better if they could do better." Providing them with simple tools and easy-to-do strategies will help them do better! The goal for yourself and for your students should be to help move them from the flight/fight and freeze states to feeling safe. Once they feel safe they are more able to change by becoming more relaxed and understand that their emotions are within their control. Through movement and conscious actions they can become more embodied and present. It is well known that energy goes where attention flows, that is why a change in focus and discovering new ways to be present and mindful can bring about radical changes in wellness. One way to help students feel grounded and calm is to incorporate frequent movement breaks into the daily routine of your class.

When you can't reach a child odds are they have shut down as a result of chronically operating in fight/flight and are in a frozen state as a way of coping. Their social engagement system is fully in protection mode. Patterns have developed and many of these patterns are unconscious. But there is help! Dr. Arielle Schwartz says, "Mind-body therapies work with the vagus nerve to help you find balance. You will find a variety of breath and movement practices aimed to stimulate and reset the vagus nerve. Through a process of self-study and mindful body awareness, you can start to learn strategies that help you restore a sense of safety and heal from trauma."[31]

---

[30] Ross Greene, PhD and author of *Lost at School* and *The Explosive Child* describes many ways to help an explosive child cope and build skills needed for thriving within a school and classroom environment. He believes the goal is to be proactive and discover lagging skills for problem solving.

Website: cpsconnection.com/dr-ross-greene or livesinthebalance.org
The scoop: cpsconnection.com/interview-dr-ross-greene
Free Resources for educators: livesinthebalance.org/educators-schools

[31] Dr. Arielle Schwartz is a licensed clinical psychologist in private practice in Boulder, Colorado. She implements a variety of practices such as EMDR therapy and Somatic Psychology for trauma recovery, attachment trauma, chronic pain relief, grief and loss. Check out her books and blog at: drarielleschwartz.com

It is possible that some students were born with low vagal tone passed on from their mothers. Mothers who are depressed, anxious or angry during their pregnancy have lower vagal activity. And once they give birth, their newborn child also has low vagal activity and low dopamine and serotonin levels.[32]

By consciously applying the tools that I describe, you will be amazed at the changes that can happen! Some of the ways to improve vagal tone and elicit a relaxation response include:

- Rub your hands together vigorously.

- Use conscious abdominal breathing to positively influence your nervous system. Take a breath in over 5 counts, hold for 5 counts, and slowly release it over a 10 count as if you are blowing fog on a mirror, slowly add in a sound like "hhh" from the back of your throat as you blow out. (This technique of constricting the back of the throat and making the "hhh" sound is a yoga technique known as Ujjayi.) Repeat until you feel calm or if doing it with a child until you notice they are calm. This changes your heart rate by slowing it down.

- Show students how to breathe properly. It's the simplest way to have balance yet so many of us do it wrong. By inhaling breath into their chest it elicits the fight/ flight response—the very thing we are trying to eliminate. Inhale into the belly to help get calm.

- Touch your face, neck, chest and arms - vagus nerve massage. This draws focus, awareness, and energy to those areas. Donna Eden, an Energy Medicine Practitioner, performs various daily energy routines that students could follow along to. Everyone could benefit by starting the school day daily with these routines.

- Hum. It is beneficial because the vagus nerve passes through your inner ear and vocal chords. You can hum something like OM or your favourite song.

---

[32] Referenced: Vagal Activity, Early Growth and Emotional Development Vagal Activity, Early Growth and Emotional Development. pubmed.ncbi.nlm.nih.gov/18295898/

Ch. 2: Honour

- Walk barefoot whenever possible. It is beneficial for grounding and calming. Take in the beauty of your surroundings with appreciation.

- Visualize what a calm relaxed body would feel like. Use all your senses.

- Focus on and repeat a word that is calming like "calm" or "peace".

- Take a cold shower in the morning. Begin with warm water then gradually cool off.

- Place ice on your face for 20 seconds, repeat 5 -10 times. This helps to reduce anger, slows the heart rate, and relaxes your body.

- Take probiotics for your gut health. Your digestive system is a big part of your overall health so keeping it balanced is important.

- Engage your sense of smell with essential oils. I like to use lavender, peppermint and a blend called Peace & Calming essential oil[33].

- Teach students to look for safety cues: speak in a calm tone of voice, friends to help them, reminder to breathe, a safe environment.

- Express yourself through your creative gifts: talk, draw, write, and move. Many students that I have worked with love to doodle. It's very calming to them.

- Yoga, tai chi, and qi gong are good practices to learn and implement.

- Sing, hum, laugh, dance, and play daily!

- Shake out your stress. Physically moving the body is so critical. Have frequent mini-dance breaks. Dance breaks alone help engage the social system, students have fun interactions, playing and laughing with each other. The result is students who develop better relationships, feel more connected and safer in the environment where they are having fun together.

---

[33] Peace & Calming Essential oil is available through Young Living. To purchase at wholesale prices contact Janet Miller at facebook.com/janet.l.miller.100/ or by email at ecstaticaboutoils@yahoo.com

Porges believes that children with Autism Spectrum Disorder have depressed social engagement systems. Imagine the possibilities for change by implementing strategies to re-engage the social engagement system! This is why relationships are crucial. Showing students unconditional love is crucial.

To feel safe at school and home children need structure and stability. As an educator, you have the privilege of providing that safety net of structure, routine, reassurance, and compassion on a regular basis within the school environment. You get to be their safe zone once you develop trust with them.

The pathways in your social nervous system are strengthened by physical activity; regular exercising increases myelination on the pathways of the nerves. Myelination is an increase of the fatty coating on nerve pathways. Having an increase of healthy myelination is important because it leads to healthy nervous system functioning.

When I discovered the polyvagal theory I was thrilled to make the connection between the benefits of a specific technique called the Morter March developed by the late Dr. M.T. Morter, Jr. and carried on in her practice by his daughter Dr. Sue Morter[34], international speaker, a master of bio-energetic medicine and a quantum field visionary.

The Morter March involves moving the upper and lower body at the same time as you move the left and right sides of your body. You create new neural pathways for balance and ease. It is helpful for resetting your nervous system and clearing subconscious blocks. When you feel more balanced and at peace you are more able to access clear thoughts and feel more positive.

---

[34] Dr. Sue Morter is an international speaker and author. She is a Master of Bio-energetic medicine and a Quantum Field visionary. Her teachings show learners how to utilize their own energy patterns to achieve higher energy frequencies through inner reflection, meditation and self-healing through implementing her techniques and strategies which are described in her book. As well you can do further learning and exploring on her website for the journey to yourself.

Website: drsuemorter.com/
Email: Info@DrSueMorter.com

Ch. 2: Honour

1. Begin in a standing position with your feet hip width apart. Stand straight.
2. Take a step forward with your right leg. Keep your left foot in place with your heel on the floor. Bend your left knee slightly as if you are in a lunge position.
3. As you are extending your right leg you simultaneously lift your left arm to a 45-degree angle. Turn your palm so that your thumb is pointing up. At this time, your right arm moves backward behind you at a 45-degree angle as well. (Thumb down) This action of your right arm moving back usually happens automatically. At this point, your left leg and right arm will be forward, and your left leg and right arm will be back.
4. Next, turn and tilt your head toward the extended left arm, look up your arm to the thumb and close your right eye.
5. In this position, STRETCH... Hold your breath for 5-10 seconds.
6. If you are a parent or an educator doing this for yourself think about an incident where you felt shame, guilt or regret. Take a deep breath and feel the feeling of forgiveness, love and acceptance.
7. Exhale, step back to centre, feet hip width apart again and switch your whole position to the opposite of what you were doing. Now it will be your left leg and right arm forward and your right leg and left arm back with your head towards your right arm. Repeat 3 times each side.

Note: If showing a student, I do not explain the forgiveness, or intentional aspect other than to simply say it's a good way to help your body feel balanced and it helps you feel calmer for learning. Adaptation for working with children with special needs: This can be done lying down, sitting, or leaning against a wall for better support and balance.

Note: Instructions for Morter March are used with permission from Dr. Sue Morter.

I love using the Morter March with students to show how they can calm themselves and feel more balanced. I have shown other students how to do both the Morter March as well as a cross lateral pattern for calmness.

Facebook: www.facebook.com/DrSueMorter/
Book: *The Energy Codes: The 7 Step System to Awaken Your Spirit, Heal Your Body, and Live Your Best Life* (New York, Simon & Shuster, 2019)

I use it to help calm students prior to reading exercises; it calms them to have better focus and read more easily. The cross lateral pattern is basically crossing over your body to the opposite side: right arm to left knee, left arm to right knee (repeat 20 times). You can do it standing or sitting, even lying down. Some students have a very hard time crossing over their body, in that case, use a coloured sticker on their hand and knee to help with focus of the action. Use two colours - one for one side, one for the other.

Along with offering courses and programs, Morter also has a bestselling book, **The Energy Codes: The 7 Step System to Awaken Your Spirit, Heal Your Body, and Live Your Best Life**, in which she describes a variety of ways to become more embodied while managing our own emotions, energy, and self-healing in order to reach our highest potential.

An engaged social nervous system improves wellbeing and health; it affects your heart rate variability in a positive manner. You will feel calm and healthy, both mentally and physically. You will shine!

E. The Six Ghosts of Fear

"Fears are nothing more than a state of mind." - Napoleon Hill, author of **Think and Grow Rich**

Along with feeling safe and protected, children should have freedom from fears. In Chapter 15 of Hill's **Think and Grow Rich**, the author outlines the six fears that we face as humans and then how to outwit them. Children may or may not consciously realize fear but might instead have feelings that they can't describe through words. Recognizing these fears can help a child feel safe, loved, and honoured in a classroom setting.

Fear of Poverty

Many children face issues of poverty. This can range from lack of food at home and no food for lunches at certain times of the month, to improper clothing for weather changes especially when transitioning from fall to winter.

There are many ways to assist children and their families in dealing with this fear. At one school where I worked, the staff got together during the Christmas season to buy clothing and special presents for students in need. The same school and many others in our city annually participate in the Joyful Socks Program where the entire school collects socks and items to

Ch. 2: Honour

fill them for men, women, and children in need. Our school also donates canned foods to our local soup kitchen and Dress Down Day proceeds are donated to a local charity. These actions create a wonderful sense of community and help those who participate develop a sense of connection and involvement.

Another way to help fight this fear is to demonstrate to children that the world is a kind and caring place. Having nourishing snacks on hand for students or starting a breakfast program are excellent places to start. When planning school activities and events that require money from parents, choose dates when you know most people get paid. (For example, consider the end of the month or near the date when government child care cheques arrive.) Schedule book fairs and bake sales around these dates and make sure to give ample time for pizza orders and milk orders to be handed in. Remember to be mindful of students whose parents simply cannot afford any of these extras. You can keep children from standing out as "less than" by slipping them money for books or offering them baked goods on those occasions.

One time, I asked the students in my class about who had money for the bake sale. About 6 out of the 24 students didn't have anything so I gave them each a one-dollar coin for a treat. It wasn't a big deal to me but I knew it meant a lot to them. The teacher that I was working with at the time got mad at me and told me if the children didn't have money, it was their lot in life and I shouldn't interfere. His words hurt me as much as fists to my stomach. How dare he say that! There were lots of reasons why children might not have money and why should a child feel left out over something that can be so easily fixed? The next time we had a bake sale, I asked again who didn't have money and gave them each a 2-dollar coin!

Paying it forward is another great way to help. I would give the ladies at the sale a $20 bill and tell them that children who came to them with goods should be charged to Mrs. Smith's bill. Once that money ran out, I would simply give the ladies more as needed. Children are not always 'without funds'; sometimes parents simply forget to send money. I've had parents bring or send me money later and be grateful that I looked after their children.

Another time at a bake sale I noticed a jar with a label on it that said: 'For the Poor'. Really? I was shocked and thought to myself that this was ridiculous. It's a nice idea to want to help children enjoy the sale—but did it have to be labeled like that? No! To be mindful and considerate of feelings it could have been labeled differently. As I mentioned above, sometimes in our busy, fast-paced world, parents simply forget to send money or haven't even had the chance to read the announcement yet.

These are just small examples about how kindness can help improve a child's world and how consideration should be given into any situation. In this kind of circumstance, be mindful when you announce that it's time for your class to go to the sale. Notice whose faces drop, who is looking sad, who hangs their head, who cries. Children speak through their actions and behaviours even if they are not using their words.

I know you can't control what goes on in the home environment, but it is possible to provide safety, security, and love at school. At home, too many children hear conversations that they shouldn't hear and have worries that they shouldn't feel it's their responsibility to figure out. If you are reading this book I am sure you are not one of the it's-their-lot-in-life kind of people. Thank you in advance for who you already are with your students. Remember to teach children they are never poor if they are rich in spirit.

Fear of Criticism

When people have a fear of criticism they tend to suppress their feelings and emotions and become people-pleasers. The effects of doing this can be life-long. Health issues can develop through the thoughts you think both consciously or unconsciously.

Criticism is one of the main sources of psychological pain and it can greatly affect you. Your self-esteem and self-worth can be affected when someone says something that was intended as constructive criticism but, for whatever reason, you take it as being something wrong with you. This can even affect your quality of life. Criticism or even the fear of criticism can cause you to lose sleep and worry excessively about what you perceive you did wrong. Fear of being criticized can affect your mood and even your ability to try something again. Efforts are halted for fear of being judged or criticized. This fear can cause you to not express your opinion as much as you would like, it can cause you to feel timid, self-conscious, shy, and nervous. It can even affect your posture and memory.

Teach your students that when you give feedback it is to help them progress and gain insight and understanding with regards to whatever you are advising them on. Encourage them to express their opinions, be confident, and believe in themselves.

Ch. 2: Honour

How you process criticism depends upon your thoughts. You can even slide into an 'I'm not worthy' mentality which can become a trigger throughout your life. This was my experience due to past failure with tests and not being able to comprehend the lessons being taught. It wasn't that I was lazy. I truly didn't understand it. I know that a left- brained person can get very frustrated and annoyed with teaching a student who isn't absorbing strategies. But right-brain learners truly learn differently, and strategies must be implemented for their understanding. Dominance profiles matter here too. I reverse numbers frequently especially when writing out a math problem. I'm thankful and grateful for calculators but I can still mix up numbers when inputting, which makes book-keeping tasks a nightmare for me.

I have seen the damage of self-criticism and the effects of it. A long time ago, when I was in high school, I was doing a math test and felt very incapable of completing the test. I could not see the value in how it would even make sense or be needed in my life. Due to my own brain dominance and learning style (which I wasn't aware of at that time, nor was my teacher, I'm certain) I got very frustrated and threw my math test in the garbage. My teacher encouraged me to dig it out and do my best. He wanted me to know that any mark was better than a zero. I dug it out, uncrumpled it, smoothed it out and attempted it again as best as I could. I felt reluctant to do so, but felt better with his encouragement. At the time, I lacked belief in my abilities and myself. When I got my test back, I had scored a whopping 14 out of 100. Well, as he said, anything was better than a zero. My teacher even gave me my course credit and made me promise never to take math again! Years later, I did find examples in my life where that math lesson could have been used. Looking back, it would have helped me immensely if the problems had been taught using real life examples of how 'x' plus 'y' equals 'z' rather than just presenting 'x' and 'y' numeral problems.

I do best with real applicable examples. Also, due to my dominant hand, ear and eyes being opposite to my dominant brain hemisphere (I'm right brain) I had no access to the logic side of my brain. When I was under stress, access to logic during new learnings and during challenging times such as a test situation, was limited and I felt incapable of performing. He was a good teacher but I was highly critical of myself and shut down, cutting off access to higher order thinking and better problem-solving abilities.

Teach your students how to respond calmly by modeling. By having a strong relationship with your student they can understand that you have their best interests at heart and that you believe in them until they can believe in themselves more. Allow breaks to help students regain their calm and gather their thoughts.

Dr. Wayne Dyer reminds us that, *"the opinion of others is none of my business"*, don't allow yourself to be influenced by how others view you. Confidence comes from within. This is an important lesson to model to students!

Fear of Ill Health

As a child, I not only had a fear of ill health, I had it. I had juvenile arthritis and my body ached daily. I had chronic nosebleeds almost daily. I slept poorly and was often extremely cold during the winter months. We lived in an old house that was heated by a woodstove and by morning when the embers were down, it was cold. We didn't have running water and therefore, didn't have an indoor toilet. We had an outhouse and a makeshift washroom in a little corner area in my bedroom. It had a door and inside a huge can with a toilet seat on it. I don't know if my teachers knew the lengths I went through each morning putting my clothes on over my pajamas because I was too cold to take them off. I craved extra layers of warmth. At night, I would put everyone's jacket on top of me too. I think if teachers had known what my life was like at that time they might have been more compassionate towards me.

Did you have a fear of illness as a child? Did you have health issues? Do you currently have any health issues or problems? Fear and worry about health may affect your mood, health, and behaviour within the classroom. Fear and worry can also cause your own health problems. Our minds are so powerful.

Know yourself and know the health status of your students, casual conversations with them regularly are important.

Fear of Loss of Love

Another common psychological fear is the loss of love. Doing things for others because you want to see them happy is one thing but doing things in order for people to like you back is another. People-pleasing is the common archetype seen for someone who holds this fear. This fear can immobilize an individual and cause them to feel anxiety, worry, and possibly depression.

Ch. 2: Honour

Loss of love is one of the most powerful fears that can cause intense feelings ranging from jealousy and lack of self-control to losing one's temper.
A student can experience the feelings of loss of love through changes in family dynamics such as divorce and additions of new family members such as siblings (new baby), step- parents and step-siblings.

When a student's home life is undergoing times of change and upheaval, there can be turmoil and mixed emotions. A student may not be able to express effectively how they are feeling because of the changes. They may feel threatened, overwhelmed and even lost. The teacher should be mindful of changes in mood, behaviour, focus, work effort and output. This is where regular open home and school communication is effective so the teacher can know why there may be changes in the child.

Fear of Old Age

Surprisingly some children might also have a fear of growing up. They are convinced that by "staying little" their parents will be here forever. That's why I think it's important to pay attention to your words — a young child can misunderstand and believe through the power of words that you want your child to stay little forever.

Fear of Death

One of the most important works of information on death and dying was written by Swiss psychiatrist, Elisabeth Kübler-Ross in 1969. Her work, **On Death and Dying**[35] is an invaluable resource for parents, caregivers, and anyone dealing with the death of a loved one. The book explains the five stages of grief: denial, anger, bargaining, depression, and acceptance.

Grief is different for everyone and the time spent in each area varies greatly from person to person. Some stages are even repeated. These stages can also occur with any other major loss: loss of a job, divorce, or poor health. Grief can be so painful and overwhelming. It can affect the child emotionally, physically, mentally, and spiritually. Children, like adults, experience a multitude of emotions, ailments, and thoughts that affect their own wellbeing.

---

[35] Kübler-Ross, Elisabeth, *On Death and Dying* (Scribner, 1 Edition, June 9, 1997).

Reactions to grief vary depending upon age as well—they can range from changes in digestion, stomach aches, constipation, diarrhea, weight loss, weight gain, headaches, to nervousness-fidgeting, pacing, and tapping. The child can experience tightness in their chest or tightness in their throat. They may have changes in appetite, eating more or eating less than before. Their body and muscles may feel weak. The child may experience a complete lack of energy. Regular sleep patterns may be affected by not falling asleep easily at night or having disturbed sleep through bad dreams and sad thoughts. The child may feel nauseous and shaky. They may be affected by sudden noises. Fearfulness and anxiety can result as part of grief as well. The child may be emotionally insecure and unsure of themselves. They may become sad more easily. You may notice them becoming more increasingly withdrawn, avoiding peers, avoiding school work tasks, even the fun ones.

At times, children may even become aggressive and angry towards peers and staff. These are big emotions. Get the assistance of your school counselors and clergy staff if you are part of a Catholic school. Keep open lines of communication with the family to discuss how to keep moving the child through their grief.

Consider the relationship the child had with the person who has passed away. If it was a close family member you can be sure they have strong feelings even if they are not able to articulate their sadness and loss.

F. How You Can Help a Grieving Child

"No one ever told me that grief felt so like fear." - C.S. Lewis, A Grief Observed

The child is in survival mode and is protecting themselves the best way they know how. Be kind, supportive, and be willing to listen to their stories.

Never force the child to tell you about their loved one. They will do it when they are ready. Allowing the child to feel safe is their comfort zone. They may not want to talk about it because it makes them feel sad.

Elisabeth Kübler-Ross was a Swiss-American psychiatrist, author and humanitarian who developed a theory that consisted of five stages of grief. She later expanded the list to seven stages and stressed that others understand that grief is not simply a linear process or a predictable process. Individuals can go through any of the stages at different times during their own grief. Stages include shock, denial, anger, bargaining, testing, depression, and acceptance.

If possible, provide a quiet reflection area for processing their thoughts, emotions, and grief. Allow mini-breaks and walks to get a drink of water.

Be mindful of their actions and words. Watch and notice the child's reactions to songs, poems, and words when mentioned. A child triggered by a memory will change body position, change their breathing, and may even appear sad and distant. Unless advised otherwise you can quietly say: *"I noticed when that song came on you looked sad. Did you know that song before?"*

Children will have questions about death; answer as honestly and as age appropriately as you can. Children find value in knowing someone understands too. I have had times where I have talked to children about how sad I felt when my grandmother went to heaven and how much I miss her. I'll tell a funny story about her and things that I miss about her and ask them what they miss about their loved one.

Young children can sometimes get confused somehow thinking it's their fault. Their fears may increase and range from fears of losing someone else or even dying themselves. Their fears increase feelings of anxiousness, isolation, and sadness. Some will even believe that they will never ever be happy again. Help them to find their happy! Be there for them with smiles, hugs, and reassurance that it all will be okay one day. Simply be there for the child, listen when they are ready to talk and encourage expressing feelings in constructive ways. Allow the child to draw pictures of memories, especially favourite times shared with that loved one.

They may not understand the permanence of death and continually wish and wait for the loved one to return. Separation anxiety may develop. The child may be afraid to leave other family members. School may become a challenging transition from home to school. Children can experience post-traumatic experiences as a result of death, especially through events they may have seen or felt at that time. Encourage parents to seek grief counseling and services of professionals to overcome the trauma.

Teenagers respond to grief like adults. They may shut down to process their loss and go into survival mode. Being there as a support for them, and as a comfort, while extending understanding and compassion will benefit them in so many ways as they adjust and find a new normal.

If you as an educator are grieving it's important to allow yourself to fully feel and go through your own grieving process. Repressed grief will express itself in other ways. Often it will express itself in health conditions and pain. Be gentle with yourself and find constructive ways to feel your own grief. Avoid destructive methods such as numbing your pain with drugs, alcohol, or punishing yourself with overeating, overspending, or over doing anything that might be destructive to yourself. Find the beauty in your good memories and focus on that.

When choosing activities for special occasions such as Mother's Day and Father's Day, keep in mind that not all children have both parents—whether it's caused by death or divorce. Many children are raised by other family members, or live in two homes. Know your students' home life situations. Their significant love may be a grandmother or nana. Give children choices in the crafts that they make, especially the cards. It is heartbreaking to see the look on a child's face when they have a card that says "Happy Father's Day" and you know they don't have a dad in their life, same for Mother's Day or any other occasion.

Children can experience the stages of grief through family separation and divorce too. They question many things including if what occurred was their fault. Always reassure them that it was not their fault and that love is forever. As Helen Keller once said, "What we have once enjoyed deeply we can never lose. All that we love deeply becomes a part of us."

G. Culture and Heritage

"Culture is the widening of the mind and of the spirit." - Jawaharlal Nehru, Indian independence activist

Many students have a richness and an identity in their culture and specific heritage. They have traditions, ceremonies, and beliefs about themselves and their world through these experiences. Learning what they have been taught to believe, treasure, and respect will give you insight to why they behave, think, and act as they do.

A classroom is enriched when students learn about the world and other cultures. Learning can be fun when you experience new things, try new foods, and discover how others live.

Ch. 2: Honour

Cultural education is essential for equality, social justice, and human dignity. We are all humans and need to be treated as the precious miracles that each and every person is.

I have always been drawn to the Indigenous cultures and only recently discovered my own true heritage and some amazing things about my ancestors. For 75 years, our family never knew where my maternal grandmother was buried. My search was on! My ancestors fought in the War of 1812 with the British army, they were voyageurs and some family members were talented carpenters who contributed incredible wooden fixtures to churches in Quebec. I find my family history fascinating and important to know. Through my ancestry research I discovered that I am Métis (which is a mix of European and First Nations). It explains why I have felt a connection to the sacred Seven Grandfather Teachings and so much more.

The Grandfather Teachings focus on seven values and each teaching has an animal totem that represents it: humility (wolf), bravery (bear), honesty (sabé or raven), wisdom (beaver), truth (turtle), respect (buffalo), and love (eagle).

Each teaching is interdependent; they are all part of living a good life. Knowing cultural traditions, spiritual beliefs, ceremonial practices, and even parenting practices of each culture enables everyone to understand and accept each other more easily and unconditionally as human beings.

Learning about First Nation and Métis cultures is a passion of mine. Have you ever done the blanket exercise? Do you know about the medicine wheel? It is important for children to learn their culture and not be shamed by it.

The residential school program was a huge tragedy and never should have happened. I am heartbroken to know what children went through during that era. Its effects have destroyed generations of families.

Parents, family and elders need to teach traditions to their children. Too many worthy traditions are not being carried over. Knowledge is being lost. Languages are being forgotten. Years ago, because natural herbs and plants and the healing power of them was an interest of mine, I had the opportunity to present my knowledge to a group of residents at a local First Nations reserve. They were amazed at the variety available in our area and their many uses. While they were impressed by what I was telling them,

I was shocked that they did not know about their uses. They explained to me that the Medicine Man was the keeper of the secrets. Which made sense, but at the same time I felt sad because the traditional knowledge was not being carried over.

I love to travel the world and see how different cultures live. I encourage anyone to travel anytime that you get an opportunity, you never know what fascinating things you will discover about the people and yourself. People need to be educated on the impact and ongoing issues related to racism, oppression, and segregation. There are many resources available to educate yourself. I'll put some resources at the end of this book.[36]

---

[36] *From the Ashes* - Jesse Thistle
I loved this book by Thistle. I found myself relating to many aspects of this book from knowing the stories of children that I have worked with and through discovering my own heritage and making sense of stories that I have heard about. The resilience of his spirit inspires a reader to know there is hope and to stay strong. It is a good reminder that we do not always know what circumstances a child is living in.

How to be an Antiracist - Ibram X. Kendi
One man's personal journey and honest reflection of racism paired with thought provoking information for self-reflection and self-examination.

White Fragility: Why It's So Hard for White People to Talk About Racism - Robin DiAngelo
This is a great "starter" book to deepen your understanding of racism and how white people benefit in our society. Where there are racial differences separation and inequality exist.

The Miners Canary: Enlisting Race, Resisting Power, Transforming Democracy - Lani Guinier and Gerald Torres
Inspires race consciousness for individuals to be proactive and work towards solidarity through teamwork for the betterment of issues ranging from education, politics to voting rights.

This Bridge Called My Back: Writings by Radical Women of Color - Edited by Cherrie Moraya and Gloria Anzaldua
It consists of stories, interviews and poems that enable the reader to gain different perspectives and better understanding of race, gender, sexuality and class issues that women of colour still deal with today in our world.

Ch. 2: Honour

All students should know and be proud of their heritage. Each student's culture should be celebrated. During the recent stay-at-home COVID-19 period, we had an online cultural lunch for students. Each student brought a food item from their heritage to our virtual classroom. The foods presented varied from pasta to pancakes. Some students and the teacher and educational assistants wore articles of clothing associated with their heritages. Then we played music from each culture—what a beautiful mix. This was one of my most favourite moments from the whole school year both online and offline! The excitement and pride that each student exhibited during their turn to share was priceless. Connection and sharing!

In 2011, I went on a 3-week humanitarian/tourist adventure to Kenya. To say that the experience was life changing for me is an understatement. We had the opportunity to assist at a school of close to 300 children. The poverty was as I had always imagined including their lack of daily nourishment. Most of the students only ate once a day and that was the lunch that they were served at school. This means that they went the rest of the day without food: no supper, no breakfast—not a bit of nourishment until lunch again the next day. The lunch consisted of corn and mush. Children had to have their own dish or they had to share out of another child's bowl. I saw one boy eating his meal out of his pocket using his red dirt covered hands.

Classrooms had no supplies except for a very limited amount of torn and tattered books that the children shared. They didn't have electricity or running water. Teachers hadn't been paid in over four months. Rather than simply give them handouts of money that would have been spent immediately, we gave "hands up" assistance of resources to empower them to be independent. We helped them get their water running again, we planted a garden to grow vegetables, refurbished their chicken coop and got them chickens to have eggs to sell. We purchased books and learning materials and paid the staff some money for their efforts and dedication—despite receiving no income for several months they continued teaching because of their love for the children. Later, we bought them a generator and hired a sewing teacher, so the students could learn skills to empower themselves in the future.

One common thing we discovered wherever we went was that despite many grim situations: death of loved ones, extreme poverty, hunger, and drought ruining their family's crops and livestock, they always appeared happy. They had rooted themselves in faith and their love of God that things would be better. Their inner resilience was inspiring and heartwarming.

Learning about their lifestyles and challenges gave me a better appreciation for all the blessings that I have. I took many pictures which I have used to show hundreds of students the differences in cultures and highlight how we are all connected and how we can help others both near and far.

Knowledge of other countries' trials and tribulations can inspire people towards acceptance, action, and change. I believe in teaching children about being of service to others in need whether it's locally, nationally, or across the world. When a child learns to be of service they learn to take the focus off their own perceived problems, they begin to understand that the world doesn't revolve solely around their needs. While having needs and having them met matters, the instant gratification that many children of the Western world expect doesn't do them any good. Learning that life doesn't always say 'yes' and learning to wait for and work for the items they want is a very positive experience. This creates resilience.

An understanding of each child's culture gives you more of an iceberg view of who they are. Through cultural projects and learning their traditions you can discover hidden treasures and answers to enhance your awareness and understanding of why each behaves as they do. Make a point of learning their beliefs, customs and parenting styles, religion, manners, and celebrations. This exploration helps each child feel included and validated for their own uniqueness and individuality.

Learning about our differences helps others understand diversity and feel appreciated and valued regardless of skin colour, intellect, talents, and abilities. It instills pride in each person's uniqueness.

H. Making Sense of Sensory Needs

"We ignore that our kids are overwhelmed with sensory input for at least eight hours a day. They can only appropriately tend to learning tasks when they are emotionally, physically, and mentally in a good place. Expecting them to do otherwise is, at best, a waste of time. At worst, it is the beginning of a chain reaction that will perpetuate sensory overload for the entire class." - Wende Parsley, Midland Reporter-Telegram

Understanding a child's sensory needs can go a long way in helping a day go smoothly.

There are many possibilities to a child's disruptive and seemingly oppositional behaviour that can sometimes be explained as a sensory integration need.

Ch. 2: Honour

Sensory integration is a neurological process where a person organizes sensory inputs from the environment that they currently inhabit.

Children can be easily overwhelmed and feel overloaded. Signs of this can include: refusing to work, saying no, crying, sweating, getting angry, repetition, impulsivity, stimming*, lashing out, changes in skin colour (pale or red), and sometimes, even a loss of balance and coordination. Physical symptom complaints include stomachaches, headaches, and nausea. *Stimming is a form of self-stimulation that is common with children with Autism. Stimming involves repetitive movements such a hand flapping, tapping on a surface. It also involves movements such as rocking back and forth, pacing, spinning, and/or repeating words. Each child is different, and their self-stimulation varies from child to child. Stimming helps the child process sensory input usually to be calm, get grounded and cope in their environment. It should be noted that it often serves a purpose for the child so if you want to extinguish it you will likely need to replace it with another behaviour.

Sensory integration researchers have called sensory integration dysfunction SPD—Sensory Processing Disorder. Noticing is an important skill with regards to children to see when it happens and how it can be prevented or lessened.

In their book **Sensory Integration, A Guide for Preschool Teachers** Christy Isbell and Rebecca Isbell state *"The child with Sensory Processing Disorder has a brain that experiences great difficulty with adjusting to or regulating responses to sensory input from the environment. The child who does not react strongly enough to sensory input is called under-responsive, while the child who reacts too strongly to sensory information is considered over-responsive."*[37]

Do you have students that do not like to write with a pencil (the noise on paper can be painfully uncomfortable to an over-sensitive child)? Children who climb on everything and jump off? Cover their ears when others are singing? How about a student who is refusing to paint, play with clay, or get their hands wet? What about the sound of chalk? Are there students who refuse to sit on the carpet or are frequently disruptive when sitting upon it? It's possible that the texture of the carpet is distracting.

---

[37] Isbell, Christy and Isbell, Rebecca, *Sensory Integration A Guide for Preschool Teachers*, (Gryphon House Inc., 1st edition, July 2009).

A watchful eye can distinguish between a perceived refusal to comply and a true sensory overload or need. Each child is different and unique in their needs. Some simple ways to manage sensory problems can include: providing a predictable and visual schedule as well as creating schedule breaks. You can create break cards to give to children. In this way the child can self-regulate and show awareness of needing a break and to empower the student to notice and speak up. It's important to have sensory equipment available. A sensory box available to all students is a great tool to have on hand. Allowing each student a quiet "fidget" toy to keep in their desk is another great idea.

Be considerate of the environment the child is in, when possible remove things that are known to be irritating or annoying to the student. An example: remove the loudly ticking clock when students are painting. Prevention whenever possible is the best strategy if you know the child's needs. Other ways to control the environment for all children and help the child can include: monitoring your voice tone and level, following a regular routine, being conscious of the noise level of the class, offering choices, respecting emotions, reducing clutter, and honouring personal space. Provide frequent movement breaks and plan ahead for smooth transitions. Remember that being consistent is key!

I. Types of Sensory Needs

"Some children may need a behavioural approach, whereas other children may need a sensory approach." - Temple Grandin, consultant and autism spokesperson

Our senses help us to learn and develop. Senses include sight, touch, taste, hearing, and smell. They also include the vestibular (movement and balance) and proprioceptive systems (sense of body position and space). When considering the whole child, there are a wide variety of needs to take into account when learning about your student:

- Are they a sensory seeker or a sensory avoider?
- Are they a sensory under-responder?
- Are they a visual seeker? Visual avoider? Visual under-responder?
- Are they an auditory seeker? Auditory avoider? Auditory under-responder?
- Are they a tactile seeker? Tactile avoider? Tactile under-responder?
- Are they a vestibular seeker? Vestibular avoider? Vestibular under-responder?

- Are they a proprioception seeker? Proprioception avoider? Proprioception under-responder?

There are many red flags that can signal which area or areas where a child might have issues. A few from the list include: Staring at bright lights, loving things that flash, being clumsy, refusing to participate in certain activities where there's too many children playing the game, getting headaches when reading or using their eyes too much, bothered by noises, bothered by movement, likes to make noise, likes to get messy, is very ticklish, always touches others and moves into their personal space, exhibits picky eating habits, takes risks, is fearful of playing and running, doesn't notice whether clothing is wet or dry. The Isbells' book has wonderful charts that may be photocopied for classroom use referencing these processing issues at a glance. This is not diagnosing, it's simply a guide for you to be alert and then notify the necessary resources that can follow up on your observations for auditory, vision and occupational therapy, as well as other services.

There is not a problem that exists to which there isn't an answer. Sometimes in order to find that answer creative thinking and brainstorming are required. There are many things you can create on a low budget to help a child cope with difficulties within the environment. Please see the Tips and Tools page for ideas. sheenalsmith.com/tips-and-tools-for-working-with-children/

A qualified occupational therapist will need to access and set up a sensory diet for the child with specific recommendations to accommodate and ease the stress they encounter through the regular routine of a day.

J. Individual Preferences and Uniqueness

"We are all equal in the fact that we are all different." - C. Joybell C., author and philosophical essayist

Know your student! A teacher once made a point of saying she kept my son right under her nose so she could keep an eye on him. She opened his desk to prove just how well she knew him. Turned out she had the wrong desk! Connect with your students by asking simple questions. What do they like to do at home and at school? What's their favourite or least favourite food? Favourite subject at school? What is their family life like? Do they have a best friend? Any friends? How many members in their family? Do they have pets? What music do they like?

Do this as a group activity near the start of the school year and take an interest at various times discussing these interests with the student. The reason for doing this near the start of the year is it quickly gives you ideas as to what you can ask your students more about, it improves communication and it helps you to know your students and what matters most to them. Great for relationship building and setting a classroom culture of diversity and acceptance. It enables the classmates to know each other better too. They can see their similarities and differences when it comes to styles and tastes.

Show your student you care. Help them to feel that you are saying 'I'm interested!'

K. Honour - It's Your Turn!

"If kids come to us from strong, healthly, functioning families, it makes our job easier. If they do not come to us from strong, healthy, functioning families, it makes our job more important." - Barbara Coloroso, author, consultant

As you can see a whole child approach truly encompasses mind, body, spirit and soul. A whole child approach that honours your students would include honouring their emotions, feelings, and fears, their cultural differences, as well as their sensory needs to enable them to experience an inclusive and equitable learning environment. As educators we work with students from a wide range of different home life experiences. It's up to us to do our part to build trust, healthy relationships and respect and show them the world is a safe place.

Self-Reflection Questions

- *What skills, insights and wisdom did you discover in this chapter?*
- *What will you implement in your classroom?*
- *What will you explore for yourself?*
- *What will you research more about for better understanding?*
- *How do you currently honour a student's culture in your classroom?*
- *Do you celebrate diversity?*

# CHAPTER 3: RESPECT

"Treat a man as he is and he will remain as he is. Treat a man as he can and should be and he will become as he can and should be." - Goethe

What does respect look like in a conscious classroom?

To me, respect is about how you treat and view others. Are you able to respect without judging them? Can you admire and appreciate differences? I always think what a boring world we would be living in if everyone were the same. Ways to show respect include being polite, listening to the opinions and views of others, encouraging others. Respecting others includes being considerate of their feelings, putting yourself in their shoes. Imagining how so many children start their day—it's not always easy for them!

Keeping in mind that we are responsible for our choices and actions is beneficial for all. They say respect is earned before it is given. I agree. But I think in many cases respect is a two-way street and it should go both ways. Children need to be treated with respect and modeled respect in order to understand it. The power of positive relationships goes a long way towards teaching respect.

Respect isn't taught by showing students "who is boss"; instead it can be taught to students by teaching them the way that they learn best. Helping students meet their needs gains respect and deep appreciation. Children do learn what they live and holding true to positive character traits enables them to develop trust and feel safe in your care.

Children who are respected and loved in all ways grow and develop in miraculous ways.

A. Judge Not! Meet the Needs!

"Everybody is a genius. But if you judge a fish by its ability to climb a tree, it will live its whole life believing that it is stupid." – Albert Einstein

Children are very in tune with how they feel even if they can't express it verbally. They have their own inner knowing and intuitive compass. They know whom to trust. Through your actions, your words, and most importantly, your energy, they will know whether to like and trust you. They can pick up on "fake nice" a mile away.

Labeling a child with judgments such as "good", "dumb" or "lazy" puts pressure on them—even if unspoken, they feel it. The effects of your negative or judgmental behaviour break a child's self-esteem internally. They end up feeling less of themselves, which often results in what you see as defiance, misbehaviour, anger, turmoil, and even destruction within the classroom.

I believe that it's extremely important to presume competence. There was one time when I was working with a nonverbal student, I was doing activities with her and she was successful at what we were doing. A resource teacher came along and saw what the student was doing and asked, "How did you know she could do that?" and added, "I never knew that she could do that!" I replied by saying, "I just assumed that she could."

Always remember that children hear what you are saying. So even though they may be nonverbal don't assume they do not understand what you are saying. Be mindful of your words around their innocent ears!

B. Mental Health Issues: A Rising Trend

"The greatest weapon against stress is our ability to choose one thought over another." - William James, American philosopher and author

Over the years, there has been a rise in mental health issues in the classrooms. It has been estimated that one in five children have mental health problems related to mood, behaviour, and thinking. There are a variety of common anxiety disorders: separation anxiety disorder, generalized anxiety disorder, social anxiety disorder, panic anxiety disorder, and obsessive-compulsive disorder. Generalized anxiety is the most common of these mental health disorders. The greatest challenge is that only one in five children who need mental health services receives them.

Ch. 3: Respect

The causes vary from genetics and brain physiology to environmental, temperament, and post-traumatic stress incidents. Left untreated these disorders can wreak havoc in a person's life. They can lead to depression, possible drug and alcohol abuse, and other issues including suicide.

A child displaying separation anxiety is often clingy, cries and has temper tantrums. They refuse to let a parent leave, refuse to attend school, and display homesickness. For this kind of anxiety, simple strategies can be employed: reassure the child, distract them with activities and to-do's with a buddy, reward independent actions, and implement a "coping" book. When the child is calm, teach some strategies for coping with the separation. I have often found that even allowing the child to draw a picture or make a card for the person they are pining for helps them to feel better. Thinking of their loved one brings positive feelings in and allows for the release of oxytocin (the love hormone that helps children feel better). For younger children, allow them to hold an object that reminds them of their parent or simply a teddy bear. Involve the whole class in relaxation techniques and calming strategies. Al's Pals[38] program has a great song for relaxation called Calm Down. It's soothing and beneficial for all. For older children, find meditation music that the whole class can listen and meditate to regularly, building up the amount of time that students can quietly sit. An ideal amount is 20 minutes but even getting 5 to 10 minutes can be beneficial.

---

[38] Al's Pals is a CASEL-approved program for younger students in kindergarten and primary grades. It is an evidence-based model prevention program. It is a resilience-based early childhood curriculum and teacher-training program that assists with developing social emotional skills, self-control, and problem-solving skills, as well as healthy decision-making techniques to children ages three to eight years old. It is designed to help children recognize and regulate their own feelings and behaviour. The lessons are fun and engaging and involve the use of character puppets, catchy music and effective teaching approaches. Benefits include children are more able to regulate their own emotions through awareness and practice. Children learn conflict resolution and ways to solve problems peacefully. It sets the stage for an environment of respect, caring, co-operation, and responsibility. Children learn about safety including dangers of household products. They will learn to appreciate differences and build acceptance and appreciation of others. They are taught the harmful effects of alcohol and other drugs. The program builds on abilities to make healthy choices and implements strategies for coping with challenges and difficulties in life. The curriculum includes 46 lessons approximately 10 to 15 minutes in length, with two lessons per week. The program can be learned through a two-day training in person or online.

Website: wingspanworks.com/healthy-al/

A coping book is a tool that you create with the student that shows drawings or actual pictures of them doing techniques that assist them in becoming calm and happy. You can add in pictures of the child doing activities that help them settle such as: deep breathing, sitting in a quiet corner, using a manipulative object such as a fidget spinner or squeezing an item like playdough.

By creating it together, the book is personalized with what works best for that child. If you use the Zones of Regulation as a resource in your class you can print out the individual tool visual that you can create with the class as a whole as you discuss the activities, techniques, and zones with them.

It can be scary for children when they are experiencing an anxiety attack. Reassuring the child that they are safe is often suggested yet not always heard by the child due to their state of mind. At the time of the panic attack, survival instincts have kicked in and the automated emotional part of the brain has taken over, blocking access to the prefrontal cortex. This means that the understanding and logic needed to determine that the fear is not real or not as dangerous as perceived, cannot be accessed.

During an anxiety attack, the first step is to get the child to breathe deeply using their preferred method of breathing. Then encourage talking about what happened. What are they experiencing at this moment? If you can get the child talking it helps with the lateral sides of the brain communicating with each other, thus stimulating left-brain and right-brain logic and language. It's useful for the child to make sense of anxiety in order to build a sense of safety and security. Learning how to take your body out of fight and flight helps you to feel more in control. By learning how to activate the logical side of your brain you neutralize the flight or fright chemicals and can more easily come back to a balanced state of mind.

To lessen the worries and help the child manage persistent worry that is causing them to feel overwhelmed, provide a safe space, a calm environment, praise appropriate behaviour responses, and have verbal and visual instructions when giving directions. You can also model positive ways to handle anxiety. Explain to the child that it's okay to worry. There are times when worry and fear are normal. Encourage deep breathing and discuss a plan for the next time—get their input as to what strategies they would like to use.

The bright side of it all is that there are answers to helping a child or adolescent cope with anxiety. Remember, however, that there is no one-

C. Anxiety and Children

"You are braver than you believe, and stronger than you seem and smarter than you think." - Christopher Robin from **Winnie the Pooh**

Sometimes it is very challenging to discover the trigger for behaviour associated with anxiety. Other times it is easy. Hoping anxiety will just go away isn't the answer, especially when an automatic response becomes ingrained as a response. When a child develops a pattern of negative response to perceived danger it takes more effort to change the response. The child assumes there is danger when there is no reason for it. The anxiety response puts the child instantly into survival mode, bringing on a cascade of emotions that can be exhibited as temper tantrums, aggressiveness, and avoidance. Some children even exhibit clingy behaviour.

Strategies for assisting a child in survival mode include: staying calm, using a reassuring voice to tell the child they are safe. If you can physically put yourself at the child's level, that is good to do too. To help manage a negative emotional response put feelings into words by saying something like "You look like you are scared about something." "Are you afraid?" And, then reassure, "Let's look at your schedule," and take out the visual schedule to see what's next (if that is the trigger). Distraction can often help pull thoughts away from the survival moment to a new focus.

"Putting Feelings Into Words" is an article about research conducted by University of California in Los Angeles. The article discusses how labeling (naming a feeling or emotion that is being experienced) disrupts the amygdala activity in response to affective stimuli. The researchers were able to measure the differences in the brain and see the pathway that the responses to labeling had on the individual. Putting feelings into words activates the linguistic processing in the right ventricle lateral prefrontal cortex (RVLPFC), the region associated with the processing of emotional information. There was greater activity with linguistic processing versus non-linguistic processing in the RVLPFC when feelings were labeled.[39]

---

[39] University of California - Los Angeles. "Putting Feelings Into Words Produces Therapeutic Effects In The Brain." *ScienceDaily*, June 22, 2007. sciencedaily.com/releases/2007/06/070622090727.htm

It is important for all areas of the brain to communicate with each other. Left to right side, front to back and even top to bottom. When the brain is in survival mode communication is limited to the dominant side, usually the right side. Logic is central to the left side of the brain. During a period of perceived stress, the child can't access and make sense of what's happening enough to even express things such as: "because this is happening, I feel...." In the right side of the brain, the amygdala perceives that survival is at stake and the systems kick in to protect.

When the child goes into survival mode, overwhelm sets in quickly and all logic is harder to access. At this moment it is recommended that you do not compromise or negotiate due to causing negative reinforcement—it will only lead to more and more compromising and negotiation, the behaviour is then rewarded rather than extinguished. An example of this could include when a child has a hard time coming in from recess and you decide to give them extra recess time. The next time they will want to stay out even longer or at least stay out for a few extra minutes each time. Eventually, it could build up to power struggles and the child upping the ante until it's never enough. Does this mean that you should never allow the child extra time outside? Not necessarily, knowing your student will help you know the right answer to that. Follow your instincts.

Assess what coping strategies the child currently employs and what is appropriate for their developmental level. Consider their expressive language and problem-solving abilities and brainstorm ideas for handling the challenge. Be mindful that signs and symptoms of stress are often seen when a child exhibits challenging behaviours. Sadly, children may be in trouble for behaviour that could just be a stress reaction rather than something done intentionally or due to the child having poor cognitive abilities.

Thankfully the brain is neuroplastic and new pathways of response can be created. Having a trusting relationship with the child and pre-planning interventions for anxiety help the child know that they are safe. This is extremely helpful when it comes to implementing strategies to help get calm and grounded once again.

One of the simplest ways to become grounded is through the breath. Breathing from the belly is the best way because often other forms of breathing may lock you in a continued state of stress. Learn what style of breathing the child prefers (the lazy eight and four-sided breathing are examples) and teach it ahead of time (visuals are useful). This may help you to avoid bigger meltdowns, less class disruptions and allow for a quicker recovery for the student. Students can also blow bubbles, a pretend feather, a pinwheel or whistles. Breathing while tracing shapes such as stars, squares, circles can also be useful.

Another way to return to a state of calm is by engaging the child with their senses and bringing them back into the present moment. Have them name five objects that surround them. What do they hear? What do they smell? You can offer food or a drink too and give choices.

A useful book for younger children is called **When My Worries Get Too Big: A Relaxation Book for Children Who Live with Anxiety** by Kari Dunn Buron.[40] You can also create a small booklet and include four to five things a child can do to get calm. Children love when it's a personalized book with pictures of themselves in it doing the suggested actions for calming. This can be squeezing a ball, making faces, blowing a feather (can be pretend), crossing the body and tapping on the opposite sides—right hand or elbow to left knee and left elbow or hand to right knee.

Here are a few more ideas to help students balance their energy and emotions, process their challenging feelings and calm themselves:

- Expanding and contracting. Stretch out your arms and express a positive "I am" statement. This has helped many others feel expanded and positive.
- Drink water (so important!).
- Count backwards from 50.
- Wear headphones to lessen noise and distraction.

When feeling anxious or stressed you can use a progressive muscle relaxation technique. It is a form of relaxation that helps an individual release tension. It can be guided by someone or done by oneself. I prefer the guided version because listening to someone's voice helps me to focus more specifically on each area being mentioned. This can be done as a group or individually. To do this you basically tense a specific area of muscles as you breathe in during a count of four to ten and relax the muscles suddenly as you breathe out. Relax 10 to 20 seconds in between muscle groups and notice how they felt before and after each exercise. I have seen it taught different ways,

---

[40] Buron, Kari D., *When My Worries Get Too Big: A Relaxation Book for Children Who Live with Anxiety* (Kansas, AAPC Publishing, 2006).

some people start at the feet, legs, thighs, and move upward. Others start at the hands, wrists, arms, shoulders, forearms, and move downward.

Movement is essential to keep your body balanced and prevent stagnation. Some movement breaks can include the use of a trampoline, playground equipment, or free play such as jumping, crawling, climbing, bouncing, rocking, dancing and running.

Put a Lazy 8 walking track on the floor with tape at the back of the class for students to have access to in order to unwind and recharge.

Sensory-need activities are important. Allow children to squeeze something in their hands: Plasticine or stress balls. Let children shred papers, cut paper, or crumple paper. Let them watch a lava lamp or glitter jars. Have balloons filled with different materials including rice, small pebbles or marbles to manipulate. All these items can be placed in a sensory-needs box (or basket) that is easy to access when children feel anxious or stressed. These items can all be created on a low (or no) budget!

Provide opportunities for time outdoors as much as possible. Nature walks, bare foot if possible.

Allow and encourage tree hugging. My son loves to embrace trees when we visit our local park. He lights up, expressing his joy as he hugs them and smiles. His anxiety dissipates when he is running through a park filled with trees.

Anxiety and PTSD (Post Traumatic Stress Disorder) may be caused by trauma. Being aware of trauma that a child has experienced can be important so that you are able to have compassion and understanding for the child rather than viewing them as simply giving you a hard time or having a hard time. Knowing this can help change your perception from "what's wrong with you?" to "what's happened to you?"

It has long been known that early adversity can have lifelong effects on children. Physical and mental trauma can affect brain development. Trauma increases the risk of maladaptive behaviours of coping that can lead to lifelong problems such high-risk behaviour, poor executive functioning decision-making, substance abuse, and an inability to delay instant gratification.

Ch. 3: Respect

This is why it is so important for educators to be educated on anxiety, mental health, and trauma-informed practices, as well as knowing how they can help students adjust and rewire their brains to create better coping skills. Children with anxiety and trauma need a safe physical, social and emotional environment that is grounded in consistency and predictability. They need help with relationship-building skills taught through caring, trust and support through inclusion. Safety is once again a key priority. I feel that I cannot stress this enough. We can learn a great deal from the child's behaviour and coping strategies:

1. Be aware. Notice when your students seem stressed and have changes in posture, breathing, emotions, and moods.
2. Respect and validate their feelings and support them with how they feel. This is the perfect time to help them co-regulate through modeling and communication.
3. Remember anxiety can be different for everyone. There isn't just one cookie-cutter approach to dealing with it. Follow your intuition and use the Zones of Regulation whenever possible.
4. Be alert to seeing if there's a pattern as to when your student is most anxious regarding making requests and experiencing situations and circumstances.
5. Try not to assume that they understand that what they are feeling is related to anxiety.
6. Encourage appropriate expression! Empower them to know they can change and control how they feel.

Sometimes we think we are the teacher, sometimes it turns out the child is the teacher and we all can learn from each other! Inclusion and being present is a gift. By boosting resilience and emotional intelligence skills children can learn to manage stress and anxiety.

D. Calming Activities

"When you're feeling anxious, remember that you're still you. You are not your anxiety." – Deanne Repich, educator

Children do need help and guidance to self-regulate more than ever. Anxiety in children is so common and we can be part of helping them feel more in control of their emotions and feelings. There are many ways to co-teach a child to self-regulate. Make the activities fun by using visuals and props. Encourage children and give them time to discover what works for them.

Earlier in this chapter, I mentioned the idea of a sensory box. I believe it's beneficial that anyone in the class can access it when they feel the need. Additionally, it's terrific if each student has one sensory item on their desk. Some children need to hold something and manipulate it to have better focus. You may think that students aren't paying attention if they are not looking at you, but they are actually listening better by using this strategy as long as they are staying present and not going off into the land of imagination.

During lessons and learning activities, I think the sensory box or basket should be near so that any student wishing to get something feels free to do so. Sometimes it takes a bit of work to see which item works best for the student, especially when items can seem like such a novelty. Eventually, through observation, you'll discover who needs to hold and manipulate something when learning.

A tool that helps children who fidget is heavy resistive Therabands® (a cost-effective alternative is pantyhose). Simply tie the bands (or the hose) around the front legs of the child's desk and the seat so they can move their feet and legs against it. This gives proprioceptive input to their muscles and joints, meeting their need to physically move to learn, increase focus and absorb new material.

If students can use a therapy ball chair it is helpful for calming, achieving improved academic work and increasing concentration. Students with ADHD have good results with use of therapy balls. They also prevent students from falling backwards because they are balancing on their chairs and on the backrests! If you can get the ball that is designed for use as a chair it is best, regular balance balls can sometimes bounce out the door!

E. Be Grounded: Meditation

"The goal of meditation is not to get rid of thoughts and emotions. The goal is to become more aware of your thoughts and emotions and learn how to move them without getting stuck." - Dr. P. Goldin, clinical psychologist and cognitive-affective neuroscientist

There are many ways to be calm and grounded and many reasons to be present, both for you, the educator, and for the students in your care. Children often have problems regulating their emotions and don't know how to calm down. Meditation is a wonderful tool, and again, this is an opportunity to model for your students.

Ch. 3: Respect

Prepare by demonstrating and practicing how to meditate properly with the whole class when the environment is calm. It can be as simple as announcing that the class will enjoy a few minutes of silence, and tap a chime or lightly ring a bell and be silent. Another option is to play music or guided meditations suitable for the students' ages. YouTube has many great meditations to choose from depending upon available time and class preferences.

F. Coping Skills

"I have learned that success is to be measured not so much by the position that one has reached in life as by the obstacles overcome while trying to succeed." - Booker T. Washington, American educator

Resilience is essential for a child to discover, learn, and thrive during their lifetime. It can be defined as having grit; it builds character and allows for a growth mindset that sees problems and obstacles as opportunities and challenges to grow, develop, and succeed. Educators can inspire students to persevere and be determined in their goals. They can empower students to believe in themselves by encouraging them to make another attempt, find alternative ways to problem solve, and discover effective problem-solving tools.

A study by CMHO (Children's Mental Health Ontario) in 2016 has shown that 10-20% of children will experience mental health or behavioural disorders, including anxiety, ADHD, depression, oppositional defiant disorder and conduct disorder during the course of their childhood.

I have seen first-hand the rise in these issues during my 18-plus years working as an educational assistant. It is sad to see how unsupported children are within the school systems. Cutbacks to school counselors do not help the situation. Nor do long wait lists at outside organizations. Children are left in limbo with no resources or very little to help them understand their feelings and how to deal with their own mental health, anxiety, and behaviour disorders. Teachers are equally unsupported in this regard.

They do not know how to help or support. Since teachers are untrained professional counselors, they are limited by what they can do. Hopefully, they will continue to make referrals and recommendations to support systems. In the meantime, strategies that support emotions and behaviours are useful. Giving unconditional love is important.

Children are more stressed than ever, and anxiety is on the rise. Helping children learn ways to become calm and relax can go a long way in supporting until additional help is in place. Children who get overwhelmed and overstimulated may become irritable, cranky, defiant, aggressive, impulsive, and overly emotional. The behaviours can vary between shutting down and bouncing off walls. All children benefit from a consistent schedule and many need advance notice of transitions. The notice can be verbal, or signaled through sounds such as timers or bells—whatever is the child's preferred mode of learning.

There are many ways to help a child to become calm but the best way is for the child to learn how to self-regulate and calm themselves. Teaching strategies ahead of time can be beneficial for intervention and prevention and for quicker recovery during meltdowns and upsets.

There are several activities that can be used for calming and toning down energy, as well as relieving frustration and excitement. One example is 4-square breathing, which I detailed in the previous chapter. Children can also be taught to ask for a "break card" and take a break in a quiet corner. As mentioned previously, students should have access to a sensory box or bin that contains items such as glitter jars, squeeze toys, play dough, toys to squish and stretch, small stuffed animals, stress balls, weighted lap bags, fruit, gum, bubbles to blow, latex free toys, strength-building items, things that are blue in colour (because it is a calming and soothing colour), small things to manipulate in their hands, a ring necklace for someone who likes to chew on things (especially clothing), and a wrist cord with a small item on it. Access to bins with sensory items such as rice, dried beans, rocks and beads, may be useful too. Whatever will help them regain their sense of calm. A quiet reassuring voice always helps too. All children are different and what works for one may not work for another; that's why it's important to have a variety available and offer choices with lots of items that a child can choose from that meets their own sensory need, whether it's touch, feel, smell, taste, or auditory.

G. Your Thoughts Can Control the Outcome

"If you knew how powerful your thoughts are, you would never think a negative thought." - Dr. Caroline Leaf, cognitive neuroscientist

You create the outcome that you see! That is why it is so important prior to, and during an activity, an event or lesson, that you are most mindful of what your thoughts are and what you are projecting.

Ch. 3: Respect

Your thoughts and expectations can even control the outcome of grades for the students—the grades become self-fulfilling prophecies. In his book, **The Seven Habits of Highly Successful People**, Stephen Covey[41] tells a story about a school in England that had a computer glitch that accidentally entered faulty data on two groups of students. They were listed as "dumb" and "bright". But what happened was the computer reversed the list and the students who were identified as "bright" were listed as "dumb" and the "dumb" were listed as "bright".

This error wasn't discovered until five and a half months into the school year, so they retested the students to see where they stood. In the group that had been mistakenly labeled "bright", the scores went up while the other group's scores went down. The mislabeled "dumb" group were seen as "mentally limited, uncooperative and difficult to teach", and were treated that way.

The new "bright" group improved because the teachers believed in their abilities and that the students could fulfill the expectations they had for them. The teachers were asked what they noticed during the first few weeks and they reported that their methods weren't working and that they had to change their methods to adapt to the group. This is such a powerful example of how our paradigms of judgment and expectation can affect the outcomes that we see.

If we can look at our students each day and see them as having unseen and unlimited potential, we can then begin to use our imagination to help them discover what's within themselves rather than project our own limited assumptions upon them.

H. Meet the Needs

"Nothing is impossible; the word itself says, 'I'm Possible'." - Audrey Hepburn, actress and humanitarian

When working with children or teens I like to keep things as simple as possible. I also like to believe in the child's potential and possibility, knowing that if they could do better, they would do better. Sometimes survival is the only thing going on in their mind—that, and trust issues.

---

[41] Covey, Stephen, *The 7 Habits of Highly Effective People- Powerful Lessons in Personal Change* (New York, Free Press, 2004).

I have experience working with many children in school settings, group homes, a detention centre and even an adolescent unit of a psychiatric hospital. Have you ever found yourself in a situation where the child or teen that you are working with is refusing to comply, is being destructive, disrupting your class and other students, shutting down and shutting you out with a bad attitude just because they want to have their own way? Engaging in a power struggle is a no-win situation. The question becomes, how can you empower this student?

The simplest technique for you to use is non-judgment and detachment. I believe that you shouldn't take their behaviour personally. It is not a reflection upon you. Although you may feel you are being kind, giving them all your patience and love, sometimes the child doesn't know how to accept or receive it. They learn to subconsciously shut others out to protect themselves. The child may just want to be seen by you. Really seen—not by imposing your perspective, or your view of why they are doing what they are doing. Instead, really try to see where they are coming from—what would it be like to be in their world? Is life easy for this child? Who's looking out for this child? Who is saying: "I may not like your behaviour, but I love you. You matter. You belong! You deserve to be happy, to be loved!"

There will be times, and maybe many times, where education and pushing curriculum on a child isn't the answer. This child is scraping the bottom of their feelings and emotions; they are in fight, flight or freeze. This child is shutting off their tears and sadness with an "I don't care" attitude. They don't know how to express themselves any other way. Put your ego aside and ask yourself in silence about what this child might need at this moment. If you are religious, pray to be shown how you can help to make a difference.

It may not be through a history lesson or a math lesson. It may be that the child needs someone to say that it's okay, that they are safe here, that someone is willing to listen and cares about how they feel. Perception is something to keep in mind. What you may view as defiance might not be that. It could be a survival instinct or feeling inadequate. Many children have trust issues, having experienced horrors that can only be imagined.

What might be viewed as giving in (being "conned" by a child/teen) may not be that at all. It may be that you can see the child is suffering in silence and simply needs someone to love, care and not add more pressure than they can handle at this moment. The thoughts of a child can be hard to figure out. But behaviour is communication. Start asking questions.

Ch. 3: Respect

I guarantee you the first answers are never really what's really going on. Keep asking questions!

It's important for all working with the child to be on the same page. What's the goal? What's the plan to support the mind, body and spirit of this human treasure? Children are our future, so their care matters greatly. Begin by looking at the basic needs. Has this child had breakfast? When I was in Kenya, it was easy to see the hard time the children had focusing upon their studies because they hadn't had breakfast yet and wouldn't be eating their first meal of the day until noon.

Remember Maslow's hierarchy of needs: air, food, and water, are top priorities under physiological needs. Clothing and shelter are also included for survival. A child can be lost and unfocused when constantly feeling the effects of unmet basic needs.

When a child doesn't feel safe they will question authority. They can rebel and seem non-compliant. It's up to the grown up to have the emotional maturity to detach from the child's behaviour and respond in a way that doesn't cause further damage to the already fragile child. The child needs to feel safe from abuse and violence. They may be suffering from post-traumatic stress due to incidents that have locked themselves into the memory of the child's cells. Health and wellbeing must be addressed. The child's level of maturity and brain development should be considered when their responses are less than what the adult expects.

What is the child capable of? How well do you know the child? Do they have underlying health issues? What are common signs of their disorder? Are they on medication? It's important for you to know the side effects of the medication. For example, children on medication for ADHD tend to have a decreased appetite and seem to drink less water than they should.
A child's behaviour could seem like its being reinforced when they are removed from a class and/or sent home. The real question is why is the child behaving this way? What do they need to feel safe? To support their learning? Do they know how to regulate their emotions, thoughts, and behaviours?

Love and belonging occurs on an interpersonal level. If the child is neglected or ostracized from their family and friends, their sense of belonging can be critically affected. Children can feel lonely and depressed when they do not feel a sense of belonging. If the child feels low self-esteem they may be searching for respect, attention and acceptance from others.

The child needs to feel confident and independent, to feel they have a sense of control over issues in their life. This is the perfect time to teach the child self-empowerment. They can learn that they have choices. The choices may result in consequences the child isn't happy about, but that's where clear rules, guidelines, and encouragement are important. With younger children, I use "red choice" and "green choice" circles as a visual prompt for my student to think about their actions. It causes the student to pause and think and hopefully consider a better option. The red and green choice circles are completely different from the colours of zones which refer to Zones of Regulation. I would suggest using one or the other not both, the Zones of Regulation and the red/green circles. (I discuss red and green choices more in a later chapter).

I. Learning Styles

"The formulation of the problem is more essential than the solution."
- Albert Einstein

My dad was one of my greatest teachers. My brother Shaun paid tribute to him when he passed away in March 2019. "He was the smartest man I ever knew. He didn't teach us just one thing, he did better than that—he taught us how to figure out how to do anything that we wanted to do." My father taught my brothers and I to think outside of the box. He taught us that there's always more than one way to do anything. Sometimes, in order to reach your goal, you have to try different ways, be persistent and never give up.

Schools are not failing us. It's really that the old ways and old systems of doing things are becoming obsolete. It's the systems that need to be changed for survival in the 21st century of education. Tony Wagner, a TEDX speaker and self-declared recovering high school English teacher, stated in his talk that *"knowledge is a commodity; it's not what you know...it's what you do with it."* So true!

Considering a child's learning style when presenting a lesson is essential. Teachers rarely have to manage an auditory learner. But visual and kinesthetic learners need more. They need visuals. Whenever possible advocate for visual and kinesthetic learners when standardized testing is required to assess abilities and knowledge. Ensure that their IEP (individual education plan) has the modifications and accommodations included for their benefit. Parents do not always know what to ask for.

J. Universal Design for Learning

"Fair doesn't mean giving every child the same thing. Fair means giving every child what they need." - Rick Lavoie, administrator of residential programs for children with special needs

I believe Universal Design for Learning is such an essential tool. It is a simple approach to curriculum that includes all students, and sets goals as well as guidelines based on multiple means of engagement, representation, and expression. This is an inclusive method that serves all students within a classroom, enabling them to reach their own potential and become valued citizens of their community. For Universal Design for Learning to be successful, the following must be happening: offering flexible instructions, being learner-centred, using digital resources, and having support from school leaders.

Planning is essential and removes possible curriculum barriers. With correct implementation learner diversity is incorporated. This allows the learner to become engaged and demonstrate their understanding as an end result. To begin it is beneficial for the teacher to believe that anything is possible and for them to begin with the end result in mind. It would be a dream come true for a teacher to see all students meet their learning goals at the end of a math lesson or series of lessons. So if thoughts create our reality it would be beneficial for the teacher to visualize the outcome of all students being successful and then plan to meet the needs through use of the principles of UDL.

There are three main principles to UDL based on the three neurological networks that educators should focus upon:

1. The recognition network involves the area of the brain involved with the "what" of learning. There must be multiple ways of representation giving the learner ways to acquire the knowledge and information. Textbooks offer a visual. Other methods can involve audio, video, and even hands-on learning.

2. The strategic network involves the "how" of learning. There must be multiple means of action and expression, giving the learner different ways to show what they now know. There is more than one way to show what you know aside from old-fashioned testing; students can orally present what they know or present their learning through a group project.

3. The affective network is involved in the "why" of learning. There must be multiple ways of engaging different interests to challenge and motivate the learner. Some ways to do this are by offering choices and allowing the student to do projects of interest that are relatable to their lives.

Are there different approaches that fit under the UDL for learning?
Yes!

Some approaches that fall under this umbrella include:

- Multiple intelligences. Allowing each child to shine in the area that they excel most at while encouraging them to build on other intelligences too.[42]
- Cooperative learning. Teamwork and collaboration, each person has a role in the group.
- Project-based learning. Meet a challenge and develop an answer to present it to others.
- Inquiry-based learning. Fosters deeper levels of understanding through discovery-learning and guided-learning.
- Gradual release of responsibility. A structured method of education that builds independence as time goes on.
- Service learning. Beneficial to experience helping in the community. It provides opportunities to develop organizational skills, build interpersonal skills, group skills, and allows for reflection of the experience.
- Reading and writing workshops.

---

[42] Thomas Armstrong, PhD, is on a mission to support the "creation of developmentally appropriate practices and rich learning environments for children, adolescents and adult learners." His website has numerous articles, blogs and resource books that he has authored to promote his goal to help others. Armstrong's website lists many keynote presentations including "Neurodiversity in the Classroom: Strength Based Strategies to Help Students with Special Needs Achieve Success in School and Life", "If Einstein Ran the School: Revitalizing U.S. Education" and "Awakening the Genius in Every Child: Discovering and Reviving the Natural Motivation that Exists in All Children" and so many more. Please note that "The Theory of Multiple Intelligences" has received criticism as part of the "evidence-based movement" in education. But, As Dr. Thomas Armstrong says it is "theory not a single classroom intervention."

Website: www.institute4learning.com
Email: thomas@institute4learning.com

Ch. 3: Respect

Knowledge is an easily obtained commodity. Thanks to technology you can resource and discover answers to anything. That's why learning what to do with knowledge is essential. The best methods use core competencies for learning.

What are the core competency skills that students need to learn?

Students' core competencies skills to know/learn include:

- Learning how to be a critical thinker.
- How to ask questions and how to ask the right questions.
- How to collaborate with others and lead by influence.
- Being able to adapt and be flexible.
- Having the mindset of an entrepreneur and the ability to take initiative.
- Learning effective oral and written skills.
- Being creative and curious, using one's own imagination.

Teamwork with your co-workers is important for success! Collaborative input from teaching peers is beneficial to support the teacher and enhance the learning for all.

A useful resource is **Teaching Every Student in the Digital Age** by David Rose and Anne Meyer.[43] It outlines the key elements for implementation of UDL. They discuss the importance of administrative support, having access to technology and infrastructure support, training and support. As well as training and support for teachers that covers curriculum planning and redefined roles.

You can also read:

Armstrong, Thomas, *Multiple Intelligences in the Classroom* 4th ed. (Alexandria, VA: Association for Supervision and Curriculum Development, 2018). Great resource with examples, templates and strategies to implement.

Armstrong, Thomas, *You're Smarter Than You Think: A Kid's Guide to Multiple Intelligences* (Minneapolis, Free Spirit, 2014).

[43] Rose, David H. and Anne Meyer, *Teaching Every Student in the Digital Age: Universal Design for Learning* (Association for Supervision and Curriculum Development, 2002).

They explain the value of knowing the students' learning preferences, strengths and abilities for success. If you can identify potential barriers in order to reduce or eliminate problems that hamper learning you increase your overall success rates and lower frustration while improving self-esteem and independence for each learner.

K. Brain dominance— Seriously, Learning Isn't All in Your Head!

"Movement is the door to learning." - Paul E. Dennison, author and founder Brain Gym®

How a child learns is a fascinating subject. Although not completely understood, science has proven many things in recent years. Historically, educators describe a student as a right-brain or left-brain learner, and have taught in a fashion that favours single-hemisphere learning.

But in reality, there is so much more that needs to be considered when teaching children in a whole brain/whole body fashion that empowers, supports, and values all learners. A left-brained, logic-dominant learner processes in a linear, analytical, detailed, step-by-step style. A right-brain, Gestalt-dominant student processes intuitively, more holistically, and tends to have better understanding through images, emotions, and rhythm.

When the learner understands what style of thinking is most natural to them and discovers how they process new information, they will learn more easily and with less stress and less self-condemnation for not "getting it".

We are all unique and shaped by our life experiences and perceptions. Along with those influences, we have innate natural factors of influence- handedness, preferences for one ear over another, one eye over another and even one foot over another!

In the book, **Smart Moves: Why Learning Is Not All in Your Head** by Carla Hannaford, PhD, the neurophysiologist and educator explains all about the brain, brain dominance profiles and how valuable movement is with regards to learning. Her book is presented in an easy to read format and is supported by scientific research that describes the body's role in thinking and learning, why we must move to learn, and how to fully activate our learning potential.

For far too long our education system has discriminated against Gestalt (right-brain) learners in many ways. Hannaford says, *"People learn differently, yet school is set up to favour certain styles of learning, and school work focuses on certain kinds of tasks. On the whole, school teaches, tests, and values logic brain tasks. Logic, sequence, computation, categorization, and verbal skills are all highly prized abilities in school. Intuition, emotion, vision, humour, rhythmic movement, image formation, and other Gestalt brain capacities are not practiced, tested or particularly valued at school."*[44]

I totally agree with her views. We all have our own gifts, talents, skills, and abilities and that should be the focus of education—to meet the student where they are at. Hannaford is also the author of **The Dominance Factor How Knowing Your Dominant Eye, Ear, Brain, Hand and Foot Can Improve Your Learning**.[45] The purpose of knowing your students' dominance profiles is to assess your students' unique styles of learning, perceiving, and responding to our environment. We each take in information differently. As a result, our dominance profile is based on our dominant brain hemisphere, as well as our dominant ear, eye, foot, and hand.

Understanding your students' characteristics of learning can help you gain insight into why they act certain ways, why they learn in certain ways, especially when under stress. By knowing this information, you can develop or set up ways to support your students' optimal learning. For example, it could be something as simple as seating placement in a classroom for ear dominance preference.

As a student, when you understand your neurological dominance pattern you can discover your strengths and grow in confidence and you can understand better why you seem weaker in other areas. It can show you why you are drawn to certain tasks and tend to avoid other tasks. When we are under stress and attempt to take in new information we access our senses that are linked to our dominant brain hemisphere. This link is formed when our dominant ear, eye, hand, and foot are opposite to our dominant brain hemisphere. But if our dominant brain hemisphere is not opposite to our dominant sense or senses then learning becomes difficult unless different strategies are used. It is true for many people that their dominant brain hemisphere isn't opposite to a certain sense or senses.

---

[44] Hannaford, Carla, PhD., *Smart Moves: Why Learning is Not All in your Head* (Salt Lake City, Great River Books, 2007).

[45] Hannaford, Carla, PhD., *The Dominance Factor: How Knowing Your Dominant Eye, Ear, Brain, Hand and Foot Can Improve Your Learning* (Salt Lake City, Great River Books, 2011).

There are 32 basal dominance profiles. These basal patterns exhibit themselves most when the learner is learning something new or is stressed. Hannaford strongly points out that these dominance profiles are not intended to label an individual. While the profile may indicate how a learner will respond, it isn't useful to apply a label as it prevents us from allowing the potential of the child to develop through strategies and activities that can assist with whole brain learning.

I am a right-brained, left-handed, left ear, left eye and left foot dominant and for me that means that I tend to learn best through movement and by focusing on the whole picture. I appreciate metaphors and examples when problem-solving. These tools help me to understand better and more easily. I am highly intuitive and often go by my gut instincts when making decisions. I have sloppy handwriting. If I were a student in a classroom, the best seating area for me would be near the front but where I could still move and not disturb others. I sometimes reverse or transpose letters and numbers; this has made book-keeping challenging for me! I am a kinesthetic learner and a big picture thinker!

Schools in general have expectations about the way that a child should learn, which includes the old-fashioned formal way of rote memorization, linear skills, sitting still and listening quietly rather than teaching children to think creatively and discover how to apply knowledge to real life situations and experiences. Carla Hannaford points out: "If we can advance to an education that balances memory and thinking, and honours each person's learning processes, agile learners with valuable thinking tools can emerge."

I love that I'm seeing more and more schools implement different approaches and theories related to learning-style differences. They are considering multiple intelligences, adding in mindfulness, raising consciousness, promoting values and upgrading our systems for living, doing and being. We are awakening!

L. Multiple Intelligence Styles

"Anything that is worth teaching can be presented in many different ways. These multiple ways can make use of our multiple intelligences."
- Dr. Howard Gardner, developmental psychologist and author

Ch. 3: Respect

Dr. Howard Gardner, a professor at Harvard University, developed what is known as the Theory of Multiple Intelligences.[46] His theory presented in 1983, helped to change the focus of educational systems from long-standing, outdated approaches such as verbal/linguistic intelligence (good at writing, speaking and memorization) and logical-math intelligence (driven by logic and reasoning) to prove that there are other forms of intelligence. IQ testing was also limiting, in his opinion, because it didn't explain the wide variety of intelligences. Beyond word-smart and number/reasoning-smart, he proposed that the other intelligences include:

- Spatial intelligence (picture smart): Good at remembering images and awareness of surroundings.
- Bodily-kinesthetic intelligence (body smart): Loves movement, has good motor skills and is aware of their bodies.
- Musical intelligence (music smart): Musically gifted and has a good ear for music and composition.
- Interpersonal intelligence (people smart): This person loves to be social and has positive interactions with others.
- Naturalistic intelligence (nature smart): Greatly appreciates natural surroundings and has a high degree of awareness of it.
- Intrapersonal intelligence (self-smart): Good at looking within for discovery and answers.
- Existential intelligence (life smart): Tackles the tough questions about life and why we die.

Knowing and understanding cognitive research on the different intelligences helps teachers understand why and how students learn, remember, and perform differently. For an open-minded teacher who refuses to be stuck in old-method styles of learning and teaching, these intelligence styles are exciting. They allow a teacher to get creative with their own class lesson plans and engage with students in the manners that they learn best. If nurtured, these new intelligences, which have existed but have not always been recognized, can have incredible effects on the learning potential as well as the self-esteem of students.

Each individual is allowed to freely express their own intelligence and learn how they learn best. With this recognition the future artists, musicians,

---

[46] Gardner, Howard, *Intelligence Reframed: Multiple Intelligences for the 21st Century* (New York: Basic Book, 2000) and *Frames of Mind: The Theory of Multiple Intelligences* (New York, Basic Book, 2011).

entrepreneurs, dancers, naturalists, and therapists are valued for their abilities and gifts rather than being labeled as having a learning disorder or being attention deficient.

Gardner's view has contributed to changes in educational theory and practice. He believes that intelligence is the ability to respond quickly to a new situation or solve a problem that is of importance to a specific culture. Culture would be related to where a child lives and based on the needs of the community decided by parents or teachers. Gardner says, *"It is the culture that defines the stages and fixes the limits of individual achievement. For example, educators have found that the Mexican American culture places a strong emphasis on community and on family; therefore, many members of this community have well-developed interpersonal intelligences"*.[47]

Let me give you an example—my son's Down syndrome needs influenced a school culture community. When he was younger, he was unable to speak well enough to be understood. Yet, when he arrived at school for kindergarten, he was able to do over 200 sign language signs that we taught him at home through videos, books, and practicing with him. The teacher used part of a math block and indoor recesses to play "Signing Time" videos[48] to his classmates. This enabled them to learn sign language, which was not part of their curriculum and helped them communicate with my son. Not only did this increase the communication skills of his classmates, it was a terrific example of inclusion and acceptance. At the time, many parents expressed their gratitude for the fact that I had placed my son in that school and in a regular classroom setting. Their children were coming home and telling their families the new words that they learned each day. It was a win-win for all.

Gardner also felt that each intelligence has its own developmental patterns and has equal potential for anyone to learn. While a learner might be skilled in one area Gardner doesn't agree with limiting their potential to just that area of expertise or skill. He believes educators should encourage growth and learning in other areas too.

Check out your strengths at this link: literacynet.org/mi/assessment/findyourstrengths.html

---

[47] To learn more, visit: www.learnenglish.de/teachers/multipleintelligences2.html

[48] Check out the videos at: www.signingtime.com/

M. Sense of Belonging and Attachment

"The idea of belonging shouldn't be considered a privilege available only to some students. It should be considered a basic human right." - Linda Mullen, executive director, Generation Spirit (formerly The Sparkle Effect)

It's critical for children to feel a sense of belonging, to feel that they are part of something bigger than themselves. Knowledge of attachment theory is helpful because it enables you to understand what motivates the individual and how they seek to have their needs met. By understanding this theory, you more clearly understand how a child relates to others, how they fear being hurt and rejected, as well as who they see as a threat. You can also develop a compassionate level of awareness of the effects a student experiences when separated from those they love—especially their mother figure.

Healthy attachments support healthy social and emotional behaviour. All kids can thrive when they know someone is completely nuts about them. What's possible? Anything is possible when the child feels they can do anything. How can you empower a child today?

Children Learn What They Live

"Even the smallest act of caring for another person is like a drop of water - it will make ripples throughout the entire pond." - Jessy and Bryan Matteo, Founders Us4You Foundation

Dorothy Law Nolte left a legacy of love in her inspirational poem, Children Learn What They Live. She was a parent educator, family counsellor and writer of a well-known poem that was first published in 1954. As a family counsellor, she taught family dynamics and parenting skills. A printed version of her poem hung on the refrigerators of many households over the years.

I hope that you take time to reflect on the wisdom in her beautiful poem. I feel that it reflects the positive values children need to experience life fully. As well, her poem reflects what the consequences can be if a child experiences life in a negative way. This is a true to life cause and effect poem. Take time to contemplate this amazing poem!

Although she passed away in 2005 at the age of 81 years old she left a work of creative thinking that can leave a lasting imprint for future generations of children.

Children Learn What They Live

- If children live with criticism, they learn to condemn.
- If children live with hostility, they learn to fight.
- If children live with fear, they learn to be apprehensive.
- If children live with pity, they learn to feel sorry for themselves.
- If children live with ridicule, they learn to feel shy.
- If they live with jealousy, they learn to feel envy.
- If children live with shame, they learn to feel guilty.
- If children live with encouragement, they learn confidence.
- If children live with tolerance, they learn patience.
- If children live with praise, they learn appreciation.
- If children live with acceptance, they learn to love.
- If children live with approval, they learn to like themselves.
- If children live with recognition, they learn it is good to have a goal.
- If they live with sharing, they learn generosity.
- If children live with honesty, they learn truthfulness.
- If children live with fairness, they learn justice.
- If children live with kindness and consideration, they learn respect.
- If children live with security, they learn to have faith in themselves and in those about them.
- If children live with friendliness, they learn the world is a nice place in which to live.

- Dorothy Law Nolte

Excerpted from the book ~ CHILDREN LEARN WHAT THEY LIVE

Copyright © 1998 by Dorothy Law Nolte and Rachel Harris
The poem "Children Learn What They Live"
Copyright © 1972 by Dorothy Law Nolte
Used by permission of Workman Publishing Co., Inc., New York
All Rights Reserved

Ch. 3: Respect

N. Respect: It's Your Turn!

"I speak to everyone in the same way, whether he is the garbage man or the president of the university." - Albert Einstein

Respect can be taught to students by teaching them the way that they learn best. Show them that you care by helping students work through their problems. Offer solutions and teach techniques and strategies that empower them, so that they will be inspired to use what they have learned when they need it. By helping students to meet their needs, you will often earn their respect and deep appreciation. It helps them to feel valued and loved. Children do learn what they live; by holding true to teaching and modeling positive character traits you will enable them to develop trust and feel safe in your care.

Self-reflection questions

- *What does respect in a classroom look like to you?*
- *What skills, insights and wisdom did you discover in this chapter?*
- *What will you implement in your classroom?*
- *What will you explore for yourself?*
- *What will you research more about for better understanding?*

 CHAPTER 4: INSPIRE

"Too often we underestimate the power of a touch, a smile, a kind word, a listening ear, an honest compliment, or the smallest act of caring, all of which have the potential to turn a life around." - Leo Buscaglia, author and motivational speaker

Encouragement can change a person's day. In fact, it can be life changing knowing that someone believes in you and has your back. Feeling supported and loved provides a confidence boost, it allows you to feel understood and inspires you to do more and be more.

In your classroom setting how do you inspire students? Does the environment matter? It is inspiring for students to be in a classroom environment that is comfortable and inviting (think progressively—not the old outdated traditional way of organizing a classroom). The learning space does matter. But beyond the clutter-free organization and the use of colour, beyond the availability of supplies for creativity projects, the flow charts, the mindset posters, the random acts of kindness bulletin board, and the leadership posters, beyond all of that, students need to be empowered and inspired through being supported with regards to their moods, thoughts, and emotions.

Inspiring students to manage these emotions through modeling and co-regulation is extremely important. All students need to feel that they matter and are loved. Inclusion is a big part of this. True inclusion—not segregation or segregated inclusion.

When everyone is included, they feel part of a community, part of a team. They understand that everyone has gifts to contribute to the environment. A welcoming community is able to show compassion and empathy, and will encourage others to grow, develop, and shine in their own way. Students build their confidence and courage so that they can be resilient and brave.

Ch. 4: Inspire

A. Courage, Confidence, Compassion and Inclusion

"Be an encourager: When you encourage others, you boost their self-esteem, enhance their confidence, and make them work harder, lift their spirits and make them successful in their endeavors. Encouragement goes straight to the heart and is always available. Be an encourager. Always."
- Roy T. Bennett, **The Light in the Heart**

Along with the courage to be yourself and take risks it's important to be confident and compassionate when working with children. Compassion and empathy are beautiful qualities and the following story, which happened a few years ago, is a perfect example of how to show compassion, love, and meet the child where they are. My son really enjoyed going to school, he was perfectly matched with an educational assistant who knew how to give the right amount of pressure to get him to comply and work hard so that he could earn his free time and rewards. He loved her so much, and rushed to school to see her. They had a very positive relationship.

On one occasion, his educational assistant was going to be away for three days. My son was not happy about it. I attempted to soften his demeanor by encouraging him to have fun and enjoy the day with the replacement assistant. He was still not pleased, and sadly I had to leave him in this state because it was time for me to get to my job as a special educational assistant at another school. I heard later that the female principal approached him and attempted to console and encourage him to go to his classroom too. What she did was exactly what a conscious classroom teacher or support staff member should do: she got to his level. She physically sat down on the dirty, winter-boot-wet carpet where he was demonstrating his right to protest the change. She talked to him, related to his disappointment and encouraged him to do his best anyway. He complied. I'm so grateful for her love and her support to be willing to do what it took. I'm sure she wasn't thrilled about sitting on the dirty floor but I know she followed her intuition to simply love him enough to be there for him exactly where he was at.

B. How to Boost Your Confidence and Build Your Courage Muscles

"The mediocre teacher tells, the good teacher explains, the superior teacher demonstrates. The great teacher inspires." - William Arthur Ward, author

To teach confidence to students you must be able to model it through your own actions. Confidence is a skill that can be developed by taking action. Holding yourself back through insecurity, fear, and doubt will only keep you where you are. Listen to how you speak to yourself when you are attempting new things.

The best way to begin to build your self-confidence is to know where you are at right now.

What are your skills, gifts and talents? Are you clear about your goals and dreams?

What do you think you are afraid of? What skills can you learn to change what you think? Sometimes just changing the way you look at things can change everything. Self-confidence is a skill that can be learned with effort and energy put into changing oneself. Here are a few suggestions when it comes to building your self-confidence muscle:

1. What do you need to learn? What would you like to master? Let's say you would like to be a better speaker but would rather pull out your teeth before ever attempting to speak in public. Don't let that fear get in the way! Take some courses or join Toastmasters. Many people learn their skills through practice, practice, and more practice. The more you do something, the better you will become at it. The same thing applies if you want to be a better writer—take a course and write, write, write. Your choices for how to begin to increase your self-confidence are limitless thanks to the Internet. You will get out of it what you choose to put into it. And, sometimes it's as easy as remaining focused and committed. Want to be a better parent or teacher? Focus on your priority and simply be a better parent or teacher.
2. Don't be so hard on yourself! Do not focus on your flaws. We all have them. We are all perfectly imperfect. Focus on your gifts and talents. Be kind and generous. Are you able to accept a compliment without an explanation or excuse such as *"Oh, this sweater? It's old"* or *"Thanks, but I hate my hair—it's too curly."* These are examples of not accepting compliments. Simply say *"Thank you!"* Put your focus on gratitude and attitude! If after receiving a compliment you say something under your own breath, think about why you are saying that and attempting to push the compliment away. Awareness of your thoughts and actions matters.
3. Look in the mirror and practice kindness with yourself. Use "I am" statements. It may seem awkward at first but stick with it until you mean what you say. Speak kindly to yourself and love yourself. There is only one you in this world. How special is that?

Ch. 4: Inspire

4. Recognize your fears and put them in their place. EFT (Emotional Freedom Technique), also known as Tapping, is a great way to get beyond fears and move forward in life. By noticing and paying attention to what you think when you are thinking negatively or having fearful thoughts, you can safely give voice to them and then replace those thoughts with positive ones.
5. Pay attention to your posture. Are you slouching and walking around with the weight of the world on your shoulders? Or, are you standing tall, smiling, looking confident and making eye contact when you have conversations with others?
6. Get plenty of fresh air and exercise. Nature helps people to stay grounded, more focused, and more energetic. It helps you to be clear with your thoughts about what you truly want out of life.
7. How are you dressed? Are you dressed for success? The way you dress can build your confidence.
8. Imagine yourself as you wish to be. Imagination is one of your most powerful allies on the road to changing your level of self-confidence.
9. Changing your thoughts and building confidence isn't an instant fix. You must practice and create new habits. New habits regarding your thoughts. New habits of being confident and taking action consistently.
10. Never allow others to put you down. Stand up for yourself. Be assertive. We teach others how to treat us by what we allow.
11. Be kind and generous to others. What you put out comes back to you. Put out kind thoughts to others. Wish others well.
12. Practice self-care. Look after yourself—drink lots of water, eat nutritious foods, and take quality supplements.
13. Stay away from drama. Avoid negativity and the negative energy of others. This energy can cause you to be down on yourself and others. Know that things are rarely as they appear to be. Think positive and find the good in everything. There is always some good in everything.
14. Ask for help when you need it. It's important for your growth and success. We all can get by with a little help from our friends and family. Feeling successful and knowing that you have people to count on builds confidence too.
15. Don't allow yourself to be discouraged when there is a setback. Let it make you stronger. Learn the lesson and get back into the game. Persistence is key. Can you imagine what would have happened if Thomas Edison had quit after 999 tries when it came to inventing the light bulb? DO NOT GIVE UP!

16. Believe in yourself! Remind yourself often why you are so great. It's not an ego thing; it's a matter of building confidence and knowing your value. Don't play small! Stand up! Stand out!
17. Take risks and step out of your comfort zone. Often the life you dream of is just beyond the light of what you see.
18. Stop holding yourself back from going for your dreams. Value yourself! Get rid of the fear of failure. Don't let the start stop you! Begin!
19. Follow your instincts. If you have a feeling or a hunch about something... listen to yourself. This builds confidence and self-worth.
20. Know that you matter and your dreams are important. Everyone was born rich and deserves a wonderful life.

As you become more confident so will your students because you are able to inspire them to be confident within themselves and their own skills, gifts and talents designed to reach their goals.

"If one advances confidently in the direction of his dreams, he will live the life he has imagined, he will meet with success unexpected in common hours." This quote by Henry David Thoreau is one of the greatest that I have ever heard and I now use it when I coach clients on shooting for their dreams. I recommend demonstrating confidence to your students as you encourage them to shoot for their dreams and as you go after your own goals.

C. Inclusion versus Integration

"Inclusion is a mindset. It is a way of thinking. It is not a program that we run or a classroom in our school or a favour we do for someone. Inclusion is who we are. It's who we must strive to be." - Lisa Friedman, **Removing the Stumbling Block**

It is quite common to find a class that thinks they are providing an inclusive environment when they are actually only providing some integration at best.

Students need to be seated where they can see and hear what's being taught. Not blocked off in a corner of a room. Their learning preferences and styles need to be considered. Knowing the brain dominance profiles of your students can assist you with proper seating arrangements.

You may have to adapt various items in a classroom to achieve inclusion, but these little tweaks truly help. For example: shorter desks, foot rests, slant

Ch. 4: Inspire

boards, slanted desk tops, spring loaded scissors, headphones, squishy cushions, timers, visual aids, pencil grips, fidget toys, and time tables are items that will benefit the classroom. Tools for success should be available to all students in the classroom, not just those with special needs.

We are moving beyond the industrial revolution age of education; we are full swing into the 21st century of learning. Recently, we got a huge taste of it through our Covid-19 quarantine time. I am sure we will see some great books coming out on the challenges and perks of educating through technology. This may impact how inclusion will look in the future. It's been a true learning curve educating my son at home with technology.

I am attempting to find balance with screen time and discovering the best ways for him to learn and complete his assignments. All while trying to avoid overload and overwhelm for him and myself. We have discovered that I'm not his favourite teacher. Lol! I am sure it has been a time of huge frustration for so many. Every day I hear others talk about how much respect and understanding parents now have for educators and their impact and experiences in working day in and day out with their child. Appreciation and gratitude are the words that I am hearing most often.

When classes resume, inclusion for all within the curriculum is still a key problem to be solved. The UDL (universal design for learning) and presuming competence are helping educators be more inclusive. Still more has to happen.

Shelley Moore is a teacher, speaker, inclusive education consultant, and author of **One Without the Other: Stories of Unity Through Diversity and Inclusion.**[49] She shares her many experiences, stories and metaphors about inclusion in her insightful and entertaining book. She highly promotes inclusion and her goal is to see inclusion as a natural part of education. There are many great videos relating to this topic on her YouTube channel; Five Moore Minutes.

One of her favourite stories that she tells is about bowling. When you go bowling, what's the goal? It's to knock down as many pins as you can to get a good score. How do you do that? You aim the bowling ball and roll it down the lane. The key question is where should you aim?

---

[49] Moore, Shelley, *One Without the Other: Stories of Unity Through Diversity and Inclusion* (Portage & Main Press, 2016).

Most people would say aim for the middle! She interviewed a professional bowler and discovered the truth. You get more when you aim for the pins that are the hardest to hit: the 7-10 split. It's one of the hardest shots to make but it is possible. How should you throw it then? On a curve, it lets the other pins help to reach the goal of knocking all pins down.

How does a classroom relate to bowling? Aim for the hardest pins to reach and you end up reaching them all through teamwork, honouring cultures and diversity, and by focusing on strengths and abilities. Everyone has something to contribute.

Should students with special needs be included in a regular classroom? That is a question frequently asked. Some say yes with certainty, others are more reluctant. I've even heard educators say, *"Well, if I wanted to teach special education, I would have been a special ed teacher."* That saddens me.

As a parent, I believe that our children deserve a place in our society and our communities when they graduate. They therefore should have a place within our school settings. Although my son is currently in a segregated class we choose that for his best interests. I truly wish that there had been better options at the time, but he needed peer interaction and friendship. When he reached Grade 5 and the differences were quite noticeable, we put him in a class that placed more emphasis on social skill-building and life skills. He is happy, well-loved, and supported. I also continue to believe that with the right supports in place, children with special needs should be in "regular" classrooms.

Dr. Gordon Porter, Director of Inclusive Education Canada says, *"That research has shown that children benefit by having a child with a disability in their class"*.[50] Not only does it help with positive learning experiences, it also enhances social skills learning through interactions with peers. Listening skills, turn taking, and assuming leadership roles are all emphasized. Prior to his switch in Grade 5, my son was blessed to have great peers who loved to do things with him such as reading, playing games and playing iPad activities.

The students with disabilities will often make improvements with communication, speech and language, while the experience also provides opportunities for peers to advocate, support, assist, and help guide each other to success.

---

[50] The Canadian Down Syndrome Society website has numerous resources for educators and parents. Visit: cdss.ca/resources/education/ An educational power point presentation on Down syndrome is available on request by emailing info@cdss.ca.

Ch. 4: Inspire

A child with a disability gives others the chance to learn compassion, acceptance and unconditional love. This is all so important for the present and future so that a person with a disability is seen as a valued member of our community. *"A true community consists of multiple abilities working together."*[51]

Students should be provided with age-appropriate activities and taught age-appropriate behaviours. An example would be: no hugging but high fives are allowed. Remember, never teach something you will want to *un-teach* later, especially with a child with Down syndrome!

Children with disabilities have a hard time when the energy in the room is high, whether it's excitement for an activity or nervousness about an event. This can cause them to act out, run away, or hide. Preparing and planning for changes is essential. Up until grade 5, my son was blessed to have amazingly caring and considerate classmates who loved him, looked out for him and always encouraged him to do his best. He was often invited to his classmates' birthday parties. He didn't always participate, but as a parent it was nice to have him invited and the other kids understood that Connor was simply being Connor.

Currently, he is a valued member of his segregated class because of his contributions and humour that he brings each day. He loves the classmates and the staff who love and care for him each day. He doesn't always participate in activities but he does what he feels comfortable doing. Sometimes, he feels the excitement and energy and it makes him want to withdraw. Once settled though, he usually participates and has a good time.

Many children with special needs are left out of after-school activities, and as a parent, I can admit it does make me feel sad. Sad because through no fault of their own, these children have a disorder or disability that prevents them from being perceived as "normal". If a special needs child is out of the classroom more than they are in the classroom, they are not being included. Students should learn the work that their peers are doing in the classroom even if it's modified to the child's level of understanding. All students have the right to be included and that means for outings and class trips as well. It's very unfair to plan any outing that doesn't include the needs of all students. Take swimming as an example—

---

[51] For more information and ideas on inclusion, visit this free resource: cdss.ca/wp-content/uploads/2016/06/CDSS-Educator-Package-English.pdf

a child shouldn't be exempt and be forced to stay behind because staff do not want to swim. This doesn't meet the requirements of an inclusive activity.

When planning activities think of the physical, safety, medical, and washroom needs of your students, also consider their focus abilities. A few common sense tips: bring supplies and things to entertain children, if necessary, and have a backup plan should something go wrong. However, don't exclude students due to your worry of what could go wrong. Plan and count on it going successfully. A few other details to consider: outdoor activities might be fine, but nature and mountain excursions for a child in a wheelchair? Any excursion that can potentially damage a child's equipment is not a good idea.

As a parent, I can't tell you the number of times I've had to point out the obvious. By the time graduation arrived for my daughter who uses a wheelchair, I was ready to take a stance again if they didn't consider the area where the students were receiving their diplomas. I was thankful and grateful that they solved that problem without my questioning. Rather than dealing with the possibility of the stage being inaccessible for some students, everyone received their diplomas in front of the stage. Inclusion means not making anyone stand out for their differences.

Know your students! As Carol Johnson, BEd, says: *"Attitude is the most critical factor related to the success of a student with Down syndrome; If you think a student will succeed, he or she will. When a student is treated like a valued learner, he or she learns."*

D. Teaching Styles and Classroom Management

"You can't teach self-discipline if the students are always looking for more treats, raffle tickets, and goodies from the treasure box." - Harry and Rosemary Wong, in **'The First Days of School: How to be an Effective Teacher.'**

There are a vast variety of teaching styles and class management styles. Clearly the way you manage a classroom will determine how effective your teaching is and how well a classroom runs. It can be smooth and peaceful, destructive and full of utter chaos, or somewhere in between.

How your class operates is often a reflection of your perception and thoughts. I realize acceptance of this idea may seem far-fetched but if you

Ch. 4: Inspire

consider the principles of success and the laws of the universe it is not far-fetched at all. With a true reflection of one's own self, you can discover how we create what we see through assumptions.

An effectively managed class can seem invisibly run. But what is going on in order for this to happen? It's not magic or completely instinctual. A classroom setting that is well managed is based upon inner authority and not ego-based power-tripping. Gone are the days of the power struggles between student and teacher, the "do this or else" mentality that defined education and discipline. For many reasons, as will be explained, don't expect perfect days all the time and learn not to get caught up in the stress and negative experiences. Good self-care and ample time to de-stress and recharge your own batteries are essential.

An overloaded brain cannot think clearly nor can it access high-level thinking for greater creativity, better resilience, and problem solving.

We all make mistakes, go easy on yourself when you make a mistake—sincerely apologize, make eye contact, and don't make excuses. Stay grounded and simply express your feelings. We all learn from our experiences and expecting perfection can be a set up for failure of yourself and your students.

A useful resource book that I highly recommend is Rick Smith's, **Conscious Classroom Management: Unlocking the Secrets of Great Teaching**.[52] I enjoy this book because he clearly describes the styles of teachers and how they can learn to manage their class in a seemingly invisible way.

E. Class Environment: How to Have a Proactive and Well-Managed Classroom

"There's a difference between trying to control your students and establishing control of your classroom. Rules are about compliance. Procedures are about coherence." - David Ginsburg, math teacher and educational consultant

It is well known that practice prevention is a more effective approach than intervention. That is why having an environment that feels safe and loving matters a great deal. Children need to feel loved and safe; a classroom that is chaotic and disorganized adds to chaos and disruption.

---

[52] Smith, Rick, *Conscious Classroom Management: Unlocking the Secrets of Great Teaching* (Conscious Teaching Publications: Writing in book edition, September 15, 2004).

If a child is behaving inappropriately, he is signaling some sort of unmet need whether it's internal or external. Behaviour is always a form of communication. Always!

Children feed on the energy around them, especially children with poor self-regulation skills. Children need to be in a respectful environment.

What would a respectful environment look like?

How would you like your class to look? Describe it in full detail.

Consider the layout, the flow, the furniture. Would you have a variety of furniture available for those that like to move? Twist and turn? Bounce? Would you have space for a student to stand?

How will desks be organized? Where will your desk be? Will you have a desk?

Could you have a sensory box corner area with a variety of items that students could choose when they feel they need to manipulate something while listening to a presentation or lesson?

Could your students have a path to follow in your class or hallway for releasing pent up energy, the need to move, the need to move to process information or simply the need to self-calm by moving.

You are the teacher! You get to set the tone for the day as students arrive to your classroom.

How do you set that tone? Do you greet them with a smile? Do you ask questions about their morning or their evenings? Do you start conversations? Do the students know what you expect as they enter the classroom? Do you allow them to run in and behave as they wish?

I have seen some cute ways the teachers set the tone for the day. Stopping students at the classroom door and greeting them, reminding them to quietly go to their desks and get set for the announcements. For younger ones, I have seen teachers have little picture squares on the wall by the door and each student chooses the greeting for the morning: hugs, high fives, "knucks"[53], and smiles are always given freely. Since the Covid-19 pandemic

---

[53] Knucks is urban slang for knuckle bumps, a gesture of greeting on par with doing a high five.

Ch. 4: Inspire

the morning greeting will need to be adjusted. Thumbs up, peace signs, Japanese bows, hands in prayer position (like Namaste), head nods and silly dances all work to bring smiles, even if you cannot see them through masks you will hear the laughter and see eyes light up.

Consider the power of focus on a daily basis. You always see more of what you focus on. In what areas is the child doing well? Take note of those actions and behaviours and know more will come.

Class rules should be agreed upon together through a group discussion with students. For younger ones I've seen the rules written out on a large piece of paper and then everyone signs it together in agreement and it's posted where everyone in the class can see it. Rules should be numbered so that they can be referred to quickly (An example, ask your student, "What's Rule #5?").

A sample list of rules could include:

1. Be responsible
2. Be kind
3. Be respectful
4. Listen when others are speaking
5. Be helpful
6. Do your best
7. Work as a team

Along with having clear classroom rules have a clear set of natural consequences when expected behaviour is not followed. By having clear rules and set consequences students can learn responsibility for their actions, choices, and behaviours.

Students need to know what to expect. So many thrive on structure and guidelines.

Simple consequences can be:

1. You break it, you fix it
2. Abuse something, you lose it temporarily
3. Loss of privileges

General guidelines should be discussed at the start of your school year and rules set with students regarding respecting other people and their time. When students help set the rules they seem to have more respect for them. Talk about respecting others and their property; teach how to apologize in a meaningful way (in person, via an apology letter). Make sure to also have no bullying and no putting classmates down rules as well. If your class follows a certain program, include loss of points into the mix. Again, students may be more mindful of their actions when clear rules, expectations, and consequences are defined ahead of time.

Here are some other expectations to discuss early on in the year:

- What will happen if homework isn't completed?
- What will happen if you do not do your work in class?
- What will happen if you hurt or bully anyone?
- What will happen if students interrupt and/or waste your instructional time?

Whenever possible frame discussions in the positive: good deeds will be rewarded. Make a point of remarking when students are doing the right thing and reward with praise, and other appropriate age-level incentives. Clearly explain how students can earn perks and free time.

ClassDojo[54] is a free resource for teachers, students, and parents for communication. It helps schools and families have better communication and keeps parents informed as to what is being taught in class. It is also a tool for sharing photos, text messages and videos. ClassDojo has ideas for positive thinking and mindset to help students learn these skills too. This resource is actively used in 90% of all kindergarten to Grade 8 schools in the U.S. and in 180 other countries. All messages can be automatically translated into 35 languages—that's pretty fantastic given the diversity of cultures that teachers teach!

Keep in mind what was mentioned in Section D (Teaching Styles and Classroom Management) of this chapter. It's harder to teach self-discipline if kids are looking for prizes for their behaviour rather than learning self-control and delayed gratification.

Also, be wary of students who are wise enough to up the ante for performing desired behaviour to the point of them running the show and you losing your power. Consider that if you use any reward program it may add to

---

[54] Class Dojo has teacher resources and videos to present the system to families www.classdojo.com/

Ch. 4: Inspire

increased low self-esteem problems and perhaps more frustration for students who have lagging skills or are victims of abuse and trauma. They are already doing their best to manage themselves and feel left out when they "never" or rarely get rewarded.

Ross Greene, author of **Lost at School**, reminds us that, *"Consequences don't teach kids the thinking skills they lack or solve the problems that set the stage for their challenging behaviour."*[55] I love the information in Ross Greene's books and wish that more training was provided around his ideas to all those who work with children and teens. What needs to happen is the *"lagging skills"* need to be identified by pinpointing the times of day or situations when the challenging behaviour is most likely to occur. Define the unsolved problem and teach the skill needed. Greene's philosophical premise has always been that *"kids do well if they can"* and that children with social, emotional and challenging behaviours lack critical-thinking skills.

It's time to change the way we look at things! Instead of thinking that a child is giving you a hard time, remember that they are having a hard time. They aren't manipulating you! That would require thinking skills such as planning and organization. Are they really accessing those skills at that moment? If it's attention-seeking behaviour, they are most likely seeking connection and looking for support. Look at these children with new eyes. See them as truly needing you, your understanding and your love.

Ross Greene highly stresses that all individuals that work with or encounter the child during the school day should be involved in a team collaborative process to discuss the lagging skills and then discover the unsolved problem.

In his book, **The Explosive Child: A New Approach for Understanding and Parenting Easily Frustrated, Chronically Inflexible Children**[56], he describes a process that is now referred to as *"collaborative and proactive solutions"*.

This is how problems get solved! He also founded Lives in the Balance, a non-profit site that has many free resources, including the ALSUP (Assessment of Lagging Skills and Unsolved Problems)[57] form for each person to fill out when your group meets to discuss the child's strengths and lagging skills. The meeting should include: teachers, principals, bus drivers, the librarian,

---

[56] Greene, Ross W. PhD. *The Explosive Child: A New Approach for Understanding and Parenting Easily Frustrated, Chronically Inflexible Children* (New York, Harper Collins, 2005).

janitorial staff, educational assistants—anyone who comes into contact with the child during the school day. Any school that does not include everyone in this problem-solving process is causing those who are not invited into the discussion to "wing it", and as we all know the results can be dangerous. The website offers a walking tour for educators and parents, directing you to priceless resources including videos and a Facebook discussion group.[58]

It is important to use empathy and problem solve together. Greene points out that, "If a kid's concern about a problem remains unidentified and unaddressed, then the kid will have little investment in working with you and the problem will remain unsolved. You don't lose any authority by gathering information about and understanding the kid's concern; you gain a problem solving teammate." Showing empathy and understanding helps the child be more coherent and more able to think through the problem for suitable answers and solutions. With repeated practice these solutions enable and empower the student to access other areas of functioning within their brain and build self-awareness and problem-solving skills. Relationships are so important! As author and speaker Brené Brown points out: "I define connection as the energy between people when they feel seen, heard and valued: when they can give and receive without judgment: and when they derive sustenance and strength from the relationship."

I enjoy reading books from Ross Greene because his programs and ideas make sense to me. I have seen the results first-hand when it comes to problem-solving using power and control compared to Greene's collaborative problem-solving. His approach involves three-steps: an empathy step, an adult-concerns step and a collaborative and mutual agreement step. Greene also has a website filled with resources aimed at ending restraints and seclusion in schools. You are encouraged to look at behaviours and students through new lenses and implement new thinking processes. The resources will help you discover how valuable and life changing being proactive can be.

Consequences do not solve the problems of lagging skills and unsolved problems. The best solution is to empower the child to be part of the

---

[57] This is the ALSUP form. Be sure to check out the guide to accompany it on the website too. www.livesinthebalance.org/sites/default/files/ALSUP%20060417.pdf

[58] To discover more about all the resources Lives In Balance has to offer, visit: www.livesinthebalance.org/. His valuable new website also has resources to implement to get rid of restraints and seclusion procedures in school: truecrisisprevention.org/

Ch. 4: Inspire

solution. This will give them lifelong skills versus temporary compliance through punishment or even rewards. Greene explains the difference between choices of problem solving in terms of baskets. Basket A, B and C. Choice A involves an imposed solution to a problem and often results in more challenging behaviour from the child. There's no joint problem-solving and it doesn't empower the child to develop problem-solving skills. With choice B you can inspire change because of collaborative efforts and discussion. It helps with prevention of future occurrences and helps you understand where the child is at cognitively. Building up the lagging skills is a useful step for prevention. A conscious classroom can benefit from using this approach. Basket C involves finding an interim solution to a problem for the time being. It does not mean that the child is getting away with something; it simply means that it is assessed as being low priority and will be dealt with at a later time.

I highly recommend his books and website for a better understanding of his methods and suggestions, especially for dealing with behaviour challenges and negativity. Greene uses an example of what he calls impulsive negativity. This is when a child is asked to do something and the child tends to respond by saying "No", yet a few seconds later without any further words from you they will comply. Greene discusses an example about a young boy he was working with. "His initial 'No' was simply his way of letting me know he needed a little extra time to organize a coherent response." Responding to this as an issue of disrespect could cause the child undue stress and possibly a meltdown.

F. The Power of Focus

"Always remember your focus determines your reality." - George Lucas, writer, producer, creator of Star Wars

You always get more of what you are focusing on whether it's your thoughts, your behaviours or your activities—the laws of attraction are always working. When working with students, always see the good in the individual. Remember that each person is usually just doing their best. If you focus on what a child is best at and what interests them, you help them build confidence and raise their self-esteem. Teach them to have a gratitude attitude. Reflect daily and get input on what each student is grateful for, whether it's by writing it in a journal during quiet time at the end of the day or verbalizing it to the class. Writing or drawing (depending upon the age of the student) is a good practice. There's power in written expression of feelings. This is a great activity to engage in at the end of day to remind students about the good things that happened during the day. It promotes feelings of positivity and establishes a desire within the student for it to happen again the next day. Begin with sentences such as:

"Today, I liked when..."
"I loved it when..."
"My favourite part of the day was..."
"I'm thankful for..."
"I'm thankful and grateful for..."
"I was happy when..."[59]

G. Behaviour Planning and Prevention

"In my world there are no bad kids, just impressionable, conflicted young people wrestling with emotions and impulses, trying to communicate their feelings and needs the only way they know how." - Janet Lansbury, **Elevating Child Care: A Guide to Respectful Parenting**

Each student that needs a behaviour and safety plan should have one in place. It should describe in detail how to interact with a student. It should tell you "triggers" to watch for and have methods for de-escalating situations and behaviour.

When a student is acting out, knowing your plan in advance is very important. There is a space between the action taken by the student and the response you take to the behaviour. It's often called the gap. The gap is an opportunity for your own self-control to make a decision that empowers you and the student to make it a win-win. If you decide to "poke the bear", so to speak, you more often than not lose. You could even end up being hurt by the student thrashing and lashing out at you in their state of fight or flight (survival mode). As the child sees it, they need to fight to get through whatever they are feeling. Always attempt to consider what the child may be feeling at this moment when there is a conflict or a possible power struggle going on.

Do not turn these situations into battles and power struggles. No one wins! Choices empower students. Using the words "first and then" or "first, next, and then" gives the student back the power of choice. Word it in question

---

[59] Create a daily gratitude journal for you and your class. You can download a free one from my website: www.sheenalsmith.com/free-gift/

form: Would you like a snack or a short break before doing your work or would you like to get started with some help?

If you insist that a child do as you are requesting before they are ready you'll lose. The child has to be ready to make a positive choice. Even if it's not a positive choice, they will learn the results of such a choice by having consistency and clear expectations. What happens, for example, when they throw books, throw pencils across the room and break items in the classroom? Once calm, the child needs to learn responsibility for their actions whether it involves cleaning up, replacing broken items or writing an apology to those hurt in the meltdown or outburst.

Respect and accountability is taught when the child is back in a frame of mind to assess and understand their actions. A child in the middle of a meltdown cannot access the prefrontal cortex, the area of the brain associated with rational decision-making.

H. The Red Choice/Green Choice Booklet

"We always have choices, and the better the choice, the more we will be in control of our lives." - William Glasser, psychiatrist

If you are working with younger students you can create a book to discuss the results of their choices and behaviours. This can be done when they've calmed down or the day after the incident. Talk about the incident in terms of red choices and green choices. I use red construction paper circles and green construction paper circles and write in the child's level of understanding what happened. What were the choices and results? What could be done differently next time? What would those results look like?

Clear rules and known consequences of actions and behaviour help a student as much as advanced detailed preparation. The tool here is to be mindful; remember that events + response = outcome. Your response to events will determine the outcome of any situation.

Consider an event. How do you handle it when a student refuses to do their math work?

You can easily believe that they just want to do their own thing or you can consider that maybe they had a rough start to their day and never had breakfast. Ask questions!

You may think their behaviour means one thing while they may be thinking the complete opposite! It's easy to misinterpret a student's behaviour. Here are some things they might be dealing with: they may not know how to ask for help, they may have difficulty expressing needs, or they may have learned to mistrust everyone in authority. Develop a relationship and rapport. Know your students. The best way to learn about them is through individual and group conversations.

How will you respond to the situation? Do you have a relationship of trust and care with this student? Relationships are important. Knowing the child is essential!

How is your own self-control? Do you easily react with anger and frustration? Are there days when your own self-control needs to be assessed? What can you do to react in a calm, non-confrontational manner?

Keep in mind that a child feels your energy! They can tell if you are angry. They can tell if you are coming from a place of revenge, anger or even hate. How sad it is for a child to feel like his teacher actually hates him. I know if you are reading this book you are not one of those educators. You are one who truly loves and cares for the students that you work with and will go to any lengths to help your students thrive and learn. I honour, respect and value you!

I believe if you truly know a child and their life you can more easily come from a place of love and understanding. You are even more easily able to accept that the child is lagging in skills, to understand and empathize with the consequences of their choices. The child has learned behaviours. They've learned to shut down, blame others, and not see their own part in how the problem developed in the first place.

I. Positive Home and School Communication

"A child educated only at school is an uneducated child. When parents and teachers work together to facilitate and inspire learning, children are the winners." - George Santayana, poet, philosopher and novelist

Healthy and consistent home and school communication is beneficial to know what's going on between each environment. Whenever possible, attempt to have consistent or comparable expectations in both environments to avoid confusing the student, especially if the child has special needs. Sending a book back and forth with a line or two about your student's day helps the parent have conversations with their child about their day. Do NOT make it a tattletale book about negative behaviour. Point out what the child did right. Of course, there are times, when parents need to be informed but complaining about a child, day after day, without offering suitable solutions is draining for the parents.

If you do not have time to write a child's day out, create a check-list or picture schedule and add in special activities or notes on lessons learned, songs sung (in younger grades). This is priceless for a parent—especially when they have a child who cannot tell them how their day went.

If the parents' view of a child's behaviour is different than yours it usually gets ignored or sometimes escalates into a "you're picking on my child battle." This type of interaction is more commonplace now. Years ago, when a child got into trouble at school they got into double trouble at home. Now, too many parents make excuses for their children and don't teach them responsibility for their choices. I say go with the facts and find out what the real story is. Even facts can be perceived differently. Keep perception in mind. Things are not always as they seem.

An educator once told me that her best tip when facing an angry, irate parent in your classroom is to ask them to sit down and then hand them a note. The sitting causes a change in breathing and the note about the child places the focus on the words on the paper and shifts the perception of it being an attack from you.

J. Goal-Setting and Class Culture

"The best education is not given to students, it is drawn out of them."
- Gerald Belcher, teacher

When it comes to team building in the classroom, it is wonderful to establish group goals and individual goals. Important attributes of class culture include providing an inclusive, safe environment where all students feel valued, respected, and honoured. Setting goals helps develop your class culture.

Shelley Moore, teacher, researcher, consultant and storyteller, strongly suggests that we get rid of S.M.A.R.T goals[60], which stand for: specific,

---

[60] Check out: See You Later S.M.A.R.T. Goals, a Shelley Moore video, www.youtube.com/watch?v=0OrntS8NrUY

measurable, attainable, realistic, and timely. She suggests, especially with an I.E.P. (Individualized Education Plan) for students, that we adopt new S.M.A.R.T goals: strength-based, meaningful, authentic, responsive and triangulated. "Presume competence, all kids can learn," says Moore. Focus goals on strengths and possibilities as to what the student can do. Word the goals as "I can..." statements. This method is empowering and helps the students understand responsibility for one's own actions. Underline the fact that as a class you are a community that should value each other's cultures, differences, and opinions respectfully. Be sure to have a "no put-down" rule and enforce it. Assign classroom jobs and class responsibilities to each student. I have seen some classes sign a contract acknowledging their role and responsibility for creating a values-based class culture.

Setting goals helps develop your class culture. Goals can be something as simple as how much time the class will meditate together and by how many minutes the sessions will increase each month. Individual goals can be set with encouragement from the teacher and peers can cheer on success as it is achieved.

Always celebrate your wins—micro and macro wins. Celebrate and cheer each other on. That is why knowing what is important to each other is good because you can encourage and support one another towards success.

If meditation is one of your class goals, here's an adaptation for increasing meditation silence if you have a student that has a hard time being quiet. Allow them to hold something like a quiet item/toy after a minimal time of silence. Gradually increase the amount of time they remain quiet. Removing the child from meditation does not teach inclusive and tolerance, nor does it help the student build up to their own capabilities.

K. Choices, Rules and Consequences

"When you take away choice, you take away empowerment. When you think you have no choice, you disempower yourself." - Crystal Andrus Morissette, empowerment coach, author of **The Emotional Edge**

To effectively run a conscious-based classroom you need to have clear goals, clear expectations, and clear rules for all. Regular routines and schedules are essential because children need structure and routine. Children need clearly posted guidelines and class rules. They need to know beforehand what consequences will result from their behaviour choices.

Ch. 4: Inspire

The class, as a group, should define the rules, whenever possible. The same with consequences, they must be clearly defined. The rules should be posted in visible areas throughout the classroom where students can refer to them. They should be simple and supported with pictures. The consequences for not following the rules should be just and fair. For example: You do not make a student lose recess for a month for not finishing a work job just as you do not have the student wash all the desks in the class when it was only on one desk that they wrote on. The student is responsible for cleaning up their own mess.

Here are a few tips:

Wherever possible give choices. Choices empower a student to take responsibility and make decisions. Choices can be offered either verbally, visually, or through the use of presenting actual objects. Only offer two or three choices at a time. Do not make the choice for the child. Avoid offering a negative choice such as, *"Do your work or no recess."*

When making requests to a child: make eye contact at their level whenever possible, use a firm but kind tone of voice, allow 20-30 seconds before repeating—especially with children with a disability. Sometimes the message takes longer to be processed before the child can respond and take action.

Avoid repeating the request too many times. Verbally praise the follow-through on the requested action. Make sure to be specific. For example, more than saying, "good job", say *"thank you for putting your books away neatly"* or *"thanks for cleaning up your mess."*

Children with special needs do not handle changes or transitions well. Whenever possible stick to your regular routine and warn ahead of time about the changes that are going to take place. You can also create a visual reminder using pictures of schedule changes so that they know what to expect. When a student is refusing to comply consider what you are asking them to do next. Is it a preferred activity? Or something they don't like? Is it a sensory issue? Is there an insecurity issue? Are they feeling unskilled and not wanting to be embarrassed? What's their skill level or interest in the activity?

I use the wording, *"first, next, and then"* verbally and as a visual for students. Students often need to see what's next to be encouraged to do their non-preferred activity first. An example of this would be: *"First, you complete one worksheet. Then, you can pick an activity that you would like to do." Or, "First, we do this worksheet, next we clean up, and then we can go to the gym."

L. Dealing with Negativity

"The art of being yourself at your best is the art of unfolding your personality into the man you want to be. Be gentle with yourself, learn to love yourself, to forgive yourself, for only as we have the right attitude towards ourselves can we have the right attitude towards others." - Wilferd Peterson, author of **Art of Living**

You must consciously choose your thoughts when interacting with others and avoid being affected by their negative energy. Notice how you feel when you spend time with others—do you leave feeling better or worse? Do you feel contracted or expanded when you are around certain people? Many people can be energy vampires. They tell you all their troubles and bad news, leaving you feeling drained and demoralized, while they feel energized and stronger for having dumped all their upset on you. Control who you allow to affect your energy; stay away from the energy vampires. Avoid them as much as possible, consciously decide how you are going to react (or not react) to them, and lastly, power up your positive emotions after spending time with them. When you are visualizing how your day will unfold be proactive and imagine a different outcome when interacting with the negative people in your life. Picture them being happy and telling you good news and an uplifting story. We do always get more of what we expect.

Tip: To be proactive and help change your work environment; do the best not to complain or talk negatively. You can even engage co-workers in a positive manner by asking questions such as: *"What's new and good today?"*

When you have students, and even staff members, that seemingly drain you of your energy you must re-energize and commit to self-care. I've had days where it wasn't fair for me to go home to my family with the mood that I was in. If I went home before unwinding and gaining my own sense of peace and balance someone in my family would be suffering within minutes of my coming through the door. I would be cranky or less patient and snap when something snarky was said to me. It wasn't fair to them. I've learned to drive around, listen to music and relax before going home. In time, I learned how to consciously change my view of the day and have less attachment to the outcome.

Ch. 4: Inspire

At school, when upsets happen you can show children that you always have a choice in how you react or respond. Especially when your "ANTs" try to kick in! "ANTs" is a term coined by psychologists to signify *Automatic Negative Thoughts*. I'm sure you've heard that the average person has over 60,000 thoughts a day and over 90% of them are negative. These thoughts are usually the same ones repeated from the previous day. Historically, through our ancestors, we have learned to watch out for trouble, be on guard, and focus on being safe. This is where we have developed the habit of thinking negatively. The problem with thinking negatively and repeating those negative thoughts day after day is that we create neural pathways with these thoughts. The repetition makes the connections in the brain stronger and we then have deeply ingrained habits such as focusing on what's wrong, talking negatively to ourselves, as well as living in fear and worry of what could go wrong. The result can even lead to stress-induced illnesses.

Debra Poneman, CEO and creator of the Yes to Success program[61], suggests that it is possible to change these habits by noticing our thoughts and then consciously choosing positive ones. When you catch yourself thinking or saying something negative say out loud or to yourself "Cancel, clear" and rephrase your perception in a more positive manner.

If your brain gets stuck in patterns of constant negative thinking and behaviour to the point of being overwhelmed, adrenal exhaustion, anger and frustration, it can lead to an overactive stress-response mechanism within the body. Sustained and chronically elevated hormones like cortisol (the stress hormone), and lower levels of serotonin and other neurotransmitters in the brain such as dopamine, have been linked to depression. An overactive stress-response can put your health further at risk with problems such as lower immune system, adrenal fatigue, chronic pain, anxiety and depression.

The systems of your body are designed to work in homeostasis. If your systems are in a balanced state, stress-free and calm, they will be working as

---

[61] Debra Poneman is an international speaker, seminar leader and business owner. She shares her cutting-edge knowledge of universal principles in an impactful and heart-centerd way. She will touch your heart and impact your life forever. She is authentic, wise and fun loving. To say that she is some kind of wonderful is an understatement. I am blessed to know her and have her as a mentor and a friend. Check out her "Yes to Success" program for true success in the 21st century. You will be inspired! Visit: www.yestosuccess.com

they should be, regulating biochemical processes such as: sleep, appetite, energy levels, sex drive, moods, and emotions.

Yet, when these systems are overloaded and overwhelmed, it becomes harder to control your thoughts and make the best decisions. Once again regular self-care and managing your thoughts is essential (lots more on this coming up!).

A common condition of unbalanced chemicals in the brain can cause anxiety and/or depression. Depression can be a serious issue. If you feel that you are suffering from depression contact medical professionals who are trained to do deeper therapy treatment such as CBT (cognitive behaviour therapy).

Be proactive! Practicing self-care to counteract stress is ideal. When possible, make it a daily habit—eat well, get a proper amount of sleep, exercise, meditate, get some fresh air and drink water.

Learning to control your "ANTs" is priceless. By "noticing" and employing simple techniques you can learn to control your thoughts. When you let negative emotions hijack your awareness, making conscious decisions to alter what you are thinking will help to put you back on the right track. Ask yourself: What's the good in this situation? What's the lesson? What is it telling me? Make a commitment to yourself to learn from these situations.

Let's look at an example. It's a simple incident; a student is playing with their bottle of water and it falls off their desk and spills all over the floor in the middle of a lesson. The teacher faces certain choices. They can take the bottle away or they can get mad and yell and be mad at the student for the rest of the day (it sounds extreme but I've seen it happen). The third option is to tell the student to get a paper towel and clean up the mess and then simply continue teaching. The student also has choices. They can be upset, have their feelings hurt by the teacher, or be embarrassed and possibly cry in front of the class. If the class does laugh at the student spilling their water, the incident can be used as a teachable moment centred on extending kindness and consideration to classmates and being respectful of the teacher who is teaching a lesson. Empowered communication is beneficial to use here. Try phrases like these: *"You handled that well, I knew you could do it, I'm proud of you for not allowing an accident to ruin your day." "That's okay; we will clean it up and get back on track with our lesson."*

You can even thank the class for not engaging in silliness at this time too. Let them know their behaviour was respectful.

Ch. 4: Inspire

How about you? Do you ever feel angry? The emotion of anger can come from a feeling of disapproval of self. This is usually a judgment. The feeling arises because you feel like a failure because you seemingly couldn't get through to the students. In his book, **Conscious Classroom Management: Unlocking the Secrets of Great Teaching**,[62] author Rick Smith describes how disconnection with a student is the greatest source of frustration because teachers take it to heart when they can't reach the child. Odds are, if you are reading this right now, you know that feeling. I've been there, I used to take it personally and its effects were damaging to my ego. Feeling like a failure is self-defeating and lowers your confidence in your ability. Having wisdom and the time to sit back and reflect on all factors and variables reminds me that as challenging as any child may seem, it's critical to teach how a child learns and know what skills are lagging so you can implement strategies to aid the child in becoming the best they can be. With that said, I'd like to add that for whole child learning to be effective, your own mind, body and spirit must be in balance. More on that in the chapters to come!

M. Resilience

"Obstacles, of course, are developmentally necessary: they teach kids strategy, patience, critical thinking, resilience, and resourcefulness." - Naomi Wolf, author

Resilience is your ability to recover from setbacks and continue moving forward.

How resilient are you? What skills do you use to pull yourself together, to pick yourself back up and bounce back from setbacks, let downs and disappointments? What helps a person develop coping skills is self-awareness, hope, strong relationships and a sense of meaning in life.

Learning how to become resilient as a teacher is essential. There are times when, although you have done your best, the things you cannot control—especially what happens in the home environment—may be the factors that affect your students' success. For example: diet and nutrition. I am a certified nutritional consultant and know that foods affect people differently.

---

[62] Smith, Rick, *Conscious Classroom Management-Unlocking the Secrets of Great Teaching* (Conscious Teaching Publications: Writing in book edition, 2004, San Rafael, California).

As teachers and educators you can't tell parents what to feed their kids but through a health curriculum you can teach healthy eating and the effects of consuming good and bad foods. Encourage healthy eating choices. Many children go home and tell their parents what they learned with regards to consuming healthy foods. You can only do what you can do. The rest is in the parent's hands.

Allergies among students are common, and often, people do not understand the ways in which an allergy can show up. For example, it's been recommended that my son restrict his intake of dairy and wheat due to the effects it can have on the intestinal and digestive tract as well as the minds of those who have Down syndrome. If a child is reacting to certain foods they may have brain fog and headaches that result in trouble concentrating. The sinus problems can cause headaches and constant nose dripping. The need to blow their nose and wipe their faces, and sanitize their hands, can all become troublesome for the child and at times disruptive for the class. Why does resilience matter in a school setting? What does stress have to do with it?

Resilience matters because you must know how to pick yourself up when life kicks you down. Educators and students all need to learn to be resilient to be able to handle what life may bring to them. No one gets through life without challenges, such as experiencing grief over the death of a loved one.

Through these moments your ability to cope is tested. And, when you let negative emotions get the best of you the effects can be disastrous, even life-threatening. Stress has powerful effects on your health. These effects can include heart conditions, high blood pressure, sleep disturbances, heart disease, and adrenal exhaustion.

With stress, you can have numerous negative feelings/emotions such as anxiety, depression, nervousness, worry, doubt, anger, judgment, and even overwhelm. I'm sure we all have experienced these emotions from time to time but it's the management of these feelings that matters most. Management needs to be timely because not dealing with negative emotions may speed up the effects upon your body.

Signs you or a child is not coping well can include: sleep problems, sadness, crying spells, depression, anger, eating problems (too much or not enough), pain, and health issues. Adults may drink excessively, use drugs or other destructive ways to numb themselves. Feeling hopeless

Ch. 4: Inspire

is discouraging! Knowing there are answers brings a renewed faith and optimism.

For children and adults it's important to know that you can heal what you feel! Louise Hay assisted thousands of individuals to discover and find their power through personal growth and self-healing. In her book, **You Can Heal Your Life**, you can read and learn about the correlation between health problems and their association with thoughts and patterns you've created. There are intentions for self-love, trust and acceptance and approval of yourself. Her book is so valuable because she lists the problem, probable cause and new thought pattern to use. For example, anxiety can be linked to not trusting the flow and the process of life. A new thought pattern and affirmation would be:

"I love and approve of myself and I trust the process of life. I am safe." [83]

Thoughts that come from worry and negative feelings like fear, regret, anger, guilt, resentment, hatred, shame, sadness, overwhelm, and frustration can all show up in an area in the body as pain, dis-ease and disability. This proves the absolute need to be very mindful of your thoughts and to teach children the power of their thoughts.

Imagine that you can go from having phobias to being fearless! You can go from having pain to lessening it and even becoming pain-free. Many of us hold traumas and stress in our body and it is expressed through pain. With the desire to change you can do anything! Believe in possibilities!

N. Inspire: It's Your Turn!

"There is no need to be perfect to inspire others. Let people get inspired by how you deal with your imperfections." - Ziad K. Abdelnour, author

To inspire a student may seem like a simple job but often it is no easy task. My best advice and wisdom through so many years of working with children is, "To believe in the student until they believe in themselves. Provide them with a sense of safety and trust by being caring and inclusive. Provide them with an environment that gives a sense of safety to the whole child physically, mentally, spiritually, and emotionally."

---

[63] Hay, Louise, *You Can heal Your Life* (New York, Hay House Inc.1984).

This happens through being grounded yourself and having consistency, predictability, and unconditional love. Empower them to be resilient through shared decision making.

Self-reflection questions:

- What have you learned about inspiration is this chapter?
- What new ways are you inspired to build your own confidence and courage?
- How will you now help your students to become more resilient and inspired?
- How will you lead and implement inclusion?
- What was your biggest take away or 'aha' moment from this chapter?

 **CHAPTER 5: VALUE**

"In order to develop normally, a child requires progressively more complex joint activity with one or more adults who have an irrational emotional relationship with the child. Somebody's got to be crazy about that kid. That's number one; First, last and always." [64] - Urie Bronfenbrenner, world-renowned child psychologist and, author

Children need to know with absolute certainty that they have someone in their corner willing to stand up for them, willing to help them grow, learn, and be accountable for their actions and decisions. My biggest reason for writing this book has been to show you that you have more power than you could ever imagine with regards to influencing a child and their learning through positive interaction, and human connection. Children are not attention-seeking, they are connection-seeking, and they are craving relationships!

Do not miss watching Ms. Rita Pierson's TED Talk *"Every Child Needs a Champion"*.[65] **In her video, this teacher of over 40 years recounts a conversation she had with an educator who stated that she, the educator, "wasn't paid to like kids only to teach them."**

Ms. Pierson responded by pointing out that, *"Kids don't learn from people they don't like."* **She also quoted veteran educator James Comer, who believes that, "no significant learning occurs without a significant relationship."**

Agreeing with these statements is one thing, let's dig a little deeper. Do you show your students that you value them? How do you show them? How do you support their growth and success?

---

[64] For more information, view this resource: developingchild.harvard.edu/wp-content/uploads/2004/04/Young-Children-Develop-in-an-Environment-of-Relationships.pdf

[65] You can view the Ted Talk here: www.ted.com/talks/rita_pierson_every_kid_needs_a_champion?language=en#t-8477

In a school environment it is important to acknowledge and value each student's cultural values and it's important to implement a class environment that enables all students to feel acknowledged, honoured and respected.

Once again, it's no surprise that this goal is achieved through knowing your students and having a connection with them. When you do what's right by your students, by valuing their strengths, skills, and natural talents, you motivate, encourage and inspire them.

They will feel worthy and deserving. Feeling those emotions gives them courage to step out of their comfort zones, try new things, and be more creative. They can learn to forgive and let go of past mistakes. They will want to do their best and learn to be more responsible for their actions. They become more curious, which in turn, leads them to become better at critical-thinking and problem-solving. As a result, they will be motivated to contribute to the school culture and community. Leaders will be developed.

One of the biggest ways to impact a student is through listening. Listening is a skill that is highly promoted in Dr. Stephen R. Covey's book, *'The 7 Habits of Highly Successful People.'* He suggests that you; "Seek first to understand, then to be understood."

A. Relationships and Connection: The Power of Thoughts

"Change your thoughts, change your life." – Dr. Wayne Dyer, internationally renowned self-development author

As you consider how you value your students, consider how you value yourself.

Dyer's quote is one of the best pieces of advice that I have ever learned. Time after time it has proven to work and improve the quality of my life. Do you have stinking thinking? Truly consider the impact of your thoughts on yourself and others. Your thoughts are like magnets—you will attract more of what you focus on. Pay attention to your thoughts; are there some that you need to change to a more positive outlook? Helping your students to understand this is important because it will aid them in understanding how they are responsible for everything that they see in their lives. It will assist them in goal-setting, learning to see the point of view of others, as well as being more proactive with regards to their own feelings, emotions, and thoughts.

Ch. 5: Value

The following tips and suggestions will help you to raise your vibration to higher levels of consciousness:

1. Be aware of what you are thinking. Are your thoughts positive or negative? Frame your thoughts using positive wording. Your thoughts become the things that you attract; make sure to focus on kindness, forgiveness, compassion, and most of all, LOVE.
2. Meditate when you can, as best as you can. There's no right or wrong way as long as you are learning to quiet your thoughts, relax, and be calm. Being still and quiet naturally raises your vibration.
3. Listen to uplifting positive music. Pay attention to the words as well. Are they uplifting? Motivating? Energizing? Or is the music bringing you down? I've listened to a lot of sad songs in the past. They kept me wallowing in my misery for longer than I should have been feeling down about any negative situation.
4. Avoid watching the news and negative forms of media, including negative posts and news on Facebook. No news when you first wake up and when you go to bed! Awaken expressing gratitude for each new day and go to sleep marinating in happy thoughts and gratitude about your blessings of the day. You get more of what you focus on. Focus on good, positive, and happy situations and occurrences.
5. Declutter your environment. Make it reflect things that you love and things that help you to feel peaceful and calm. Your home should be a place to energize and recharge.
6. Be of service to others. Help those less fortunate than you, whenever you can. Be compassionate and do random acts of kindness daily.
7. Eat healthy nutritional foods to energize and cleanse your body. Avoid foods that make you feel sluggish a short while after having consumed them. Eat fresh organic fruits and veggies. Eat a variety of nuts and healthy fats, not saturated fats. Avoid white sugar and white flour.

It is important to pay attention to how you feel after eating food. I discovered when I eat foods with sugar and white flour that I tend to get more headaches, neck, and shoulder pains. I used to run to the chiropractor thinking I had put something out in my neck or back. Once I began eating less of these foods my pain lessened. I also noticed around Christmas when I ate more white flour sweets and baked goods that my body ached horribly a day or two later. The white processed food caused inflammation in my body. I've noticed that children who consume high-sugar snacks have runny noses more frequently.

B. The Value of Play, Movement, and Exercise

"Play is often talked about as if it were a relief from serious learning. But for children play is serious learning." - Mr. Rogers, creator and host of *Mr. Rogers' Neighborhood*

There is a considerable amount of value in play and movement when it comes to happiness and stress relief as well as emotional wellbeing and development. If a person is under stress, they literally *"flip their lid"* and have less access to their prefrontal cortex where higher order, problem-solving thought processes take place. They tend to handle the stress through the most dominant side of their brain.

For optimal benefit, it is best to use both sides of your brain. When a child is dysregulated they need assistance to calm down and regain control. Through movement they are easily able to settle and regulate and have improved self-control.

Once settled they then have more access to improved focus. When using your whole brain your learning skills are increased. These skills include; improvements with memory, reading, writing, comprehension, and math skills. Many have also noticed improvements with their concentration, vision, verbal, and creative expression. People have even discovered that their abilities with sports have improved, especially their coordination, stamina, and energy. It's good for your health to practice movements that engage your whole body daily.

Whole brain learning can be achieved through balancing the three dimensions of human brain function. These dimensions are centering, laterality, and focus.

The Centering Dimension is associated with the top and bottom structures of the brain. Centering helps us to balance emotions with rational thinking. Stress can throw us out of balance and often cause us to function in fight, flight and/or freeze mode.

The laterality dimension relates to both sides of the brain – left and right, as well as the midfield. Many skills associated with laterality include use of both sides for optimal listening, reading, writing, and even speaking. It is also essential for the ability to think and move at the same time.

Ch. 5: Value

The focus dimension is associated with the back and front parts of the brain. Focus is important for comprehension. Many children with ADHD have difficulties with the focus dimension.

Performing simple exercise activities in schools can be easy to incorporate into the schedule. They can be done in classrooms on a daily basis. There are some schools that even start their day in the schoolyard with a 10-minute assembly of staff and students performing movement exercises to enhance learning. Other schools do their daily exercises during morning announcements. Numerous classes start each new session of learning new material by doing movement exercises first. Many classroom teachers have reported improvements in behaviour, attitude, attention, focus, homework completion, as well as progress in all around academic performance for the whole class when they allow their students to have frequent movement breaks.

Repetitive movement builds new neural pathways, enabling children and adults to improve their speech, memory, coordination, as well as skills that some of us may even take for granted such as the ability to jump, balance on a beam, or the ability to cross over the midline of our body. The midline is an imaginary line down the centre of the body that divides it into left and right sides. Being able to cross over the midline is important for the arms and legs to do specific activities and tasks. As examples: if the child is drawing a line on a piece of paper he should be able to draw the line across the page without switching hands, when playing a board game the individual should be able to use their right hand to place a game piece on the left-hand side board (naturally crossing over the body), they should be able to sit crossed-legged. Cross-lateral movements are a developmental process that when inhibited or not fully developed can lead to difficulties in activities such as crawling and skipping. Children may have a hard time doing star jumps, putting on socks and shoes and may switch hands during writing tasks when crossing over the body is required.

Educators may notice low fine motor skills such as weakness and poor grasp when holding a pencil, difficulties tracking text when reading, and challenges when kicking a ball. Students with difficulties crossing over the midline often need assistance with dressing skills—buttoning clothing, and shoe tying, for example. They will avoid certain tasks or get easily frustrated. Beneficial activities for skill-building can include: cutting paper (involves the use of each hand), beading crafts, folding paper, ribbon dancing (have a ribbon in each hand, play music and mirror actions using both arms to move the ribbons both at the same time.) Games like Twister and Simon

Says are useful for actions that involve the use of both sides of the body. Marching is another fun way to build this skill.

Skill-building is beneficial for your whole class. When doing stretching with your class during movement breaks and Simon Says activities add in movements that encourage crossing over that imaginary line. The cross crawl movement is one of the best exercises that I like students to do. I'll often use it and say, "Copy me." This can be done standing, sitting, or even lying down depending upon the child's capabilities. The movement here is to put the left hand on the right knee then switch up and place the right hand on the left knee. This can be varied according to the child's capability. A variation: when putting the left hand to right knee the child can lift their knee towards the hand.

Children with midline processing difficulties will have a hard time with this activity until their coordination improves to guide them. I have put stickers on their knees and hands so they can match colours with the movement. For example, red stickers on the left hand and right knee, and blue on the right hand and left knee. If you are working with a child with special needs you can assist them by helping them physically do this movement to build new pathways. Never force a child to do this or any movement, instead invite them to join in and see how it feels for them. An occupational therapist can suggest movements for you to do with your students as part of their care.

Exercise has numerous benefits for the body and the value of movement should never be underestimated with regards to development of intelligence and learning ability. Years ago, when children with cognitive deficits and physical disabilities were put in institutions their full potential was never known. They were placed in isolated institutions where they lacked attention, physical touch from loving caregivers, and the opportunities for actual physical movement. Connection and movement are essential for brain development and firing of neurons. That is why the brain is so fascinating. Intelligence is inborn and with assistance it can be drawn out— **energy flows where attention goes**.

For more than 80 years it has been accepted that movement enhances learning. Its importance is made even more relevant as we witness more and more children getting less physical activity than ever and experiencing greater struggles with educational skills. I wholly believe that everyone should understand the critical link between exercise and learning. It is important that everyone realizes that achievement of academic skills can be improved through purposeful movements that enhance whole brain learning. As founder of Brain Gym®, Paul Dennison frequently states, *"Movement is the door to learning."*

Frequent movement breaks are essential—stop, drop and dance! Test out different styles of music to see what energizes your class most of all. A variation is to have one or two students demonstrate dance moves one at a time at the front of the class and get the others to copy the movements. Children really enjoy this!

MeMoves[66] is another easy and effective way to increase attention in as little as 2 minutes of movement. It works wonderfully for calming children with ADHD, Autism spectrum disorder, anxiety, and depression. It is a terrific activity for the whole class. Children mirror movements, emotional expressions and actions in concert with music that is calming and appealing to children of all ages. Changes that have been noted along with increased calmness include: increase in positive social interaction, an increase in expressive language and in attention, as well as better organization and imitation skills.

MeMoves has received praise by Patricia Wilbarger, MEd, OTR, and FAOTA.

Wilbarger is an occupational therapist and clinical psychologist who developed the concept of the sensory diet. She also designed the Wilbarger Deep Pressure and Proprioceptive Technique (DPPT) and the Oral Tactile Technique for sensory defensiveness. These techniques should be implemented by a qualified occupational therapist.[67]

---

[66] MeMoves is an easy and effective way to increase attention in as little as 2 minutes. It is a patented award-winning DVD multimedia program for self-regulation. It is designed to activate the parasympathetic nervous system. It is organized into three categories: joy, focus and calm. You can watch MeMoves in the classroom here:
www.youtube.com/watch?v=55OGz8PVrRI

[67] Please remember that this technique can only be practiced by a trained OT or if a teacher has been trained by an OT. For more information about the Wilbarger Protocol, please visit: www.nationalautismresources.com/the-wilbarger-protocol-brushing-therapy-for-sensory-integration/

There is also a link with a list of changes to notice to determine if the technique is working or not working: sensoryprocessingdisorderparentsupport.com/wilbarger-brushing-compressions.php

Wilbarger has said: *"I've been involved with neuroscience as a base of activity for a very long time and I'm so impressed with the foundations that MeMoves brings. This is a very subtle way to calm and change peoples' brains and behaviour, and they don't even have to know it! I strongly recommend MeMoves, and I think as we go forward we're going to compile a lot more of the neuroscience that relates to this work. It looks like such a simple activity, but it's really not."* I believe that it is a valuable tool for mind, body and heart connection, especially for younger children.

On a side note, I have used the Wilbarger technique with a few children after being trained by an OT on how to implement it with my students. This tool is calming for those that need a certain amount of deep pressure to feel relaxed and in better control of their actions and behaviours in order to settle down for learning. Benefits include: ease in transitions, increased attention, and better self-regulation. A specific brush is used for this technique. I highly recommend that you have a trained specialist implement this or properly show you how they want this used on a specific child.

C. Rhythmic Movement

"The keystone of the entire structure of the spiritual and physical universe is the rhythmic balanced interchange between all the opposites." - Walter Russell, author

Rhythmic Movement Training™ (RMT) "is a system of gentle rhythmic movements and reflex integration activities for developing emotional balance, learning ability, ease of movement and sensory integration." [68]

It is a motor development program based on spontaneous rhythmic movements that you would normally see babies attempt. It was developed by the late Dr. Harald Blomberg. After working with severely motor-handicapped children, he concluded that the spontaneous rhythmic movements that babies make are of fundamental importance both for motor abilities and for the development of many faculties including speech, emotions and vision. The movements are also necessary for the maturation of the infant's brain. He based most of his program on rhythmic exercises that he learned in 1985 from Swedish body therapist, Kerstin Linde.

---

[68] Bloomberg, Dr. Harald, *Rhythmic Movement Training: Level One (RMT and ADD/ADHD)* (Stockholm Sweden, 2008). For more information, please visit his site: haraldbloomberg.com

Ch. 5: Value

When Rhythmic Movement Training is used with children and adults with less severe challenges it improves motor abilities and motor control such as coordination, muscle tone and integration of primitive reflexes. Additionally, many people have noticed improvement in different areas such as speech, vision and difficulties with attention, hyperactivity, reading and writing. According to Dr. Blomberg's hypothesis this improvement can be explained by the stimulation and linking up of different parts of the brain caused by the rhythmic exercises.

To be effective the rhythmic exercises need to be done regularly at least five days a week. Depending on the progress of the client the exercises need to be developed or replaced by follow-up movements on a regular basis.

The effects caused by the rhythmic exercises may sometimes be noticed after a short period but the changes may not be lasting until the different parts of the brain have been sufficiently stimulated and linked up. This usually takes at least three to six months. In children with more severe challenges it may take a year or more. **Some children, especially those with Autism spectrum disorder (ASD), need to be on a gluten and/or casein free diet to get optimal effects from Rhythmic Movement Training.** *Some children and adults get emotional reactions during the training and may not want to do the exercises. If this happens the training program usually needs to be changed.*

I have taken Dr. Bloomberg's course a couple of times and my learning has expanded each time. I found this was a course to be "experienced" for best understanding and application. I realize not all educators have time for this type of therapy nor do schools have personnel to teach children these valuable techniques.

But please keep in mind that the value of movement is priceless and its effects extend way beyond the immediate into the long term.

D. Top 10 Signs Your Brain is Running on a Paradigm

"Whether you think you can, or you can't—you are right." - Henry Ford, American industrialist

A whole body approach to learning includes not only your physical (body) efforts and movement; it includes your mind and spirit—thoughts, beliefs and paradigms. When you can value and appreciate and understand yourself, you are more able to help others. There might be certain paradigms that are holding you back from your dream life, your dream classroom, and the true reason you went into teaching and working with children.

But, wait! Before I tell you what these paradigms are, I feel like I should begin by giving you a definition. It wasn't too long ago that I had no idea what the term meant or even how to spell it! I didn't understand the influences paradigms were having on my life. I soon discovered they were causing me a great deal of grief. In fact, these paradigms were holding me back from the life of my dreams!

Simply put, paradigms are merely habits. These habits are exhibited through our thoughts, beliefs, and actions. The paradigms that you model will give you the results that you have in your life in all areas: health, wellness, career, relationships, and even your finances. And they can be defined by the following equation:

How we think + How we behave = Our results (life experiences). Period.

For years every time I attempted to make big changes in my life my plans seemed to fall through. I had paradigms that affected my health and caused me extreme pain. As a result they caused me much unhappiness and dissatisfaction. I felt like a failure. I was working so hard to make changes and as soon as I advanced a few steps, I would be hit with a challenge and then, bam, I'd be right back to square one.

Your paradigms can stem from your genetics and the environment that you were raised in. The good news is that if you are not currently living your dream life it is possible to shift your paradigms with focus, gratitude, and commitment. Many paradigms are unconsciously patterned into our systems. Awareness is a key!

I mentioned Debra Poneman's technique in the previous chapter and it applies for paradigms too! Whenever you catch yourself thinking a negative thought that doesn't serve your highest good, whether it's a complaint or disempowering thought, you can simply say "cancel/clear" and reframe that thought or comment with a more positive and empowering one.

Ch. 5: Value

If we can discover, uncover, and notice our paradigms, we can access what works for us and what doesn't. This awareness can assist us in making decisions that lead us to more fulfilling lives and happier classrooms. You are in charge, you must decide and commit to developing new habits!

Here are the top 10 paradigms that affect many people and could possibly be holding you prisoner in your mind:

1. Self-esteem: Do you believe that you are worthy of every goal, vision, and dream that you can imagine? Do you reject yourself? Do you know that your life cannot outperform your own self-image?
2. Time: Do you use the excuse that you cannot do something because you don't have enough time? We all have the same 525,000+ minutes each year to spend how we choose. The choice is yours. This is important within a classroom because there is only so much time within a day, but by being organized and making the best use of the time you have, you will see your day run more smoothly. Set a solid foundation of rules and expectations and follow through for your students and yourself.
3. Money: Have you ever said 'no' to something immediately because you currently did not have the money? Teachers and educational workers are skilled at coming up with alternative ways to do activities, crafts, and events when funds are limited, but imagine if you expanded your consciousness about money and found it to be flowing more easily into your life and your classroom budget. What would happen?
4. Health: Could you do more if you felt better but you seem to be constantly experiencing one health issue after another? Did you know there is often an association between thoughts, feelings, and wellness?
5. Fear: Have you ever felt stuck, unable to make any decision out of fear and worry about what might happen? Even though you have no way to know something awful may happen, you quickly assume everything that can go wrong, will go wrong and stop thinking about how things could be different or better.
6. Resignation: Have you felt hopeless when presented with a setback or a failure? Do you quit after a few attempts at something? Do you resign and give up? Do you hold back on trusting how the situation will unfold and picture disaster instead?
7. Avoidance: Have you felt it's easier to not do something than experience or take a chance of experiencing negative emotions from your past? Perhaps you have experienced painful failure in the past and vowed never to do it again without a guarantee that next time would be different. Maybe you have already shut down and are not willing to take a chance.

8. Age: Do you say 'no' to adventures, opportunities and use your age as an excuse? Age is a matter of mind. There are an endless number of personal stories of individuals that accomplished great success after the age of 50.
9. Judgment: Do you avoid being yourself for fear of others judging you? Are you a people-pleaser at the cost of yourself?
10. Success: Are you one of those individuals that actually fears success? Some people fear success because of what they imagine the result or cost will be to their lives. Success isn't envisioned as a positive thing, it is viewed as too great a cost and then life gets put on hold.

There are so many examples of thoughts that can be considered paradigm-limiting beliefs. These thoughts cause feelings that affect your performance, your life and your success. The thoughts are coming from your perception of things. Notice what comes up the next time you are faced with a decision, a choice, or an opportunity. Then, ask yourself, what will the cost be if I do not do this? How can I look at it another way? What have I done in the past that has held me back? What could I do differently this time?

In schools, students can benefit from learning to assess their performance, their work efforts, and even their habits. By having honest discussions you can empower students by complimenting them when they show leadership, good work habits, and initiative.

When you lovingly address students' successes and setbacks you can assist them in learning how to modify, adjust, and change their thoughts, beliefs and actions. Students will feel more valued when they are coached by you, knowing and feeling that you have their best interests at heart.

Just as you change your perception of the situations, adjust your current thoughts and challenge yourself to find empowering thoughts, new ideas and new ways of acting, you can model and allow them to do the same. This shows them to never give up!

E. Value Yourself: Self-Love

"Love yourself first and everything else falls into line. You really have to love yourself to get anything done in this world." - Lucille Ball, actress

To work more effectively with students you have to first begin with yourself. You've only got one you! You must make self-care and self-love a priority! Without your health, vitality, and energy you won't exist. Do you find it hard

Ch. 5: Value

to put yourself and your needs first? You are not alone. Many of us weren't raised that way.

If you have been a people-pleaser, have a hard time setting boundaries, and continually put others ahead of yourself you will crash at some point and if you are like me it's going to be painful, disheartening and maybe even embarrassing. The most crushing part is when you realize that you must take responsibility for everything that you see. We create what we believe. It can be a hard pill to swallow at times but it is part of how we grow, learn, and develop new ways of being.

This is my story; I am not proud of it, but it was a huge lesson on many levels. For many years, I was a "super" mom. I did everything for my kids, especially my two youngest ones with special needs. I made promises to them when each was born to do my best to help them have the best life ever. I would go to the ends of the earth to find things to enable them to live a life of health, wellness, and happiness. I took courses, programs and certifications to learn about health and nutrition. I went or took them to specialists that taught alternative modalities. For over twenty years, I frequently took my daughter to SickKids Hospital and a children's rehabilitation centre that was eight hours away from our home. I stayed up way too late on school nights searching for answers or studying. I lacked sleep, proper nutrition and my only exercise was running all day long meeting the needs of others. I burned the candle at both ends many times. During these crazy days, I was also working full time as an educational assistant. Work became tense: there was drama, challenging dynamics and I felt like I had a complete lack of support.

I hit the point of being frustrated and angry daily at work. It was not good for me to go straight home from work because I was easily angered or annoyed with the people that I love the most—my family. They would innocently say something that I would take the wrong way and I would snap at them for no or little reason at all. I am sorry for that. I felt like such a lousy mom. I would zone out and play mindless games on the computer to avoid life and avoid reality. It became clear that things had to change, tough conversations and communication had to happen, and I had to accept that sometimes in life you do not have control over what happens. My friend, Marianna was fighting for her life at this point in time. That added to the stress and anger that I was feeling. I felt so helpless and angry that life was not fair. I knew my life had hit an all-time low when our dog lunged at me and bit me. I hit an all-time high of anger when my husband did not really believe that our dog bit me, despite an actual bite mark on my skin near my hip. My life felt like the dog bite: so painful!

I was in a job that was draining my soul and spirit, my life was a daily struggle, financially we were struggling to make ends meet, my relationship with my spouse was rocky and my whole future seemed like there was nothing to look forward to. Add some chronic pain into the mix from arthritis and daily headaches, neck and shoulder pain from a car accident. I wanted to quit and give up. Life seemed pointless and depressing!

But, I knew that I was not a quitter! I searched for answers for me, for my sanity and understanding. As time went on I continued learning and taking self-development courses, learning essential tools including Ho'oponopono (a Hawaiian practice of reconciliation and forgiveness) and other emotional freedom techniques (more details on these amazing techniques in the next chapter!), and other empowering courses that proved to me that we create what we believe. So with the discovery of learning that our thoughts create our reality I knew that I had to make changes, and fast.

My miracle was finding that my answers were already within me, and at the same time, finding a tribe of like-minded souls that were all searching for what I was looking: for peace, love, and happiness. I practice these techniques and I offer them to you in this book for your own self-discovery and growth. Through lots of self-care, self-discovery, and awareness I can thankfully say I am happier at my job, I have more abundance and it increases regularly. My relationship with my spouse is better and we talk and laugh more often. My children are thriving despite me not finding every answer that I wished I could for them. I have learned to allow them to be themselves. I have learned to let go and forgive. I have learned to be less angry, less sad, and to choose happiness more often by looking for the good, I have learned to look for the lesson or simply to find some humour in the struggles and challenges of everyday life. I have learned most of all to forgive myself, practice self-care and love me more.

Love yourself first! Starting right now. Say and repeat often: *"I love myself, I love myself!"* It's not selfish to love yourself, to value yourself, and tend to your self-care needs. In order to give to others, you must first give to yourself. By honouring yourself you give yourself a chance to grow through awareness and change. When we don't give our own needs attention, we feel more stressed and burnt out. Our energy is zapped. Our coping skills deteriorate. Tolerance is limited. Even our own attention and focus is affected. Health and illness can take hold in your weakened state.

Ch. 5: Value

Know the A-B-C's of you - Awareness, Behaviour, Consequences

A. What causes you stress, anger, frustration, or other negative emotions?
B. What is your behavioural response to your emotions?
C. You know the consequences because you likely have seen the patterns of fallout after you succumb to negative reactions. How can you change the pattern?

Honour and value yourself! Know that you are a gift to our world, and that you matter. Your work is so important and you have chosen this line of work because you want to make a difference; you are reading this book because you are awakening to new possibilities, new strategies, and new ways of helping children grow and be inspired.

Honour and value who you are and where you are without judgment and with love, and honour each of your students in the same way. Steve Jobs said, *"Have the courage to follow your heart and your intuition. They somehow already know what you truly want to become."* And that is to be the best teacher ever!

F. Thoughts Are Things: How to Love Yourself

"The truth is to love yourself with the same intensity you would use to pull yourself up if you were hanging off a cliff with your fingers. As if your life depended upon it. Once you get going, it's not hard to do. It just takes commitment." - Kamal Ravikant, author

To consciously love yourself, you must choose your words and thoughts with great care, love and awareness of how powerful your words can be.

In his book, **Love Yourself Like Your Life Depends On It**[69], Kamal Ravikant talks about his life and his struggle to find the secret to life. He describes how he sorted through a variety of methods to get to the point of loving himself and why it's essential for peace and happiness. One of the simplest strategies is to repeat, *"I love myself"*. Make it a mantra—repeat often, over and over. Do it when you are drinking your coffee, sitting at stoplights, at a time where you do something regularly, like making dinner.

---

[69] Ravikant, Kamal, *Love Yourself Like Your Life Depends on It* (Kamal Ravikant, ©Kindle Edition 2012).

With practice you can choose to be mindful and present with your thoughts. Here's how: Take a deep belly breath—expand your belly, breathe in love and say, *"I love myself"*. Then breathe out and let go of whatever thoughts and sensations come to you. Thoughts will come and that's okay, but continue to focus on taking in the love and feeling heart-centred and grounded. Repeat. You may want to hold your hand on your heart as well if you choose. I find it gives a fuller connection to my heart. Make this a daily habit for inner peace and quiet. This can be done silently anytime you feel that you need a quick sense of calm. Before your day begins, before you have to have a challenging talk with a student or a parent. The amount of time that it would take to do this could vary depending on how long it takes you to become centred. The more frequently you practice it, the more quickly you will become centred.

In the classroom, your students could do this, "I love myself" practice as a pre-meditation statement. Teach them the process prior to meditation and invite them to begin silently repeating the mantra in their minds. After 10-15 seconds, listen to music or have a continued period of silence. Meditation time will vary based upon your students' age and ability. The amount of time can increase with frequent regular practice.

Another self-love technique that Ravikant, Dr. Wayne Dyer, and many other motivational speakers recommend is daily mirror work. Author and teacher, the late Louise H. Hay has a book called **Mirror Work: 21 Days to Heal Your Life**. She describes the benefits to developing confidence, overcoming resistance to change, and boosting self-esteem. The Mirror Principle, which is one of her core teachings, shows us that what we see in our lives mirrors back what we believe about ourselves. Loving ourselves is critical to living a life of happiness and fulfillment. *"Doing mirror work,"* Hay tells readers, *"is one of the most loving gifts you can give yourself."* [70]

---

[70] Ms. Hay was a powerhouse lady for change. She changed the lives of millions and left a legacy of love for the world and all who knew her. She created a publishing company Hay House Inc. and a non-profit, Hay House Foundation, to encourage and financially support diverse organizations for food, shelter, counseling, and hospice. She truly made a difference in her lifetime and continues to do so through her organizations.
Hay, Louise, *Mirror Work: 21 Days to Heal Your Life* (Hay House Inc., 2016).
About Mirror Work: www.louisehay.com/what-is-mirror-work/
Free 400+ Affirmations: www.louisehay.com/hay-foundation/

Ch. 5: Value

Mirror work, or mirror play as she calls it, is simple and easy to learn. The simplest way is to look at yourself in the mirror in a nonjudgmental manner. Be mindful of the thoughts that come up and let them go. Spend about 3-5 minutes daily. You may feel uncomfortable doing this at first, that's okay, you can build up to a longer time. You can say "I love myself" or you can practice affirmations that start with the following phrases: *"I am....", "I love...", "I can...", "I like..."*

I received the cutest video from Dr. Wayne Dyer a few years ago. It's called, *"Jessica's Daily Affirmations"* and you can find it on YouTube[71]. It shows a little girl in action doing her affirmations. This video went viral because of her enthusiasm, positivity, and cuteness. An affirmation is anything we say or think. Speak positively and lovingly towards yourself. Repeat often. Know that you are worth it. If you were asked what and who do you love, how long would it take before you added yourself to that list? This is a great question to ask your students. It makes for a perfect discussion about self-esteem and self-worth.

All too frequently I hear students putting themselves down. Letting students know that you believe in them, respect them, and value them is priceless.

G. Self-care

"Be gentle with yourself, learn to love yourself, to forgive yourself, for only as we have the right attitude towards ourselves can we have the right attitude toward others." - Wilferd Peterson, author

This quote by Wilferd Peterson, author of **The Art of Living**[72], makes sense no matter whether you are a man or a woman, a teacher, an educator, or a para-support staff member. To have the right attitude you must be positive, loving, and compassionate towards yourself. The best way to be loving towards oneself is through self-care. Too many of us let ourselves reach the point of burnout, depression, and overwhelm before we admit we are overloaded. The expectations put on educators these days are often unrealistic and that is why many of us advocate for better circumstances through proactive interactions and involvement with our unions, letters to school boards, and letters to those in power within the education areas of government.

---

[71] Check it out here: www.youtube.com/watch?v=qR3rK0kZFkg

[72] Peterson, Wilferd. A., *The Art of Living* (Galahad Books, December 1993).

We must stand our ground, stand in our power, and look out for our own wellbeing.

I know many teachers, educational assistants, and counselors who, like me, appear to have it all together. Even when we are drowning and floundering in overwhelm on the inside, people look at us and believe that we're having so much fun, because this is what we are projecting on the outside. This is where I am going to say it's critical to ask for help. Use your support team. Collaborate with co-workers to find answers to your challenges. This is more important than ever with the potential of more online teaching. Brainstorm together. There is always more than one answer to any problem.

At the same time, practice self-care daily, in as many ways as you can. Our lives are challenging, from raising our own children and managing our homes, we have many responsibilities. Teachers spend endless hours at home preparing for the school days and school months ahead. Educational assistants often work two and three extra jobs to make ends meet financially. All of these responsibilities need to be balanced with regenerative self-care practices that give us energy and peace of mind.

I'm not sure how your day starts but I've had many days where I can barely drag my body out of bed. I've never been a morning person; I'm a night owl. I love to sleep in and used to have a hard time understanding how people could wake up and be so chipper at 5, 6 or even 7 a.m. I have discovered over time that the foods I consume at night really affect how I feel in the morning. I tended to get a 'grain brain'. I've never been tested for a gluten allergy but I know how I feel the next day after eating foods with gluten the night before. It's like a severe hangover and includes a major headache, brain fog, occasional blurred vision and complete body pain. What a relief to finally get this message through my head! Once you learn that something affects you, it is loving to stop consuming these foods and value yourself and your health.

What forms of self-care do you currently practice? Firstly, if you are overwhelmed, make sure to take some proactive steps to help yourself such as: breath work, taking your regular breaks, having frequent movement breaks, meditating, and, if possible, getting fresh air on your lunch break every single day.

Signs of being overwhelmed can include: sleep problems, anxiety, depression, lack of energy, as well as feelings of anger and frustration. Since everyone is different and unique you must discover your own ways

of becoming grounded and recharge your own batteries often to avoid overwhelm, health problems and to experience true joy on a daily basis.
The following steps are highly recommended for students and educators alike—following them is an essential step to improving your quality of life.

1. Go to bed at a regular time each evening. Preferably before 10 pm. Enjoy quiet calming activities before bed. Avoid watching the news before bed or being on your computer or phone screens. Avoid eating after 7 pm.
2. Limit caffeine intake (this includes soda and energy drinks)—particularly later in the afternoon and evening. Choose non-caffeinated beverages instead.
3. Limit alcohol intake before bed as it can often cause a person to wake during the night.
4. Eat foods that nourish you, that are full of nutrients, vitamins, minerals, proteins, and essential fats. Avoid sluggish foods like processed carbs, refined foods, potato chips, artificially sweetened snacks, and desserts. Reach for more fresh fruits and vegetables!
5. Drink water daily - It is essential. Encourage the students that you work with to drink water too. So many do not drink enough water and our brains need it to function optimally.
6. Body wise, your body needs to move daily. Make time for fun activities: take karate lessons, ski, skate, roller blade, roller skate, skateboard, golf, run, jog, or walk, join a gym, swim, join Zumba®, tai chi or dance class, bike ride, stretch, hug and cuddle with spouse, kids and pets.
7. Get creative by doing right-brain activities that get your creative juices flowing like painting, drawing, colouring, arts and crafts activities.
8. Pamper yourself! Shower with lemon body wash, it's so refreshing! Take long bubble baths, soak in Epsom salts and lavender. Use essential oils for calming. Lavender is great! Treat yourself to new hairdos and a new outfit consisting of each season's colours. Get regular massages, manicures, and pedicures. Have spa days alone, with your friends, your mom, your daughter—whoever brings you joy!
9. Practice self-compassion activities that restore your energy and vitality. Create your own list and ask yourself often— *"What is the most loving thing I can do for myself in this moment?"* Teach this practice to your students!
10. Express gratitude daily—Write it down. Journal each night before bed. Reflect on everything that was good about the day. Have a Gratitude Attitude.
11. Stay present—be where you are without judging others and yourself.
12. Learn to say 'No' to others.

13. Learn to say 'Yes' to yourself.
14. Engage in positive self-talk. Would you talk to others the way that you talk to yourself?
15. Look after your inner child. What does he/she need to feel safe, loved, valued and respected? Sometimes the answer includes many of the suggestions in this section. Other times, it's simply standing up for yourself, avoiding negative people, and protecting your own energy.
16. Realize you are not alone. You are truly never alone when you realize that we are souls having a human experience. We have guides and angels all around us waiting to be asked for their guidance and assistance.
17. Count on co-workers to encourage and support you. Be a team player. We are all in this together!
18. Spend time with family and friends laughing and enjoying life's adventures. Have dinner and movie dates with your spouse regularly. Watch comedy shows that make you laugh out loud. Go to concerts, plays, and local entertainment venues. Get friends together for potlucks, weekend getaways, friendship and shenanigans. Nothing recharges me more than a crazy fun weekend with my best friends. Time with friends on social media can be energizing too. Stay away from energy vampires. Take regular holidays. Celebrate life!
19. Drop expectations of perfection. We are perfect in our own imperfections and that's truly okay. Dare to be yourself!
20. Love yourself more—self-acceptance is critical. To fully love another you must be able to love yourself first.
21. Forgive often and let stuff go. We all know that holding grudges and staying angry can affect us deeply. Don't let your health suffer because of a refusal to forgive or drop an incident that bothered you, upset you, or caused you to have hurt feelings. Each day is a new day, begin again.
22. Practice receiving. As educators, we tend to be givers yet have a hard time accepting from others. When we won't receive with ease we are pushing away our own good. Energy is everything! Accept compliments without excuses; accept offers that will help make your day run more smoothly. Avoid always trying to be superwoman or superman.
23. Be mindful of the power of focus. Energy grows where focus goes!
24. Cultivate relationships! We all need our tribes! Regularly spend quality time with people that you can easily relate to. Share your similarities and celebrate differences.
25. Celebrate the miracle of life; know that life is not meant to be hard.
26. Learning can be part of your self-care. Read self-development books that are of interest to you. It's relaxing and easier to learn something if it is of interest to you. I love books by Dr. Wayne Dyer, Louise Hay, Lisa Nichols, Brené Brown and many others. Listen to inspirational TEDX

Talks. Find and cook new recipes, bake a special desert, visit a museum, check out local attractions, take a road trip, start a new hobby, learn a new language, learn to play an instrument for fun, do crosswords, puzzles and other brain games, join a book club. Explore!

27. Develop your own daily happiness habits for empowerment. Here's what Marci Shimoff, author of **Happy for No Reason: 7 Steps to Being Happy from the Inside Out** suggests when you have a problem: 1. Focus on the solution. 2. Look for the lesson and the gift. 3. Make peace with yourself.
28. Make time for mindfulness daily. If you can make time daily to practice mindfulness your life will change beyond what you could ever imagine.
29. Make it a habit to appreciate! As my mentor Marci always says, "What you appreciate, appreciates."
30. Learn how to ground yourself. Being grounded is such an empowering feeling; you feel balanced and more in control of your day-to-day life. I personally love two tools taught by Dr. Sue Morter. The first is called the Morter March developed by her father, the late Dr. M.T. Morter, Jr. (See Chapter Two for details on how to perform the march). The second tool is a yoga activity called, 'mula bandha,' which translates as, *the root lock, used to calm the nervous system*. In her work, she brings together ancient wisdom and quantum science. She teaches seminars, webinars, and events to teach others practices and principles designed to embody your higher consciousness. These principles are explained in detail in her book **The Energy Codes: The 7 Step System to Awaken Your Spirit, Heal Your Body and Live Your Best Life**. Visit her website to learn more about her amazing energy practices: drsuemorter.com
31. Environment: Create beauty in your living space. Surround yourself with beautiful items that uplift you when you look around. When you declutter, get rid of items that do not bring you joy. Ask yourself..."*does this bring me joy?*" If the answer is 'no', recycle it, give it away or throw it out. If an item is broken throw it away. You do not need the negative energy that it brings.
32. Learning about feng shui and making small changes can create amazing shifts in the flow of energy, abundance and happiness. No sharp edges! Have natural objects (wood, stones, rocks) in your surroundings. Consider the colours of paint in each room, the colours of your bedding and sheets, the colours of clothing that you wear.
33. My friend Marianna appreciated so much about life; even when she was battling cancer she found a place that brought her peace and a feeling of Zen. She knew to appreciate the little things in life. My Zen moments are spent drinking my morning coffee at my deck in the sunshine looking at a clear blue sky, listening to the birds joyfully singing to each

other and anticipating what good the day will bring. Look at each day as a gift and find your own Zen. Be authentic and be you! Know that you are worthy. *You are enough!*

H. Burnout

"We stay in productivity, running on adrenaline for as long as we can, but finally this buildup of stress fires the amygdala, the alarm system in the brain. Subjectively, this means there are no more creative ideas, we feel mentally and physically exhausted. This phase of breakdown is characterized by decreased energy systems in the body, specifically decreased ATP output."
- Daniel Schmachtenberger, Founder of Neurohacker Collective

When you hit this point of overload, overwhelm, and over-focus, your body becomes out of balance, blood sugar levels are affected, poor sleep patterns appear, memory and concentration problems become apparent, your energy decreases, pain levels increase, and mood levels are at an all-time low. This all leads to discouragement, frustration, maybe even depression and loss of interest in something you once loved, such as teaching children and teens.

This happens to the best of us, and when it does, know that it is not a sign of weakness. It is a request from your body to slow down, listen to what your body is telling you, follow your instincts, ask for help, and practice radical self-care. This kind of stress throws your body out of whack and your brain needs to be rewired to prevent your nervous system from going predominantly into a sympathetic state where you are feeling constantly on high alert in a state of flight, fight or freeze.

Many people used to believe that the brain was in the driver's seat of intelligence. Research now shows it is really the gut and the heart that are driving and communicating to the engine called the brain. The vagus nerve, the nerve that connects the brain to the heart and the gut is one of the main pathways in which the parasympathetic system gets activated in the brain.

HeartMath Research Institute in Santa Cruz, California, offers a wide variety of tools for emotional management and inner balance to reduce stress and increase resilience through science-based intelligence, while transforming stress, worry, letting go of anger, rage and frustration.

Ch. 5: Value

At HeartMath they access the interactions between the parasympathetic and sympathetic systems by measuring heart rate variability patterns. When an individual is calm, relaxed and in a state of happiness, joy or love, the patterns are smooth. If the individual is angry, anxious, or frustrated, the patterns show incoherence and chaotic wave patterns of heartbeats. They have a tool that has a heart rate variability sensor that works from a smart phone app called Inner Balance®[73].

Another simple way to help you rebalance is calmly breathing with your hand over your heart for a few seconds then asking, *"What's the most loving thing that I can do for myself at this moment?"* Listen, and then take action on the answer.

Can you see how valuing yourself and your students through your own self-care and relationship-building will ensure that you create a legacy of students who will never forget you or the lessons that you taught them: to be better citizens, to know themselves and to know how to self-regulate when they are on their own in this world?

A study conducted by Aspy and Roebuck (1983) involved investigating the impact of a teacher exhibiting acceptance, genuineness, and empathy on student effectiveness. Their research involved over 3,700 classroom hours of instruction from 550 elementary and secondary school teachers. They concluded that, *"students learn more and behave better when they receive high levels of understanding, caring, and genuineness than when they are given low levels of them. It pays to treat students as aware and sensitive human beings."*[74]

I. Value: It's Your Turn!

"Consciously integrating the wisdom and support from our Soul into our life's interactions releases the unconditional love, compassion, and heart intelligence that we already own. We become more inclusive of the whole of humanity, with whom we are energetically connected." - Doc Childre, Founder of HeartMath

---

[73] For more information about HeartMath and its programs, visit: heartmath.org

[74] Mortiboys, Alan, *Teaching with Emotional Intelligence: A Step by Step Guide for Higher and Further Education Professionals* (Psychology Press, 2005).

We all come here with a knowing, a knowing that we are here for a reason. We may not consciously remember why we came but the reason we come is to serve and make a difference in some way. When we choose a path that involves educating children who will be our future it's our responsibility to do our best, follow our intuition and lead with our hearts. As pointed out in this chapter and throughout this book, I cannot stress enough how invaluable it is for a child to feel unconditionally loved and valued simply for being one's own self. Let these precious human beings know how much you value them, let your eyes light up when you see them, and create fun memories together. Listen to them attentively.

Find balance in your own self-care and self-love so you have energy and wisdom to inspire them to become the greatest version of themselves, full of their own self-worth, and knowing that they are enough. Teach them to love themselves and respect the world around them. Everyone has value simply because they exist and we are all one. We are all in this together for the betterment of mankind.

Self-reflection questions

- *Moving forward, how will your interactions with students change?*
- *What about your interactions with parents? Co-workers?*
- *Are you willing to become a better listener?*
- *How will you show more empathy?*
- *What do you value most about your students?*
- *What does "value" mean to you?*
- *How will you value yourself more?*
- *In what ways will you increase your own self-care?*
- *Do you see how everything changes, when you come from a place of love?*

# CHAPTER 6: ELEVATE AND EVOLVE THROUGH HOPE

"Bless the world with your mind, heal the world with your heart, lift the world with your soul, and elevate the world with your life." - Matshona Dhliwayo, philosopher, leadership expert and columnist

How do we elevate ourselves? Our students? We do it by realizing, knowing and accepting that energy is everything and we are energy. Period. What you put out is what you get back. Knowing, understanding, and believing that energy matters will enable you to find balance, joy, calm and love in your life, and the same in your classroom. The higher the energy vibration the better everything flows.

We elevate ourselves through self-care, consciously choosing and empowering thoughts, leading with our hearts, being aware, proactive, and by being a living example of kindness and compassion.

Are you still wondering how to do it? How to find balance, calm, joy, and happiness in your class and your life? Considering that energy is everything and everywhere, it's essential that we vibrate at higher frequencies—the frequencies of love, joy, gratitude and happiness. When we are operating in lower frequencies like fear, worry, doubt, shame and sadness we draw more of that energy to ourselves. It's the law of attraction at work. It's always working! Consciously, and most often, subconsciously.

We see what we believe. We create our own reality through what we believe and the easiest way to change our reality is to change our thoughts. In circumstances where you may be feeling like you have no control, keep in mind that what is affecting you is not so much the circumstance as your thoughts about the situation. These thoughts trigger emotions, which create feelings, and those feelings are put out to the Universe in the form of energy, which may affect your present circumstances and your perception. The feelings that you express and experience within; you may think that you are not expressing energy about them just because you are only thinking them. Guess what? Those thoughts are things and they do affect what you see ... even if you never speak them out loud.

The reason is that there is energy in thoughts. Peace Pilgrim said, "If you knew how powerful your thoughts were you would never think another negative thought."

An example of this could be that it is raining and outdoor recess is cancelled. You immediately jump to feelings of disappointment, convinced that indoor recess will be chaotic and noisy, and the students will be wound up for the rest of the day. And, if that's what you are looking for, that is usually exactly what you will see. Instead, consciously call up the perfection of the situation (feel that feeling of it truly being perfect). Suddenly, you're inspired; it's a great chance to do that dance party you've always wanted to do. Have music planned in advance, divide the class, maybe even have prizes on hand. An activity like this raises the vibration. The students are usually happy, laughing, and tired when recess is over. They're more willing to settle and get back to work. The benefits of movement, exercise, and dancing can never be overstated especially where positive effects can happen within the brain and for the whole body. Through your commitment to seeing the perfection of the situation, you have created a memorable and fun activity that benefits both you and your students!

A. Begin Where You Are With What You Have

"Do not wait; the time will never be 'just right'. Start where you stand, and work with whatever tools you may have at your command, and better tools will be found as you go along." - Napoleon Hill, American self-help author

At times we may find ourselves complaining that we don't have the right program, funding is missing for extras and we don't have the necessary resource tools. In my opinion, all you can do is control what you can control and begin where you are with what you have. It's a simple strategy to dream-building. Know that what you dream of is possible. You have to look beyond your current circumstances. Your current circumstances may not be exactly as you wish your classroom or experience to be. There may be things that you wish you had to use to help your students manage emotions—a quiet place for a student to regulate themselves, time to co-regulate with your student, extra book resources that a child can read for better understanding of emotions and big feelings, counselors available to help your student through trauma.

Ch. 6: Elevate and Evolve Through Hope

By not focusing on lack you can appreciate with gratitude what you do have at this moment. If you choose to focus on lack, including fear, worry and doubt, you will ultimately draw more of that into your experience. You have to have faith!

When I'm putting dreams and wishes out to the universe or God I say, *"This or something better,"* and I truly expect this wish or something even better than my wish to come true. Then I take steps towards the goal that I wish to manifest. This can mean talking to my principal or teacher about the requirements that I see the student or the classroom needing for support. Often it's the start that stops us. Have faith, take baby steps, and move forward. When you step into the light of the unknown the path becomes clearer, answers and ideas will come to you and you will be shown what to do next.

Remember that taking steps when you are not sure what to do next can involve letting your faith be bigger than your fear, it can also take a whole lot of creativity. Brainstorm with your team, your co-workers and even your students about achieving the goals you want for your classroom. Students can have great ideas or ways to do something that adults might overlook.

B. Raise Your Vibration

"If you want to find the secrets of the universe, think in terms of energy, frequency and vibration." - Nikola Tesla, inventor, engineer and futurist

Elevating your vibration involves accepting it is all an inside job that revolves around your thoughts, your self-care and your habits. When you take full responsibility for these areas it shows students that they can do it too. Leaders are developed through positive relationships and positive interactions, mutual respect, understanding, compassion and love. Every child can lead in some way.

Some effective actions for raising your vibration include your thought processes:

1. By staying present in the now and using the power of focus will help you achieve success for yourself and within your classroom. Everything begins with you, that's all that is in your control and the effects of your self-control emanate outward. If you don't like what you see, change your thoughts. Think of when you are helping a child master something such as balancing on a beam in gym class. At first, the student can't do it and needs your hand to help as they balance. You help and you

keep encouraging and imagining your student being able to do it. You cheer them on and you get excited about their potential. With practice and consistency, the student masters the skill and is able to do it by themselves. If you focused on negativity, convinced that they would never master the skill, odds are they wouldn't. Believe!
2. Stop saying things to yourself like *"I'll be happy when ..."*, or *"Someday I'll ..."* Be happy NOW!
3. Develop a sense of allowing. Things are what they are; be at peace with that. Become aware and limit judging about how anything should be. There's never only one way to do anything, nor ever only one right way.

That is why it's so important to be mindful of your thoughts, emotions, and feelings. Manage them with a variety of tools including diet, breath work and meditation.

C. Happiness: It's Truly Your Choice

"Taking ownership of your happiness has two aspects: Accepting that being happy is up to you and that you have the ability and power to be happier by changing your habits. Taking "response-ability": responding to all the events in your life in a way that supports your happiness." - Marci Shimoff, bestselling author of **Happy for No Reason**

The stress in our lives these days can be overwhelming. We really have to be mindful and aware of how we create our own happiness just as much as we can create our own unhappiness. The quickest way to unhappiness is comparison. If you find yourself jealous and sad when you see others having things in life that you want for yourself, you may find yourself falling into the unhappiness zone.

If you find yourself feeling like things never go your way, then it's time to change your focus. Remember, you always get more of what you focus on.

Here are some of my favourite ways to make happiness my choice:

1. Spend quality time with family and friends doing fun activities where you can share laughter and love.
2. Get enough sleep. You'll be more productive and happy when you are well rested.
3. Go outside and enjoy plenty of fresh air. Being in nature can help you feel grounded and energized.

Ch. 6: Elevate and Evolve Through Hope

4. Exercise—there are so many benefits to exercise. Find something that you love to do and do it often.
5. Meditate and/or find time to relax, unwind and listen to energizing music. It can restore your soul.
6. Dance. Dance. Dance.
7. Play. Especially if you have children—get out and play with them. You'll feel younger for it.
8. Find ways to be of service to others. Giving back promotes a feeling of wellness and belonging. You can definitely make the world a better place somehow. We all have our gifts.
9. Smile and laugh daily, even if it means turning on a comedy channel.
10. Have plans and goals and take steps toward them each day. Your success depends upon it.
11. Travel and have adventures, experience life to its fullest!
12. Last, but certainly not least, make it a priority to express your gratitude daily. Throughout the day consciously be thankful. Each night write out all the things you experienced throughout the day that you are thankful and grateful for. Dr. Robert Emmons at the University of California, Davis, conducted an experiment. He noted that, *"People who kept a gratitude journal (a weekly record of things they felt grateful for) enjoyed better physical health, were more optimistic, exercised more regularly, and described themselves as happier than a control group who didn't keep journals."*[75] Try this for yourself. Write five things in your journal each night before bed for best results. Practicing gratitude daily is a habit that will add great value to your life. As author and speaker Bob Proctor[76] says, *"Gratitude is an attitude that hooks us up to our source of supply. And the more grateful you are, the closer you become to your maker, to the architect of the Universe, to the spiritual core of your being. It's a phenomenal lesson."*

As you go off to sleep each night in your gratitude mindset you will marinate in that positivity throughout the night. Sweet dreams and keep smiling!

---

[75] For more information, visit: *health.ucdavis.edu/medicalcentrefeatures/2015-2016/11/20151125_gratitude.html*

[76] Bob Proctor is a world-renowned speaker, motivational coach and author of many best-selling books including: **The Secret, ABC's of Success** and **The Science of Getting Rich**. For more information, visit his website: www.proctorgallagherinstitute.com/

D. Letting Go

"Renew, release, let go. Yesterday's gone. There's nothing you can do to bring it back. You can't; 'should've done something.' You can only; DO something. Renew yourself. Release that attachment. Today is a new day!"
- Steve Maraboli, author, speaker and behavioural scientist

As educators we all go through events and situations that require us to either forgive, let go or reframe a situation in order to move beyond it. One of my toughest lessons was how to move beyond anger, sadness and the loss of a loved one. I used to have a blog and the following is a copy of one of my most popular articles. It's relevant because it deals with grief. I find it to be a very challenging emotion: the processing and letting go parts.

When life gives you strawberries what can you do?

One summer, I ordered freshly picked strawberries from a farm. When I picked them up and tasted one I felt instant gratitude for how delicious it was. I do not recall enjoying strawberries that tasted that great for over 25-plus years. The place where I enjoyed some like that was when my now deceased grandmother, Jean Barber, grew them in her backyard garden. Sweet memories!

On that particular warm and sunny summer day, I decided to go and see my grandmother and bring her some of the delicious fresh berries. She lives in a nursing home now; she's frail, weak, and quite blind. But she still remembers and speaks of times and things from long ago. It was wonderful to visit with her. I washed and cut up the berries and helped feed them to her. She could do it herself a bit. Although there were fewer struggles for her if I assisted to feed her. I was honoured to do that for her. She was overjoyed in how delightful they tasted. She definitely loved them.

I couldn't help but smile and recall the days so long ago when she was fiercely independent, the toughest and one of the kindest women that I know. She had the best sayings and greatest stories. She was 101 years old at this time. Imagine the changes she has seen over the years. She's had a hard long life with many good times and many sad and heart-breaking times too. Her attitude and her faith were her best allies. She ate well and worked tirelessly every day. We are all blessed that she has and is with us still. It's sad to see someone so energetic aging and knowing one day she will be gone. I will forever remember the "good old days" and be grateful for the sweetness that she brought to our family.

Ch. 6: Elevate and Evolve Through Hope

As I continued on my journey home, I dropped off some flats of berries at my dad and stepmom's for them to enjoy as well. They so often gave to us. I thought it would be nice to give them some of their sweetness back. Clare, my stepmom, makes great jam!

I then hurried to visit my friend Marianna in the hospital. Her health condition wasn't good. In my heart of hearts I refused to believe it could be as bad as they were saying. She was only 50 years old. She had so much more living to do. How do you ever say goodbye to someone you love? Adore? And shared so many laughs and good times with? I couldn't let go. I refused to believe that a miracle wouldn't happen. I'd read too much about miracles. I believed in them. She believed in them too. She deserved one. She was one of the most beautiful, loving, kind, and generous individuals that anyone could ever meet. She brought sunshine to the lives of so many. I brought her some strawberries too. She loved how they tasted too, but even more so during that week, her father had brought her the party sandwiches that he made for her every year since she was a little girl for her birthday. She was thrilled to be able to see them and loved how decadent they tasted. More sweet memories! Bittersweet too! We didn't get our miracle. I never got to say goodbye to her. I'm sure I couldn't have anyway. Life makes me think about death and death makes me think about life. The days and years go by in a blink and at times it seems like life stands still. Memories of long ago feel like yesterday and it seems impossible that someone I've loved could really be gone forever. This past year a lot of my favourite earth angels passed away. Not good, not sweet!

I have to focus on the fact that I have been blessed to have had so many memories, so many good times and so, so much laughter in my life. To focus on sadness makes me want to withdraw and be angry at the world. It often doesn't seem fair. I try to find the good in things—last week I realized something that made sense to me. Clare brought me some homemade strawberry jam from the summer berries. A thought came to me right away—**when life gives you strawberries—make jam.**[77]

I couldn't have the strawberries back, nor have the good part of summer stand still forever, nor could I have my friend, Marianna, and the others that have left this earthly world back. But I can choose what I do with my berries (my memories). I can turn them into jam—into thoughts that make

---

[77] This essay was originally published in 2014 on my personal blog "SpiritandSoulTimes.com". My grandmother has since passed away, on June 7, 2015 at the age of 102.

me happy, thoughts that bring me back my smile. Things will never be the same, but they can be okay, and even good!

We always have to live each day to the fullest and make the best of things as they are.

When life gives you strawberries, make jam.

How do **you** move beyond your sadness? Loss? Anger? Grief?

E. Ho'oponopono

"The practice of forgiveness is our most important contribution to the healing of the world." - Marianne Williamson, author and spiritual leader

Through my experiences I discovered an amazing and powerful ancient Hawaiian technique called Ho'oponopono. It is designed to help the individual to get rid of any judgments they are holding. It is a method that involves aspects of forgiveness, repentance, gratitude, and love. The best part is that it's simple to do and you don't need an expert to achieve results! A Hawaiian healer, Morrnah Nalamaku Simeona, originally taught Ho'oponopono. She founded a version called "Self I-dentity through Ho'oponopono". A student of hers shone the spotlight on this technique when he cured a ward of criminally insane inmates at a Hawaiian State Hospital using Ho'oponopono.

This student's name is Dr. Ihaleakala Hew Len. He worked as a staff psychologist at the hospital from 1984-1987. What was so astonishing was that he never met any of the inmates face to face.

How is it possible that he had results you may be asking? What kind of results? It was very straightforward. Over a period of a couple of years, he read over each patient's file and practiced Ho'oponopono upon himself. As he read the patients' files he noticed that something would come up within him. So he did the process of Ho'oponopono within himself and miracles occurred. Patients changed and were eventually let loose of their shackles and got to leave their confinement in the hospital. It is a simple prayer made up of four sentences: *"I am sorry. Please forgive me. Thank you. I love you."*

Ch. 6: Elevate and Evolve Through Hope

The prayer is repeated for several minutes, and it can also be done continuously throughout the day.[78]

It seemed strange to me, and it likely must seem strange to you, but to heal others you must heal yourself. This requires a deep understanding of how everything is created in your mind. We create our reality by our thoughts, feelings and actions.

You are responsible for what you *"see"*. If you found yourself getting angry with that statement that's okay. It's a common reaction. When you are ready to accept it, you will understand it. The bright side is you are more in control than you may realize. That's powerful!

Sometimes, with this technique, it is easiest to begin with a problem that you know you created. Being overweight from overeating is a good example. That's easy to understand. Sometimes the reasons for a condition in your life go deep, but if you are willing to admit your own responsibility for overeating or any other bad habit that is causing you stress and illness, this technique can truly help! Through acceptance you can transform.

If you are interested in knowing more about this practice, Dr. Hew Len has written a book called **Self I-Dentity through Ho'oponopono**[79]. Also, Joe Vitale, an author of self-improvement and self-healing books co-wrote a book called **Zero Limits** with Dr. Hew Len[80] and discussed in further detail the work of Dr. Hew Len and the miracle of the inmates going from shackled with wrist and ankle restraints to living on non-violent wards or released completely. When Vitale asked Dr. Hew Len about healing them, Dr. Hew Len corrected him, *"I didn't heal them. I healed the part of myself that was responsible for creating them."*

Everyone is different and that is why I present so many different methods and modalities in this book. You must test and see what helps you most based upon your own learning styles and preferred methods to implement.

---

[78] I am a Certified Ho'oponopono Practitioner. If you would like to become a certified by Dr. Joe Vitale, check out this information: joevitalecertified.com/hooponopono/

[79] Vitale, Joe and Ihaleakala Hew Len, PhD, *Zero Limits-The Secret Hawaiian System for Wealth, Health, Peace and More* (Wiley: 1st edition, May 18, 2009).

[80] Simeona, Morrnah Nalamaku and Ihaleakala Hew Len, PhD., *Self I-dentity Through Ho'Oponopono (Basic1) The Foundation of I*, (9th revised edition, 1989).

If any of these suggested techniques are interesting to you be sure to check out the resource section for further learning.

I've presented the information very simply and in a manner to pique your interest to go on and learn more. Many of these kinds of energy techniques offer courses, programs, training and even certification to enhance your skills and knowledge. Happy exploring!

F. Emotional Freedom Technique

"The cause of all negative emotions is a disruption in the body's energy system." - Gary Craig, founder of the EFT technique

A favourite tool that I highly recommend and love to use with children and adults is called the Emotional Freedom Technique. It is simple and easy to learn. It is also known as *"tapping"*.

EFT is an extremely powerful self-help technique that anyone can learn easily and quickly. For true health and wellness to exist the mind, body and spirit must be in balance. Due to the high costs of healthcare and wellness, I can see EFT being very useful now and in the future. This technique is growing quickly in popularity. I have seen amazing results through my own use of it and the use of it by others. I have shown many students how to do this too. One time I showed a student this prior to her usual expected meltdown. She loved it and when her next meltdown occurred she completely relaxed as if to say, *"Ahhhh, this is exactly what I needed at this moment."*

When I visited my friend Marianna in the hospital before she went to hospice care, she was in extreme pain. I asked if I could do some tapping on her. Of course she agreed and had instant relief. A nurse came in that had seen her in extreme pain minutes before and was completely blown away with the change in pain levels and stress that Marianna was experiencing. The nurse was so impressed she asked more about it and thought nurses everywhere should be taught this, especially when a nurse is left feeling frustrated because she doesn't know how to take the pain away and help her patient.

Emotional Freedom Technique (Tapping) can:

- Stop food, cigarette, and alcohol cravings
- Lower pain in the head, back, neck and shoulders
- Lower stress levels

Ch. 6: Elevate and Evolve Through Hope

- Aid in neutralizing emotional pain, trauma (lessen sadness, increase your joy, eliminate anger)
- Improve physical performance
- Eliminate physical allergies
- Calm and help children if they have nightmares and fears
- Change negative thought patterns
- Increase intuition
- Help children get calm and refocused

EFT was developed by a now retired man named Gary Craig in the 1990's. Since then, many variations of his technique have appeared. The technique is so simple to implement, his website offers more detail and explanation on how to do it. Check it out![81]

My dear friend, Sue Busen is a practitioner, speaker and best-selling author. She has written many wonderful books about EFT including **Tap into Balance** and **Tap into Success**. She has a specialised way of doing EFT and it is simple and easy to learn. It's called the GetSet™ Approach. Sue says, *"When you change your vibration, you change your life. Literally. Everything in the Universe is energy, whether it's a human or a rock, a thought or emotion. It's all energy. And energy is in a constant state of vibration. It's the speed at which the energy vibrates that makes the difference. When you raise your vibration, you resonate at a higher frequency. This is the key to optimizing your life. And it's surprisingly easy to do! We are living in a very exciting time. The trials of life can be transforming if we allow them to be."* Her book **Tap into Balance** has scripts to go along with each area that you are working on.

She recently released a book on tapping for children **Tap in to Joy: A Guide to Emotional Freedom Techniques for Kids and Their Parents**. Like all her other books, its chock full of useful information.[82]

G. Being an Empath and Expressing Empathy

"Our innate capacity for empathy is the source of the most precious of all human qualities." - His Holiness, the 14th Dalai Lama

---

[81] To learn more about EFT and all its benefits, visit: https://www.emofree.com/nl/eft-tutorial/tapping-basics/how-to-do-eft.html

[82] Visit the website for lots of different resources: www.tapintobalance.com

Are you an empath?

An empath is someone who has the ability to sense the mental and emotional states of other people. These people have a high social intelligence and are very good at helping others through their problems. Unfortunately, in doing so, empaths tend to take on a heavy emotional burden as they end up feeling what others around them feel. Many teachers and educators are empaths. Empaths are strongly aware of the feelings of others; they can actually feel another person's pain. For example, I am a *"sad magnet"*. If you are sad, I instantly pick that up and often burst into tears, seemingly out of the blue. If I'm feeling happy and this happens, I will look around to see whose energy I may have just picked up.

This happens to me on a regular basis. One time in a bookstore in Toronto, a middle-aged lady walked past me and I burst into tears. Normally, I do not ask strangers weird questions, but this was one of the strangest instant feelings that I ever experienced. I turned around and went up to her and asked if she was okay. She immediately burst into tears and told me that she had recently moved to Canada and missed her family and friends so much. She was lonely and sad ('No kidding!' I likely said in my head). We chatted for a few minutes and she seemed to be feeling happier. Hopefully, I left her feeling better. I felt better too because the incident helped me realize how easily I can pick up on the feelings of others. It helped me understand that I needed to figure out how to lessen my susceptibility to taking on the sadness and emotions of others without losing the gift of understanding others.

Like empaths, teachers and educators are overall caring, compassionate, and understanding people. They choose this career to help others. They are inspired! They need to be continually learning and discovering ways to motivate their students to be motivated and driven to succeed. It's a challenge when some of the students in the class seem unmotivated, lost, or even completely shut down.

Those students are my favourites, you know the ones—hoodies over their heads, their heads on the desk, shutting out the world, avoiding eye contact, poor posture, stooped shoulders. Not surprisingly these are the ones that need you and often they seem to be the hardest to love. Not for me, I am drawn to them.

These are the students that likely have experienced unspeakable traumas and have learned to just shut down and withdraw as a coping survival strategy. If you think forcing them to do schoolwork is the way to go about things, you are dead wrong. Drop the power struggle! These students need love, nourishment and they need their needs met so they can get out of flight, fight, or freeze mode. Then the learning can happen! They need to feel safe. They need secure relationships. They need you to inspire them. And for them to be inspired, you need to be inspired too.

For you to be inspired, you need to be confident, courageous, and compassionate for yourself and to yourself. Everything begins with you! So much of teaching and self-development is an inside job.

How many of the following characteristics do you relate to?

You feel the emotions of others around you and you get feelings about others even if they are not near you. An example is that you may be feeling tense for an inexplicable reason and later discover a person in the room next to you was angry or tense at the same time. It is even possible to feel the emotions of people in other countries.

You have an inner knowing about people and places and you can pick out a liar a mile away.

Being in a crowd can feel overwhelming. You'd rather be anywhere else. You like solitude and places where you can feel grounded.

You don't like small talk. You even find it draining to experience.

Clutter weighs you down. You declutter frequently in order to feel light and grounded. Be sure to declutter your surroundings frequently.

You may have had challenges with addictions: food, alcohol, drugs, etc.

You avoid violence on TV. You avoid the news and negative movies because of how you feel from being exposed to them.

People often say you are sensitive. You have a sensitivity to other people's energy and also to the environment around you (smells, sounds, etc.).

You pick up on the physical symptoms of others and experience "pain", often in the lower back.

You often feel drained and have low energy, especially if around negative and/or narcissistic people.

As an empath you are drawn to help others and have interests in alternative therapies in order to lower stress, limit the drain on your energy, and be happier.

H. Tips for an Empath on Achieving Balance and Happiness

"Living as an empath may not always be easy, but living as an empath with a victim mentality is a sure-fire way to put the keys to your happiness in the hands of the world around you. You are more than just an energetic sponge. You have willpower, choice, and volition. Don't be afraid to step into your power and take back control over your energy field." - Steven Bancarz, Christian and former new ager

There is no doubt that life as an empath can be very draining. It's hard work because it drains you physically, mentally and emotionally. Gaining understanding of what an empath is can provide relief because it explains a great deal about you and how your life has played out. Knowing can bring a sense of peace, as long as you become proactive and discover which strategies are best for you to keep yourself grounded and protected from the negative energy of others.

As an educator you are exposed to such a variety of emotions (and energy) throughout the day ranging from happiness and joy to anger and rage. Compassion fatigue can easily set in, leaving you feeling physically, mentally and emotionally exhausted. Being exposed to so much energy makes self-care more important than ever; there are many ways to look after your wellness. Choose what works best for you and have a regular self-care routine.

Protective and wellness strategies include:

1. Visualize yourself surrounded by a protective light (most people chose a white light). It's not to keep all people out. It's designed to create safe boundaries, enabling you to choose whom you share your energy field with. I sometimes explain it like this: *"Pretend you are in a phone booth, you can open and close the door, allowing you to decide whom to let in or keep out. If you are frequently around negative people that you can't avoid or whose behaviours are unpredictable, put the white light around you and feel the confidence of its protection. It might seem strange but I've seen it happen many times that those negative people will walk away from you or avoid you when the protective light practice is used."*

Ch. 6: Elevate and Evolve Through Hope

2. Do not take on everyone's problems. It doesn't help them to grow if you are solving everything and not allowing them to discover their own answers. There isn't a problem to which an answer doesn't exist. You can support, listen and encourage, but it is important that you direct them to find their own answers in the quiet of their own minds. Empowered people feel successful!
3. Learn about chakras and find what helps you most to advance and be balanced when it comes to your mind, body, and spirit. There are activities, food and colours that assist with balancing each chakra.
4. Stay grounded. Spend time in nature: be close to water, trees, and fragrant flowers. Practice yoga, meditation, tai chi, or visualization. Dance and play daily! Sing daily!
5. Breathe. Be conscious of your breathing. Do you hold your breath when learning new things? When around others with negative energy? When you are feeling tense or anxious? Breathe it out. There are many different breathing techniques and styles. A simple and easy one that I find effective is to breathe in to the count of 4, hold it for the count of 4 and then breathe it out for a count of 4. Blow your breath out gently with pursed lips as if you were blowing through a straw, or attempting to keep a feather in the air.
6. Clear the negative energy away by smudging. Sage is perfect for this. Other choices for smudging include: frankincense, Palo Santo and copal. The simplest way to smudge is to open windows and doors and place your sage bundle in a fire-proof bowl. Light it and then blow out the flames so that you have embers that are glowing. Thank Spirit/Creator or God (whomever you believe in) and with both hands fan the smoke to your heart, over your head, as well as the front and back of your body to cleanse yourself. Then, working one room at a time, starting at the lowest point in the room, with your hand or a large feather, guide the smoke around the room to corners, ceilings and walls. Then steer the smoke towards the windows and doors to send the energy out. Put your smudge bundle in sand or dirt to extinguish the embers. Don't wet it or you won't be able to light it again! Express gratitude to the smudge bundle for its healing and send love to each room. Maggie Harrsen, the founder of Puakai Healing, says, *"When I'm in a space after it's been cleansed, I feel peace, joyful, safe and energized, creative, and able to deeply rest."*
7. Spend time in solitude to recharge yourself. Being happy and balanced helps you remain calm, peaceful, and less influenced by the energy of others. Make self-care your priority! Take a moment to review my self-care tips in the previous chapter.

I. Advice for an Empath: How to Help Yourself be Less Affected by Others and Manage Your Anxiety!

"Empaths are not overly sensitive. They have a gift but must learn to manage their sensitivities." - Dr. Judith Orloff, psychiatrist and author

If you are an empath, anxiety and depression can become a vicious circle if emotions are not managed properly. The best thing that you can do for yourself is to know yourself. Learn what sets you off or sets you back into a downward spiral. How can you be balanced and fulfilled?

Empaths have now been scientifically proven to be more prone to anxiety, especially social anxiety, as well as depression. While having the intuitive ability to interpret the emotions of others, empaths also have a tendency to take those emotions on and become negatively affected by them. Soon, anxiety and depression set in, and life gets way harder than it needs to be. Learning to manage those emotions can be a lot of work, as well as a whole new learning curve because of our upbringing. Many of us have not been taught how to process and release our emotions.

When I was growing up, expressing negative emotions was somewhat taboo around our house. I felt as though our feelings were often suppressed. As children, many of us were told to stop crying, be quiet, and sit still. When we expressed our emotions, we weren't always acknowledged. Years of this behaviour can lead to our natural expression being stifled, and in time, we become disconnected from our true selves. Then, the work of getting re-connected to our true selves begins again.

As I mentioned earlier, as an empath I have found that I'm very sensitive to sadness. If someone enters the room or walks by me and feels sad I instantly suck in that energy and quickly feel sad, even to the point of crying for an unknown reason. Learning how to manage these connections and emotions has been a blessing. I can still use my gift to relate to others and I protect myself for balance in my own energy field.

Vision architect and business coach, Amateo Ra, suggests that you identify your feelings and carry out a dialogue with yourself about how you are feeling. It could go something like this:

"I am feeling angry and upset ... Hmm, this is trying to show me something. Anger, what are you trying to show me?"

Ch. 6: Elevate and Evolve Through Hope

(Pause and see what answer comes up to your question).

"Oh I feel secretly sad. Why am I sad?"

(Pause and see what answer comes up to your question).

"Oh, I am missing something. What's missing?"

(Pause and see what answer comes up to your question).

"I am not getting enough time to be creative in my own space. I need to be alone and be creative. How do I feel?"

(Pause and see what answer comes to you).

Place your hand on your heart and then ask the following question: *"What is the most loving thing that I can do for myself at this moment?"*

(Listen for the answer).

Then do it immediately, or as soon as possible. While working on this book, I recently got very frustrated due to the lack of quiet in my home. The television was on, dogs were wandering in and out of the house, my daughter was practicing her piano, my son and husband kept coming in and out of the house—it seemed everything was going on all at once. I couldn't focus and I was getting more and more frustrated by it. Even after expressing my need for quiet it still continued. I pressed on, attempting to achieve clarity in the chaos, until I hit the point of "flipping my lid". My reaction was to flee and escape. I was beyond accomplishing anything in my agitated state. As I was self-regulating I contemplated how students must feel when they flip their lids; shutting out others and unable to access their prefrontal cortex for problem-solving and the language centres to use words to express their feelings. That's why it is so important to be proactive and watch for triggers and catch students, or yourself, before they/you blow a gasket and lose it. Another thing that I noticed in my frustration and anger was that my husband tried to console me by expressing his understanding by touching my arm. I turned away as if to say get out of my space. Students do that too. At that moment, we are in full protective mode. We want our space. Once again, knowing your students and recognizing their need for space and alone time is important.

Empaths tend to like to be alone when they are facing issues. That space gives them a chance to recharge when necessary and gain focus. However, when facing a challenge, make sure to ask for help when you know you need it. We all can get by with a little help from our friends.

J. Seek First to Understand Through Active Listening Skills

"Listening problems are at the root of many learning and communication problems, and learning how to listen well greatly improves our abilities." - Pierre Sollier, educator of the Tomatis Method.[83]

Noticing and listening to what is going on in a classroom is extremely important so that you can be on top of interactions between students and also be present enough to notice trigger-reactions that students may be expressing long before a full blown melt down or outburst. Listening intently shows students that you care and that they matter.

As author Stephen R. Covey points out, "Most people do not listen with the intent to understand; they listen with the intent to reply." There are a few important but simple ways to attentively listen with the intention to gain a better understanding and awareness of what the individual is attempting to communicate to you. Although you know how to do this well, modeling this skill for students and teaching them how to do it is a beneficial skill for them to have for their entire lives.

Commonly known tips include maintaining eye contact, facing the person who is speaking, maintaining an open body stance or posture, and avoiding having crossed arms (which is indicative of being closed off and blocking the other person out). Listen with the intent to understand and develop an understanding as to where the student is coming from, how they are feeling, what their thoughts are. Genuine communication can be a challenge. It is important to listen with an open mind and an attitude of non-judgment. Be present and do not interrupt the person who is speaking.

---

[83] Pierre Sollier studied under Dr. Tomatis. He opened the Mozart Centre in California and he has authored many articles on the subject. The Tomatis Method helps those with ADHD, Autism, learning problems, Down syndrome and so many other issues. Visit: integratedwellbeing.com.au/services/tomatis-method/

Ch. 6: Elevate and Evolve Through Hope

As discussed previously, remember to avoid problem-solving, you want to empower the student to solve their own problem. Most students don't want you to give them advice (they usually already know their own answers), they simply want to discuss the problem out loud to gain clarity. Some students, however, simply want you to agree with them. If you disagree they are angry and resentful. Realize it's their problem, not yours. It could be that they want to have someone confirm their victimhood, whether they are conscious of it or not. Many students who feel like victims develop that stance early in life because of the meaning they have assigned their experiences, circumstances and thoughts. Helping them increase their self-esteem and feelings of empowerment is beneficial.

Give empathy not sympathy. With sympathy you are pitying someone or feeling sorrow for them. With empathy you are expressing that you understand what it is like to be in their shoes. This requires skill and a high level of thoughtfulness. While it can be developed with the best intentions, in some instances one can't truly ever know the fears, worry, pain and/or shame that the student or other person is feeling. The most important thing is to just be there for someone and let them know you care, to listen to what they are saying. You don't have to solve all of their problems; simply be there, listen and focus.

When the student has finished talking, clarify what you have heard by paraphrasing key words. Begin with: "What I hear you saying is …". If there was something that was unclear, say: "I wasn't sure what you meant by …". Ask open-ended questions (How did it make you feel? How are you planning to resolve this? What could you do next time?) to obtain more details and bring the conversation to a deeper level. If the conversation gets side-tracked, pull it back by paraphrasing the issue you were originally discussing and saying, "Tell me more about …".

When discussing a situation or problem you can ask, "Has this problem helped you learn anything?" or "What could you do differently next?" Consider that problems are opportunities for learning and growth.

Other actions that you can do to show that you are listening include nodding and saying things like "uh huh or "hmmm". Facial expressions are another way to show you are listening. Rarely has anyone been taught how to communicate and listen effectively. Now, more than ever, these skills are essential. Model and practice with students whenever you can, through your example they will learn.

K. Be Present. Develop Mindfulness: It's Your Gift to Yourself and Others

"Unease, tension, stress, anxiety and worry—all forms of fear - are caused by too much future and not enough presence. Guilt, regret, resentment, grievances, sadness and bitterness and all forms of non-forgiveness are caused by too much past and not enough presence." - Eckhart Tolle, author of **The Power of Now**

The most perfect gift that you can give your students is to be present. Be in the moment of whatever is going on. Forget about being off in your mind thinking, worrying, and wondering about issues that are not at hand. Your grocery list can wait. You can send your texts later. Stop thinking about how your morning went before you arrived at school. The reality is that things happen every morning: juice gets spilled, you might be late dropping your children off, and someone might cut in front of you on the way to work.

By being present you can see, hear, and feel what's going on in the moment and respond to your students appropriately.

Parent tip: At home, be present as well. It's easy to get caught up in housework, zoned into emails or online activities but it's important to be there for your children. I'm raising a guilty hand here; this is something I've learned the hard way. Once, as I was absorbed in some online business my daughter approached me and said *"Hey Mom, can I go to England?" "Just say uhhmm,"* she continued. (That was my signature zoned out response when not actively listening).

Me: "uhhmm....what?"

I came into awareness of what she was attempting to do, knowing how I tend to zone out. I laughed out loud, "Nice try!" She laughed too and likely said "ugh" under her breath because her plan didn't work out.

L. Mastering Your Emotions to Empower Yourself

"No one can make you feel inferior without your consent." - Eleanor Roosevelt

Ch. 6: Elevate and Evolve Through Hope

You can master your emotions and empower yourself to creatively transform your classroom environment and your life. Peggy McColl, goal-achieving mentor and author of numerous books including **Your Destiny Switch**[84] offers a variety of tools to empower her readers to discover how they are in control of their life through their emotions and thoughts. You require discipline and determination to accomplish your goals and it all begins with a decision and knowing what you want. She explains how every positive emotion has an opposite negative emotion and how it's possible to dial up or dial down these emotions. Like so many of us, Peggy originally thought her emotions were controlled by the events outside of herself and the people around her. Once she discovered she was the one in control, she found her power. We can all have this power. Peggy discovered she could attract situations that mirrored her feelings of happiness, abundance and confidence—you attract what you put out!

Having control of your life and emotions doesn't mean that negative events will never happen to you or in your class during the day. It does, however, give you the strength to know that whatever happens, you have the tools to recover more quickly, forgive easily, and move forward without judgment. Are you clear on your goals and expectations for yourself, for your class, and your students as individuals? Avoid judging and never focus on what you do not want. Focus on that which you wish to see and experience. You must clearly know what you wish to see and send that wish out to the Universe, then detach from the outcome allowing the Universe to unfold. It's the law of expectation. Hold onto the belief and know that if it's meant to be, it will be.

Throughout my training in Mary Morrissey's, Dream Building Coaching Program[85] (I'm a Certified Dream Builder Coach), I learned that you need to imagine and create from the place of your desired feelings and emotions. There are specific questions that you can ask yourself. They include:

- *What do I want?*
- *What would I love to experience?*

---

[84] McColl, Peggy, *Your Destiny Switch: Master Your Key Emotions, and Attract the Life of Your Dreams* (Hay House Inc.: United States of America 1st edition, May 2007).

[85] You can get Mary's free e-book, Stronger Than Circumstance, and find more information on her coaching program here: marymorrissey.com

- *What would I love to see in my life, in my classroom, and in my school environment?*
- *How would my ideal day unfold?*
- *How would I feel?*

Imagine your day from start to finish using all of your senses. Write it down.

Where do you begin? Begin with the end in mind. That is a simple statement that requires great clarity and decision-making. I learned from Mary Morrissey that we need to begin with the end in mind because all things are created twice; First in thought, and then in form. The extent to which you succeed can depend upon how clearly you have defined what you are going to accomplish. What do you want to see from your students as each day unfolds? How about at the school year's end? When they are grown and on their own?

You are blessed because you get to choose whether you will live your life by default or by design. You have to be self-aware enough to use your own consciousness and imagination to choose your thoughts. If you are not self-aware you could end up living out the scripts that others have planted in your mind. It's up to you to design your life!

The best part of being the creator of your life comes from understanding and knowing that whatever you design in your imagination can be filled with infinite possibilities beyond your current circumstances.

Once you have clearly decided what you would love to see in your life, it is suggested that you write it down using as many details as possible; make sure to include all of your senses in the exercise. Many coaches are now using power-scripting for recording their goals in order to listen to them daily. Peggy McColl highly suggests this strategy; she calls it your Power Life Script™.

Whether you listen to them or read your goals, remember that repetition is the key. As Napoleon Hill, author of **Think and Grow Rich**, says, *"Repetition or affirmation of orders to your subconscious mind is the only known method of voluntary development of the emotion of faith."* Review your goals a minimum of three times a day—morning, afternoon and evening.

I believe it's important to write out your goals by hand. There's said to be much power in the written word. As my mentors, Marci Shimoff, (best-selling author of **Chicken Soup for the Woman's Soul,**

Ch. 6: Elevate and Evolve Through Hope

Love for No Reason and *Happy for No Reason*[86]) and Debra Poneman (creator of *The New Success Revolution*[87]), advise, adding the phrase "this or something better" to the end of each intention. Then move forward with faith knowing that which you desire will come true. Expect! Believe! Know it will happen!

M. Elevate: It's Your Turn!

"Turns out that loving yourself is the greatest way to improve yourself, and as you improve yourself, you improve your world." - Dr. Joe Vitale, spiritual teacher

Teachers of the future will be more like coaches - we are the embodiment of HOPE (Help Other People Evolve). As educators, we can make a huge difference, especially when we have the faith and a belief that all things are possible. Trust that if you lead with your heart your path will become clear. Heart-centred teaching isn't just a way to teach; it's the way to discover yourself, and the hidden talents and gifts of your students.

The world is waiting for you to discover and explore, to seek to understand and develop connections and relationships, to help your students feel honoured, safe, and loved.

Know that through what you teach, how you honour and respect them, you will inspire their own greatness within them. Value yourself and your students—they will be elevated by love and will evolve to be the next generation of doers; successful in all their endeavors. As Marci Shimoff says, *"Love is your job description—no matter what you do for a living. If you ever feel unsure of what you're supposed to do in a situation, here's a good rule of thumb: always do what leads to greater love."*

Love yourself first and then love the students you work with. It's that simple! Love is all that matters. All kids can thrive!

---

[86] To learn more about Marci, visit: happyfornoreason.com

[87] To learn more about Debra, visit: yestosuccess.com

Self-reflection questions

- *What are your favourite ways to find your smile and be happy?*
- *What was your biggest take away from this chapter?*
- *How will you implement the strategies in this chapter?*
- *What teachers have been good role models for you?*
- *What do you remember most about them?*
- *How can you love more—yourself and others?*

— REFERENCES —

Armstrong, Thomas. *Multiple Intelligences in the Classroom*, 4th edition. Alexandria, VA: ASCD-Association for Supervision and Curriculum Development, 2018.

Armstrong, Thomas. *You're Smarter Than You Think: A Kids Guide to Multiple Intelligences*. Minneapolis, MN: Free Spirit, 2014.

Bennett, Roy T. *The Light in the Heart: Inspirational Thoughts for Living Your Best Life*. Self-published, 2016.

Bloomberg, Dr. Harald. *Rhythmic Movement Training: Level One (RMT and ADD/ADHD)*. Stockholm, Sweden, 2008.

Buron, Kari D. *When My Worries Get Too Big: A Relaxation Book for Children Who Live with Anxiety*. Shawnee, KS: AAPC Publishing, 2006.

Busen, Sue. *Tap into Joy: A Guide to Emotional Freedom Techniques for Kids and Their Parents*, 1st edition. Bloomington, IN: iUniverse, 2007.

Busen, Sue. *Tap into Joy: A Guide to Emotional Freedom Techniques for Kids and Their Parents*, Special Expanded Edition Featuring Eli Bear ™, 2020.

Busen, Sue. *Tap into Balance: Your Guide to Awakening the Joy Within Using the GetSet™ Approach*. New York, NY; Morgan James Publishing, 2015.

Carrington, Jody. *Kids These Days: A Game Plan for (Re)Connecting with Those We Teach, Love & Lead*. Impress Books, 2020.

Coloroso, Barbara. *Kids are Worth It: Raising Resilient, Responsible and Compassionate Kids*, First Edition. Toronto, ON: Penguin Canada, 2010.

Covey, Stephen. *The 7 Habits of Highly Effective People - Powerful Lessons in Personal Change*. New York, NY: Free Press, 2004.

Davidson, Cathy N. *The New Education: How to Revolutionize the University to Prepare Students for a World in Flux*. New York, NY: Basic Books, 2017.

Delahooke, Mona. *Beyond Behaviors: Using Brain Science and Compassion to Understand and Solve Children's Behaviorial Challenges*. Eau Claire, WI: PESI Publishing & Media, 2019.

Dennison, Paul E. and Gail E. Dennison. *Brain Gym: Simple Activities for Whole Brain Learning*, 31649th edition. Ventura, CA: Edu Kinesthetics, 1992.

Dweck, Carol. *The New Psychology of Success*, Reprint, Updated Edition. New York, NY: Ballantine Books, 2007.

Dyer, Wayne. *Change Your Thoughts - Change Your Life: living the Wisdom of the Tao*. Carlsbad, CA: Hay House Inc., 2007.

Freeman-Koester, Cecilia. *I am the Child: Using Brain Gym ® with Children with Special Needs*. Reno, NV: Movement Based learning Inc.,1998 and 2010.

Frontiers. "How self-regulation can help young people overcome setbacks." ScienceDaily. sciencedaily.com/releases/2017/05/170529101502.htm (accessed March 4, 2021).

Gardner, Howard. *Intelligence Reframed: Multiple Intelligences for the 21st Century*. New York, NY: Basic Books, 2000.

Gardner, Howard. *Frames of Mind: The Theory of Multiple Intelligences*. New York, NY: Basic Books, 2011.

Garr, Lisa. *Becoming Aware: How to Repattern Your Brain and Revitalize Your Life*. Carlsbad, CA: Hay House Inc., 2015.

Ginott, Haim G. *Teacher and Child: A Book for Parents and Teachers*, Rei edition. Scribner Paper Fiction, 1993.

Goleman, Daniel. *Working with Emotional Intelligence*. New York, New York: Bantam Books Paperback, 2000.

Greene, Ross W. *Lost at School: Why Our Kids with Behavioral Challenges Are Falling through the Cracks and How We Can Help Them*. New York, NY: Scribner-A Division of Simon & Shuster, Inc., 2009.

Greene, Ross W. *The Explosive Child: A New Approach for Understanding and Parenting Easily Frustrated, Chronically Inflexible Children*. New York, NY: Harper Collins, 2005.

Hannaford, Carla. *Smart Moves: Why Learning is Not All in your Head*. Salt Lake City, UT: Great River Books, 2007.

Hannaford, Carla. *The Dominance Factor: How Knowing Your Dominant Eye, Ear, Brain, Hand and Foot Can Improve Your Learning*. Salt Lake City, UT: Great River Books, 2011.

Hay, Louise. *Mirror Work: 21 Days to Heal Your Life*. Carlsbad, CA: Hay House Inc., 2016.

Hay, Louise. *You Can Heal Your Life*. New York: Carlsbad, CA: Hay House Inc., 1984.

Hill, Napoleon, *Think and Grow Rich*. First Copyright 1937, ©2010 Simon & Brown.

Hoffman, Kent, Glen Cooper, Bert Powell and Christine M. Benton. *Raising a Secure Child: How Circle of Security Parenting Can Help You Nurture Your Child's Attachment, Emotional Resilience, and Freedom to Explore*. New York, NY: The Guilford Press, 2017.

References & Resources

Isbell, Christy and Rebecca Isbell. *Sensory Integration A Guide for Preschool Teachers*, 1st edition. Beltsville, MD: Gryphon House Inc., 2009.

Kemp Guylay, Kathryn, *Give It a Go, Eat a Rainbow*. Sun Valley, ID: Healthy Solutions of Sun Valley LLC, 2016.

Kuypers, Leah. *The Zones of Regulation ®: A Curriculum Designed to Foster Self-Regulation and Emotional Control*. Santa Clara, CA: Think Social Publishing, 2011.

Kübler-Ross, Elisabeth, *On Death and Dying*, 1st Edition. New York, NY: Scribner, 1997.

Lantieri, Linda. *Building Emotional Intelligence: Techniques to Cultivate Inner Strength in Children*. Boulder, CO: Sounds True, 2008.

Law Nolte, Dorothy and Rachel Harris. *Children Learn What They Live*, 1st edition. New York, NY: Workman Publishing Company, 1998.

Lewis, C.S. *A Grief Observed*, 1st edition. New York, NY: Harper Collins Publishers, 2001.

McColl, Peggy. *Your Destiny Switch: Master Your Key Emotions*, 1st edition. Carlsbad, CA: Hay House Inc., 2007.

Moore, Shelley. *One Without the Other: Stories of Unity Through Diversity and Inclusion*. Winnipeg, MB: Portage & Main Press, 2016.

Morter, Dr. Sue. *The Energy Codes: The 7 Step System to Awaken Your Spirit, Heal Your Body, and Live Your Best Life*. New York, NY: Simon & Shuster, 2019.

Mortiboys, Alan. *Teaching with Emotional Intelligence: A Step by Step Guide for Higher and Further Education Professionals*. United Kingdom: Psychology Press, 2005.

Nichols, Lisa. *Abundance Now*. New York, NY: Dey Street Books, 2016.

Orloff, Judith. *The Empath's Survival Guide: Life Strategies for Sensitive People*. Boulder CO: Sounds True, 2017.

Peterson, Wilferd. A. *The Art of Living: Thoughts on Meeting the Challenge of Life*. Galahad Books, 1993.

Porges, Stephen W. *The Polyvagal Theory: Neurophysiological Foundations of Emotions, Attachment, Communication, and Self-regulation*. New York, NY: W.W. Norton & Company Publishing, 2011.

Proctor, Bob. *The ABC's of Success: The Essential Principles from America's Greatest Prosperity Teacher*. New York, NY: TarcherPerigee, 2015.

Ravikant, Kamal. *Love Yourself Like Your Life Depends on It*. Self Published. 2012. Kindle.

Rose, David H. and Anne Meyer. *Teaching Every Student in the Digital Age: Universal Design for Learning*. Alexandria, VA: ASCD-Association for Supervision and Curriculum Development, 2002.

Rousseau, Dr. Barbara, *Your Conscious Classroom: The Power of Self-Reflection*. Bloomington, IN: Balboa Press, 2013.

Shimoff, Marci, *Happy for No Reason: 7 Steps to Being Happy from the Inside Out*, Illustrated edition. New York, NY: Atria Books, 2009.

Shimoff, Marci. *Love for No Reason: 7 Steps to Creating a Life of Unconditional Love*, First Free Press Edition. New York, NY: Atria Books, 2010.

Simeona, Mormah Nalamaku and Ihaleakala Hew Len. *Self I-dentity Through Ho'Oponopono (Basic1)*, 9th revised edition. The Foundation of I,1989.

Smith, Rick. *Conscious Classroom Management-Unlocking the Secrets of Great Teaching*, Writing in book edition. San Rafael, CA: Conscious Teaching Publications, 2004.

University of California - Los Angeles. "Putting Feelings Into Words Produces Therapeutic Effects In The Brain." *ScienceDaily*, June 22, 2007. sciencedaily.com/releases/2007/06/070622090727.htm

Wolfe, Patricia. Brain Matters: *Translating Research into Classroom Practice*. Alexandria VA: ASCD-Association for Supervision and Curriculum Development, 2001.

Wong, Harry K. and Rosemary T. Wong. *The First Days of School: How to be an Effective Teacher*, 4th edition. Mountainview, CA: Harry K. Wong Publications, 2009.

Vitale, Joe and Ihaleakala Hew Len. *Zero Limits-The Secret Hawaiian System for Wealth, Health, Peace and More*, 1st edition. Hoboken, NJ: John Wiley & Sons, Inc., 2009.

References & Resources

— RESOURCES —

A-B-C (Antecedent-Behaviour-Consequence) — a simple model that can be used to explore behaviours and triggers to change behaviour. Find out more at their website: betterhelp.com/advice/behavior/understanding-the-antecedent-behavior-consequence-model/

Al's Pals - a CASEL-approved program for younger students in kindergarten and primary grades. It is a resilience-based early childhood curriculum and teacher-training program that assists with developing social emotional skills, self-control, and problem-solving skills, as well as healthy decision-making techniques for children ages three to eight years old. It is designed to help children recognize and regulate their own feelings and behaviour. The lessons are fun and engaging and involve the use of character puppets, catchy music and effective teaching approaches. Benefits include children becoming more able to regulate their own emotions through awareness and practice. Children learn conflict resolution and ways to solve problems peacefully. It sets the stage for an environment of respect, caring, co-operation, and responsibility. Children learn about safety including dangers of household products. They learn to appreciate differences and build acceptance and appreciation of others. They are taught the harmful effects of alcohol and other drugs. The program builds on abilities to make healthy choices and implements strategies for coping with challenges and difficulties in life. The curriculum includes 46 lessons approximately 10 to 15 minutes in length, with two lessons per week. The program can be learned through a two-day training in person or online. Find out more at: wingspanworks.com/healthy-al/

ALSUP Form — see Assessment of Lagging Skills and Unsolved Problems

Armstrong, Thomas - is on a mission to support the "creation of developmentally appropriate practices and rich learning environments for children, adolescents and adult learners." His website has numerous articles, blogs and resource books that he has authored to promote his goal to help others. Armstrong's website lists many keynote presentations including "Neurodiversity in the Classroom: Strength Based Strategies to Help Students with Special Needs Achieve Success in School and Life", "If Einstein Ran the School: Revitalizing U.S. Education" and "Awakening the Genius in Every Child: Discovering and Reviving the Natural Motivation that Exists in All Children" and so many more. Please note that "The Theory of Multiple Intelligences" has received criticism as part of the "evidence-based movement" in education. But, As Dr. Thomas Armstrong says it is "theory not a single classroom intervention."
Website: institute4learning.com
Email: thomas@institute4learning.com

Assessment of Lagging Skills and Unsolved Problems – This website offers a detailed form that can be used as a discussion guide to help educators and parents identify lagging skills and their attendant behavioural challenges. It is comprehensive but not exhaustive and it's a great place to start problem solving. It is part of the Lives in the Balance website: livesinthebalance.org/sites/default/files/ALSUP%20060417.pdf

Bloomberg, Harald (1943-2020) - the founder of Rhythmic Movement Training, a highly effective technique that uses body movement to help stimulate mind, body, brain connections which can help in the treatment of many types of developmental disorders such as ADD, autism and even more severe conditions such as psychosis and schizophrenia. For more information, please visit his site: brmtusa.com/our-founder See also Rhythmic Movement Training.

Bowlby, John (1907-1990) - a British psychoanalyst with a keen interest in understanding the distress infants have when separated from caregivers, especially mothers. For further reading about the Bowlby Attachment Theory including information about the stages visit: simplypsychology.org/attachment.html Another link which discusses the theory is: psychology.sunysb.edu/attachment/online/inge_origins.pdf

Bowlby Attachment Theory – see Bowlby, John

Brain structures - This short video of Dr. Dan Siegel's Hand Model of the Brain offers a unique way to envision the various parts of the human brain and how they are interrelated. It is a very useful tool for understanding terminology about parts of the brain. Check out the video here: youtube.com/watch?v=f-m2YcdMdFw

Canadian Down Syndrome Society - their website has numerous resources for educators and parents. Visit: cdss.ca/resources/education/

An educational power point presentation on Down syndrome is available on request by emailing info@cdss.ca

For more information and ideas on inclusion, visit this free resource: cdss.ca/wp-content/uploads/2016/06/CDSS-Educator-Package-English.pdf

Carrington Connections Network for Educators - offers a training program for educators that specializes in connecting with kids, especially those who have experienced trauma – "How to Connect with Kids These Days". This organization provides a network for educators to share experiences and support each other based on shared goals and values and a common field of expertise. I took this course in April and May of 2020. It was informative and educational with the opportunity to access a VIP Course with 20 hours of extra audio inspiration. It was filled with many useful tips and strategies to consider when working with students who have experienced trauma. Carrington offers educational opportunities for school-wide training and learning about trauma, grief and loss, connection and relationships.
Course: How to Connect with Kids These Days.
Website: drjodycarrington.com
Email: jody@drjodycarrington.com
Facebook: facebook.com/drjodycarrington

CASEL – The Collaborative for Academic, Social, and Emotional Learning is an organization that is focuses on identifying and sharing programs that support SEL (Social and Emotional Learning). To find out more visit: casel.org/guide/

Circle of Security is a training and intervention system that is geared towards helping parents guide their children towards age appropriate independence. It focuses on helping parents and caregivers read the behaviour of children and respond appropriately. This is a great resource for understanding how to protect, nurture and parent your child to feel safe and secure while exploring their own independence and self-discovery. You can learn what a toddler is expressing through difficult behaviour. You will also learn how your own upbringing has influenced your parenting style. circleofsecurityinternational.com/cos-books/books/

ClassDojo - a free resource for teachers, students, and parents for communication. It helps schools and families have better communication and keeps parents informed as to what is being taught in class. It is also a tool for sharing photos, text messages and videos. ClassDojo has ideas for positive thinking and mindset to help students learn these skills too. This resource is actively used in 90% of all kindergarten to Grade 8 schools in the U.S. and in 180 other countries. All messages can be automatically translated into 35 languages—that's pretty fantastic given the diversity of cultures that teachers teach! Check it out at: classdojo.com

Coloroso, Barbara - an international speaker and author recognized for her works designed to assist parents and educators with discipline, parenting, and non-violent conflict resolution. She offers much wisdom for stopping bullying at home, schools and communities through the many books she has written.
Website: kidsareworthit.com
Email: info.kidsareworthit@gmail.com

Covey, Stephen (1932-2012) - author of *The 7 Habits of Highly Effective People*, as well as several books about leadership, parenting, and education. Time magazine named him as one of their 25 most influential people in 1996.

EFT - Emotional Freedom Technique, also known as Tapping, is a self-soothing practice that involves tapping with your fingertips on specific meridian points of the body while talking or thinking through stressful memories or experiences. To learn more about EFT and all its benefits, visit: emofree.com/nl/eft-tutorial/tapping-basics/how-to-do-eft.html

Emotional intelligence (EI) or emotional quotient (EQ) - defined as "the capacity of individuals to recognize their own, and other people's emotions, to discriminate between different feelings and label them appropriately, to use emotional information to guide thinking and behaviours, and to manage and/or adjust emotions to adapt to environments or achieve one's goal(s)" (quoted from Wikipedia). The concept of emotional intelligence began to gain popularity after Dan Goleman, a science reporter at the *New York Times*, released his book *Emotional Intelligence i*n 1995. Teaching the skill of living with emotional intelligence is good for students, and learning how to teach with emotional intelligence is a priority skill for educators.

Essential Oils – The use of aromatherapy for stress and calming has been around for centuries. Inhaling and the topical application of essential oils are popular ways to improve one's state of mind. It is important to work with the highest possible quality oils when you consider that you are ingesting them into your body through your lungs or skin. I personally use the Young Living Brand of oils in my home and life. I especially like a blend called Peace and Calming Essential Oil which I purchase through a local (to me) representative: Janet Miller: facebook.com/janet.l.miller.100/

Explosive Children – see Greene, Ross.

References & Resources

Daily Gratitude Journal – my free gift to you. On my website you'll find a template and instructions of how to create a daily gratitude journal. Create one for yourself. Use it to create journals for your students. It's a wonderful tool to self-discovery. sheenalsmith.com/free-gift/

Gardner, Howard – an American developmental psychologist who created the theory of multiple intelligences, essentially purposing that there are more than one way to learn. It is discussed in broad strokes in Chapter 3, Section L. His theory is also discussed on learnenglish.de/teachers/multipleintelligences2.html

Gratitude – the act of appreciating what you have in your life at this exact moment. Research has begun to support the notion that teaching yourself to be appreciative of the things and people in your life can have profound and lasting positive effects on your life. To learn more visit: health.ucdavis.edu/medicalcentre/features/2015-2016/11/20151125_gratitude.html

Greene, Ross - author of Lost at School and The Explosive Child which describe many ways to help an explosive child cope and build skills needed for thriving within a school and classroom environment. He believes the goal is to be proactive and discover lagging skills for problem solving. To find out more check out: livesinthebalance.org and cpsconnection.com/dr-ross-greene
Free Resources for educators: livesinthebalance.org/educators-schools

Guylay, Kathryn – an author, speaker, certified nutritional counselor/coach, podcaster, and media personality. She hosts an interesting and informative podcast called Mountain Mantras: Wellness and Life Lessons Podcast where she interviews leaders in the wellness and leadership worlds. She has authored two books on nutrition and children – *Give it a Go, Eat a Rainbow* and *Make Nutrition Fun: End Food Fights* and *Find Family Peace in Just 30 Days*.
Website: makeeverythingfun.com
Email: kathryn@guylay.com

Hay, Louise (1926-2017) - generally acknowledged as one of founders of the self-help movement, Hay was an author, speaker, publisher (Hay House Inc.) and philanthropist (The Hay Foundation). She was a fierce proponent of the transformative power of positive thinking and over the years wrote 18 books that focus on the healing power of affirmations and positive thinking. To find out more check out her website at: louisehay.com

HeartMath Institute - founded in 1991 with the aim of providing scientifically validated tools to help people "listen" to their hearts and their intuition. It is a form of biofeedback that helps to improve your emotional strengths. To find out more, visit: heartmath.org

Ho'oponopono – a technique that utilizes a mantra of forgiveness and gratitude to self-heal and to help others around you heal from emotional trauma. I am a Certified Ho'oponopono Practitioner. If you would like to find out more visit: joevitalecertified.com/hooponopono or laughteronlineuniversity.com/hooponopono-4-simple-steps/

Kohn, Alfie - the author of 13 books on education and human behaviour. They include eight on issues in education (e.g., homework, standardized testing, grades, teaching styles), two on parenting, and four on general topics (e.g. human nature, competition, motivation). He is a well-known critic of the education system's prioritization of grades and test scores. He has also written for mainstream publications including *The Atlantic, The New York Times, Harvard Business Review, The Chronicle of Higher Education,* and *Parents.*

Kübler-Ross, Elisabeth – (1926-2004) a Swiss-American psychiatrist, author and humanitarian who developed a theory that consisted of five stages of grief. She later expanded the list to seven stages and stressed that others understand that grief is not simply a linear process or a predictable process. Individuals can go through any of the stages at different times during their own grief. Stages include shock, denial, anger, bargaining, testing, depression, and acceptance.

Lives in The Balance - a non-profit organization founded by child psychologist Dr. Ross Greene, originator of the empirically supported *Collaborative & Proactive Solutions* (CPS) approach and *New York Times* bestselling author of the influential books *The Explosive Child, Lost at School, Lost & Found,* and *Raising Human Beings.* The aim of this organization is to foster collaboration and empathy, and inspire change for all children (especially the most vulnerable) through heightened awareness of the detrimental and counterproductive effects of punitive interventions when children appear to be acting out. They offer resources and programs to caregivers of behaviorally challenging kids through their website, podcasts, Facebook groups, training programs and conferences. Check them out at livesinthebalance.org

References & Resources

Leaf, Caroline – Dr. Leaf is a cognitive neuroscientist with a PhD in Communication Pathology and a BSc in Logopedics and Audiology, specializing in metacognitive and cognitive neuropsychology. Since the early 1980's she has studied and researched the Mind-Brain connection and has done research on the neuroplasticity of the brain. She has developed an original theory of the science of thought, as well tools and processes based on this research which are becoming popular as a research tool, and a way to help people develop and change their thinking and subsequent behavior. Her techniques have transformed the lives of patients with Traumatic Brain Injury (TBI), chronic traumatic encephalopathy (CTE), learning disabilities (ADD, ADHD), autism, the dementias, emotional traumas and mental health issues and has shown thousands of students of all ages, and adults and corporations how to use their minds to detox and develop their brains. She has presented her unique Switch on Your Brain with the 5-Step Learning Process® and the Metacognitive-Map™ learning tool to thousands of students and corporations worldwide. There are many YouTube, Vimeo and Podcasts of her teachings available.

Maslow's Hierarchy of Needs - a theoretical model outlining the most basic and vital human requirements for healthy survival. It is most often illustrated using a pyramid with the basic and most foundational of all human needs being the physical requirements for survival - food, water, warmth and rest, and culminating at the apex of the pyramid with the need for self-actualisation.

Mind Body Therapies – Unresolved trauma has been proven to have a measurable consequence to the mind and body, especially childhood trauma. I have quoted Dr. Arielle Schwartz in this book. She is a licensed clinical psychologist in private practice in Boulder, Colorado. She implements a variety of practices such as EMDR therapy and Somatic Psychology for trauma recovery, attachment trauma, chronic pain relief, grief and loss. Check out her books and blog at: drarielleschwartz.com

MeMoves - based on Stephen Borges' polyvagal theory this is a patented sequence of music, moves and visuals that helps those who struggle with self-regulation in the classroom, at home or other environments. It is an easy and effective way to increase attention in as little as 2 minutes using an award-winning DVD multimedia program. It is designed to activate the parasympathetic nervous system. You can watch MeMoves in the classroom here: youtube.com/watch?v=55OGz8PVrRI

Moore, Shelley – teacher, speaker, inclusive education consultant and author of *One Without the Other: Stories of Unity Through Diversity and Inclusion*. She offers insight suggestions and opinions on her website: fivemooreminutes.com/about/ where she features videos instead of typical written blog posts.

Morrissey, Mary - speaker, author, personal development coach, creator of the dream building system, The Dream Builder. To find out more about her coaching program and to get her free e-book Stronger Than Circumstance, check out: marymorrissey.com

Morter, Sue - an international speaker and author. She is a Master of Bio-energetic medicine and a Quantum Field visionary. Her teachings show learners how to utilize their own energy patterns to achieve higher energy frequencies through inner reflection, meditation and self-healing by implementing the techniques and strategies which are described in her book. Website: drsuemorter.com
Email: Info@DrSueMorter.com
Facebook: facebook.com/DrSueMorter/

Morter March – described in detail in Chapter 2, Section D

Non-violent communication is a powerful four-part process for communication and connection developed by Marshall Rosenberg PhD. This system stresses the importance of being specific about your observations, feelings, needs and requests when discussing challenging situations. A free pdf download is available on their website along with other valuable information:
nonviolentcommunication.com/aboutnvc/4partprocess.htm

Pierson, Rita - a professional educator since 1972, she taught elementary school, junior high and special education. She has worked as a counselor, a testing coordinator and an assistant principal and now she educates the educators, specializing in 'under resourced learners' with the aim of helping to impact the higher than average dropout rate, especially among African-American boys. One of my favorite of her TED Talks is called "Every Kid Needs a Champion":
ted.com/talks/rita_pierson_every_kid_needs_a_champion?language=en#t-8477

Polyvagal Theory - posits that there is essentially a third type of nervous system in the human body which can be called the social engagement system. This system helps us to navigate relationships. It is linked to the vagus nerve which is a primary part of the autonomic nervous system, a nerve that runs from the brain through the neck and chest to the abdomen. This nerve linked to the regulation of emotions, social connections and fear responses. See Also Porges, Stephen.

References & Resources

Poneman, Debra - an international speaker, seminar leader and business owner. She shares her cutting-edge knowledge of universal principles in an impactful and heart-centred way. She will touch your heart and impact your life forever. She is authentic, wise and fun loving. To say that she is some kind of wonderful is an understatement. I am blessed to know her and have her as a mentor and a friend. Check out her "Yes to Success" program for true success in the 21st century. You will be inspired! Visit: yestosuccess.com

Porges, Stephen - a distinguished scientist at the University of Indiana. He is the leading expert in developmental psychophysiological and developmental behavioural neuroscience and the founding director of the Traumatic Stress Research Consortium. He developed the polyvagal theory that supports our desire and quest for safety and understanding of the workings of our social engagement system. He links the ANS (autonomic nervous system) to social behaviour. His wisdom has given me great insight and understanding of how children and adults get locked into set patterns and are simply unable to free themselves from autism, anxiety, depression, trauma, and other mental illnesses. His work enables others to understand the unconscious connection between psychological experiences and physical manifestations within the body.

He has also created SSP (Safe and Sound Protocol—a listening program designed to reduce stress and auditory sensitivity while at the same time enhancing social engagement and resilience. I reference his book *The Polyvagal Theory: Neurophysiological Foundations of Emotions, Attachment, Communication, and Self-regulation*. Website: stephenporges.com See also Polyvagal Theory

Price, Hal – an international speaker and the author of a series of children's book including Eli Benjamin Bear and other animal heroes. The books are intended to reinforce positive self-esteem lessons for children while at the same time strengthening the bonds between parents and children as they enjoy the stories together.

Rhythmic Movement Training – a technique developed by Dr. Harald Bloomberg based on the work of Swedish body therapist Kerstin Linde. It focuses on a specific sequence of body movements which are based on the earliest most fundamental physical movements that infants make as they are learning about their bodies. These movements help to integrate our physical reflexes and at the same time activate critical links between the cerebellum, limbic system and prefrontal cortex. According to Bloomberg this "whole-brain linking" creates optimal functioning which explains why the movements are so helpful for a large variety of conditions such as ADD/ADHD, learning disabilities, developmental delay, autism and even severe psychiatric disorders such as psychosis and schizophrenia.

SEL – Social and emotional Learning, also referred to as Social-Emotional Learning, is the process through which individuals learn what they need to develop healthy self-identity, manage emotions, achieve personal and group goals, feel and show empathy for others, create and maintain supportive relationships, and make responsible caring decisions. See **CASEL**

Shimoff, Marci - if you've ever picked up any of the widely popular 'Chicken Soup' books you've probably encountered her work. She is has co-authored six of those ubiquitous titles, including *Chicken Soup for the Woman's Soul, Love for No Reason* and *Happy for No Reason*. She is a popular speaker on topics included self-esteem and peak performances. You can request her free e-book The 5 Secrets to Deep and Lasting Happiness from her website: happyfornoreason.com

S.M.A.R.T. GOALS – This acronym usually stands for Specific, Measurable, Achievable, Realistic, Timely. It is a short form for an often used way to measure concrete goals intended to be achieved within a given period of time. Shelley Moore, a specialist in the field of inclusive learning offers an alternative version – Strength-based, Meaningful, Authentic, Responsive, Triangulated. Check out her video at youtube.com/watch?v=0OrntS8NrUY

Tapping – see EFT – Emotional Freedom Tapping.

Theory of Multiple Intelligences – created by Dr. Howard Gardner this theory purposes that there are many different ways that children and adults learn. This means that those with brain injuries can learn and be taught, it must just be approached in a different way. The theory is discussed in more detail in Chapter 3, Section L.

Tomatis Method - a form of sound and listening therapy developed by French ear, nose and throat specialist, Dr. Alfred Tomatis. It is works by stimulating parts of the ear which correspondingly stimulates parts of the brain and nervous system. It has been found to be effective in treating a range of auditory processing disorders (APD). To find out more visit: integratedwellbeing.com.au/services/tomatis-method/

Wilbarger, Patricia – an occupational therapist and clinical psychologist who developed the concept of the sensory diet. She also designed the Wilbarger Deep Pressure and Proprioceptive Technique (DPPT) and the Oral Tactile Technique for sensory defensiveness. It is a technique that combines the tactile sensations of brushing with deep muscle massage to assist in calming and re-programming the body and mind. These techniques should ONLY be implemented by a qualified occupational therapist.

References & Resources

Wilbarger Protocol – also called the The Wilbarger Deep Pressure and Proprioceptive Technique (DPPT), a specific pattern of physical stimulation delivered using a special type of brush and gentle joint compressions. It is believed to facilitate the coordination of mind-brain-body processes in a manner that influences positive change. It was developed by Dr. Patricia Wilbarger. It is a highly specific technique which should only be attempted by a properly trained occupational therapist. To find out more visit: nationalautismresources.com/the-wilbarger-protocol-brushing-therapy-for-sensory-integration/

Young Children Develop in an Environment of Relationships – a report prepared by the National Scientific Council on the Developing Child. Available at developingchild.harvard.edu/wp-content/uploads/2004/04/Young-Children-Develop-in-an-Environment-of-Relationships.pdf

Zones of Regulation – a cognitive behavioural approach to teaching others to self-regulate. It can work at the classroom level or be scaled up to encompass the entire learning environment. On the website there are links for free educational resources to use such as Zones of Regulation bingo and Zones Moment of the Week. I highly recommend buying the whole book which includes a DVD with colour printables. The website also has pre/post data collection self-assessment worksheets. The company is progressive and always adding more to their site as well as having studies in the process of gathering quantitative data. They also now have a game that teachers or educational support staff can play to enable group collaboration and problem-solving skills and strategies with visual support, "Navigating the Zones: A Pathway to Self-Regulation", for cooperative learning. For more information, visit: zonesofregulation.com
Email: info@zonesofregulation.com

— BOOKS I RECOMMEND —

Conscious Classroom Management: Unlocking the Secrets of Great Teaching by Rick Smith.
I enjoyed this book because he clearly describes the styles of teachers and how they can learn to manage their class in a seemingly invisible way.

From the Ashes by Jesse Thistle
I loved this book by Thistle. I found myself relating to many aspects of this book from knowing the stories of children that I have worked with and through discovering my own heritage and making sense of stories that I have heard about. The resilience of his spirit inspires a reader to know there is hope and to stay strong. It is a good reminder that we do not always know what circumstances a child is living in.

How to be an Antiracist by Ibram X. Kendi
One man's personal journey and honest reflection of racism paired with thought provoking information for self-reflection and self-examination.

Kids These Days: A Game Plan for (Re) Connecting with Those We Teach, Love & Lead by Jody Carrington.

Multiple Intelligences in the Classroom 4th edition by Dr. Thomas Armstrong.
It is a great resource with examples, templates and strategies to implement.

On Death and Dying by Elisabeth Kübler-Ross – a thought provoking book that details Kübler-Ross's stages of grief. This book was written in 1969 and she later went on to expand her theory to include seven stages rather than the original five.

One Without the Other: Stories of Unity Through Diversity and Inclusion by Shelley Moore.
An insightful and entertaining book where she shares her experiences and opinions about working as a teacher and in support of truly inclusive learning environments.

Sensory Integration A Guide for Preschool Teachers by Christy and Rebecca Isbell. Students who are over stimulated because of sensory overload are struggling to cope and learning to identify the cues can help you help them and your other students. I touch on this topic in Chapter 2.

The Energy Codes: The 7 Step System to Awaken Your Spirit, Heal Your Body, and Live Your Best Life by Sue Morter.

References & Resources

The Miners Canary: Enlisting Race, Resisting Power, Transforming Democracy by Lani Guinier and Gerald Torres
This book inspires race consciousness for individuals and encourages them to become proactive and work towards solidarity through teamwork for the betterment of issues ranging from education, politics to voting rights.

This Bridge Called My Back: Writings by Radical Women of Color, edited by Cherrie Moraya and Gloria Anzaldua
It consists of stories, interviews and poems that enable the reader to gain different perspectives and better understanding of race, gender, sexuality and class issues that women of colour continue to deal with today in our world.

When My Worries Get Too Big: A Relaxation Book for Children Who Live with Anxiety by Kari D. Buron. The book is filled with ideas for helping young students cope with anxiety and the resultant stress related behaviours.

White Fragility: Why It's So Hard for White People to Talk About Racism by Robin DiAngelo
This is a great "starter" book to deepen your understanding of racism and how white people benefit in our society. Where there are racial differences separation and inequality exist.

You're Smarter Than You Think: A Kids Guide to Multiple Intelligences by Dr. Thomas Armstrong.

— ACKNOWLEDGEMENTS —

I would like to acknowledge my greatest teachers, all the children and students that I have ever had the pleasure of working with over my 40 year career.

To my own children; Meagan, Garry, Tessa, Connor and my stepdaughters, Sasha and Britney. Along with being my greatest teachers, you are my greatest treasures. May you always have the freedom to be yourselves. You are my "why", the reason that I strive to learn more, to do better and to be better. Each of you inspires me to have hope and pursue possibilities through my unconditional love and desire to help each of you become the person that you are destined to become.

To my grandchildren: Kenzi, Hunter, Harlyn, Reese and Landin. You remind me of the value of play, humour, and laughter. You light up my heart with your unique, sweet and wonderful personalities. I love you all beyond measure.

To my Mother, Elizabeth Leonard, you are the woman that I admire most in the world. Your resilience, your kind heart and your quiet strength inspire me to believe in myself and to keep keeping on when times are tough. You taught me more about life and love than you will ever realize.

Chris, my spouse, my love, my rock; you are truly the wind beneath my wings. You have kept our home and life together when I was immersed in putting this book project together. I am deeply grateful for your patience, understanding and for always being a safe place for me to land after a challenging day.

Shauna Hardly, the book doula, thank you for putting your whole heart into assisting me with giving birth to this dream book project. Your editing skills and input are appreciated beyond words.

I am extremely grateful to Beth McBlain for her final edit and proof-reading expertise, her valuable input, suggestions and final layout that has helped to make this book the treasure that you are reading. Special thanks to her team, Lisa Crandall and Eddie Chan, for making it a reality.

Sweet Debra Poneman, I am in awe of your achievements and your kind and caring heart. Thank you from the bottom of my heart for your support, your belief in my abilities and your incredible forward for this book.

Acknowledgements

Marvellous Marci Shimoff, I am honoured by your generosity, encouragement and years of teaching me so much valuable wisdom and support through the Year of Miracles program.

Suzanne Lawlor, coach extraordinaire whose encouragement and gentle guiding wisdom empowers me to make intentional and insightful decisions that lead to my own happiness and personal growth.

To everyone who has crossed my path in one way or another I would like you to know that I am grateful and appreciative of our shared experiences. I especially love the adventurous encounters that were filled with laughter and love. I am honoured that you shared your life and/or story with me. Please know that I hold you in a piece of my heart. May everything that you dream of become a reality.

Image Credit: Dorothy Brunner

I have a dream...My dream is to see hunger end in my lifetime through my efforts and the efforts of others. I truly believe that this is possible when we collectively as human beings say, "NO MORE!"

A portion of the proceeds from my books sales will be donated to the following two places, the Sault Ste. Marie Community Soup Kitchen and Tumaini Afrika Sault Ste. Marie.

Our local Soup Kitchen relies on donations to support its programs to valued members of our community. They will issue tax receipts for donations over $10.00

They have a great resource that lists 25 ways to help the soup kitchen. soupkitchencommunitycentre.org/25-ways-you-can-help-the-soup-kitchen.html

I am sure that Soup Kitchens in your own communities need your support too. Consider helping them out whenever you can, however you can as well.

Contact information: soupkitchencommunitycentre.org/
Sault Ste. Marie Soup Kitchen Community Centre
172 James Street
Sault Ste. Marie, ON P6A 1W3

Acknowledgements

The second charity dear to my heart is Tumaini Afrika Sault Ste. Marie, a non-registered Sault Ste. Marie based group of volunteers dedicated to working with children and women in Kenya.

Our vision: "Tumaini Afrika focuses on education as the key to empowering children and women to become confident, creative, self-reliant people whose personal growth and success will enable them to inspire others and become agents of change in their own communities."

Website: tumainiafrikassm.com/
Email: tumainiafrikassm@gmail.com
Facebook: facebook.com/TumainiAfrikaSSM

THANK YOU FOR YOUR SUPPORT!

— NOTES —

— NOTES —

— NOTES —

— **NOTES** —

NOTES

Empowering Solutions for Educators of Children with Special Needs

All Kids Can Thrive will help you understand your key role in the future of education to guide, motivate and inspire students to achieve their own level of greatness through their skills, natural gifts, and talents. By applying the tools you will be inspired, knowing that you made a difference by enriching your students' lives—and by being the best version of yourself.

"As exemplars for teaching students about life, moral values, education, and unity consciousness you have a tremendous opportunity in your hands. I know you will enjoy this resource filled with valuable wisdom, useful tools and insights for teachers, educational assistants, and support staff alike. Thank you Sheena, for your wonderful insights for our youth."
—**Dr. Sue Morter**, bestselling author of *The Energy Codes*

"Sheena Smith offers a powerful system for helping students live happy, thriving lives by discovering how to be self-reflective, resilient, and empowered. 'All Kids Can Thrive' is a valuable resource to help guide your students to shine brightly in their own unique ways."
— **Marci Shimoff**, #1 *NY Times* bestselling author and featured teacher in *The Secret*

"Neuroplasticity is more than a buzzword; It is a blessing to know that learning potential is endless with the application of re-patterning and brain enhancing exercises. Sheena's book provides you with an introduction to some of the many proven and effective techniques for improving the functioning of your brain to consistently rewire your brain for lasting positive changes. Sheena has the beautiful gift of being able to see children as whole and complete, exactly the way they are which enables her to help them reach their full potential. I believe there are angels on this planet tapped to do the work that Sheena naturally does in this world, and her work is very needed at this time."
—**Lisa Garr**, host of The Aware Show and Being Aware, author of *Becoming Aware*

Sheena L. Smith has helped children to reach their full potential for over 40 years, including 20 years in the educational system. With this book she hopes to inspire you to believe in yourself in your efforts as an educator, parent, or childcare worker and to have inner knowing that there is always hope.

Photo credit: anna@kevanna.com

A portion of proceeds from all book sales will be donated to the Sault Ste. Marie Community Soup Kitchen & Tumaini Afrika Sault Ste. Marie.

ISBN: 9781777621902

www.ingramcontent.com/pod-product-compliance
Lightning Source LLC
Chambersburg PA
CBHW081409080526
44589CB00016B/2508